Teaching Writing with Computers
An Introduction

Pamela Takayoshi
University of Louisville

Brian Huot
University of Louisville

HOUGHTON MIFFLIN COMPANY   BOSTON   NEW YORK

Editor-in-Chief: Patricia A. Coryell
Senior Sponsoring Editor: Suzanne Phelps Weir
Development Editor: Janet Young
Editorial Assistant: Becky Wong
Cover Design Manager: Diana Coe
Manufacturing Coordinator: Florence Cadran
Marketing Manager: Cindy Graff Cohen
Marketing Assistant: Sarah Donelson

CREDITS

Blythe, Stuart. Chat room. "Stu's Room." 31 March 2000. LinguaMOO.
22 June 2001. <http://lingua.utdallas.edu:7000/3894/>.

Printed in the U.S.A.

ISBN: 0-618-11526-9

123456789-CRS-06 05 04 03 02

Contents

Section III: Teaching Beyond Physical Boundaries

Section IV: Teaching and Learning New Media

Section V: Assigning and Assessing Student Writing

Introduction

PAMELA TAKAYOSHI AND BRIAN HUOT

As the new academic year approaches, a program administrator at a large public university plans the orientation meeting for instructors teaching writing in computer classrooms. Because the staff ranges from novices to experienced teachers, the administrator is looking for first-day readings—articles which will provide the novices with an overview of the issues they will be facing as teachers using computer technologies, readings which will lay a groundwork for understanding the more complicated, nuanced issues involved in teaching writing with technology which the teaching group will read about later in the semester. She looks at several articles which have worked in the past as good first-day, introductory articles:

> Thomas Barker and Fred Kemp's "Network Theory: A Postmodern Pedagogy for the Writing Classroom" (1990); Nick Carbone's "Trying to Create a Community: A First-Day Lesson Plan" (1993); Janet Eldred's "Pedagogy in the Computer-Networked Classroom" (1991); Gail E. Hawisher's "Electronic Meetings of the Minds: Research, Electronic Conferences, and Composition Studies" (1992); Cynthia Selfe's "Redefining Literacy: The Multilayered Grammars of Computers" (1989) and "Preparing English Teachers for the Virtual Age: The Case for Technology Critics" (1992); Richard Selfe's "What Are They Talking About? Computer Terms that English Teachers Might Need to Know" (1992); Patricia Sullivan's "Taking Control of the Page: Electronic Writing and Word Publishing" (1991); Robert Yagelski and Sarah Powley's "Virtual Connections and Real Boundaries: Teaching Writing and Preparing Writing Teachers on the Internet" (1996).[1]

Every semester, the administrator has more difficulty finding current articles (current in terms of theory *and* technology) which address basic questions about a first-time experience teaching in a computer classroom. The articles that worked in the past continue to raise important issues such as the need for the teacher's pedagogical theories to inform the shape technology takes in her curriculum, the ways in which contemporary writing theories are supported (and not supported) by computer technologies, and an introduction to

1

the language and concerns involved in teaching writing with technologies. Although these issues remain important for an instructor entering a computer classroom in 2002, the scholarship produced ten or fifteen years ago is not as relevant as it might have been when it was first published. The specific technologies have evolved, and the software discussed in such articles is quite different from that loaded on the hard drives of the machines that the teacher and students will be using.

Technology develops very rapidly. An industry standard seems to be that a newly purchased computer will be obsolete in three years since technological developments (i.e., programs, web applications, and peripherals) will require newer machines to support them. Some of the technologies we considered important ten years ago are no longer available or have been metamorphosed into forms no longer relevant to their original function. For example, although hypertext as a type of reading and writing no longer garners the attention it once received, the emergence of the World Wide Web as a hypertextual space requires a new understanding of the principles first introduced in the use of hypertext. Scholarship on computers and composition is similarly positioned—technological developments in writers' lives require new, evolving understandings of the place of technology in contemporary writing theories. So although early scholarship on computers and composition is certainly relevant in terms of its larger claims, it is no longer current in terms of the existing technological and theoretical realities of many writing classrooms. The technologies described ten or so years ago are no longer new to most in the culture, and technologies not available then are now ubiquitous (i.e., the World Wide Web). While the authors in this collection return to the basic concern of applying computers to composition—how do I best use computers in my writing classes?—they also explore technologies in which contemporary writers are actually engaged.

Similarly, scholarship which introduces teachers to writing technologies needs to be updated in terms of what we now know about the place of writing technologies in writers' lives and in classrooms. Although more teachers every day are facing the (forced or embraced) integration of writing technologies into their curriculum, current scholarship does not address very well the needs of teachers new to a computer teaching environment. The field's current scholarship largely assumes an audience familiar with the ongoing debates and issues that shape current conversations in the field. This broader and more detailed exploration of the many facets of writing with technology grew out of a basic concern for teaching with technology. In their thorough history of computers and composition, Hawisher, LeBlanc, Moran, and Selfe provide evidence of the roots of teaching composition with computers in the early eighties as writing teachers worked out the place of technology in their curricula. Writing technologies entered composition studies through the classroom as teachers struggled to learn how to teach with these new machines. Articles published in the early eighties focused on the relationship between computer technologies and writing processes; in these articles, researchers and teachers were defining the role writing technologies might play in writing pedagogies. From these initial explorations which focused on broad questions (Why teach with technology? How do we teach with technology? How does technology affect writing, writing instruction, and writers?), we developed answers that led us to more tightly and closely focused investigations of a wide range of relevant issues—the ideologies (gendered, racialized, classed) of technologies that intervene in classroom practices, the processes of developing critical technological literacy (processes which build upon the acquisition of basic computer literacy), and, more recently, the interaction between technologies and our work as compositionists. These discussions—important and necessary for building a complete vision of what happens when writers engage with writing technologies—are questions for sophisticated users and scholars of technology. Teachers approaching the integration of technology into their writing curricula for the first time have more broadly defined needs based in the materiality of technologically mediated writing practices.

So where do new teachers begin? Many of us have been the administrator in the scenario we have just described, and we imagine the same scenario playing out across the country in other writing programs. Whether teachers are involved in a teaching group or working individually to transition writing instruction into a computer-mediated environment, they will find the chapters in this collection a good place to start. During the last ten years, computer technologies have been applied to composition teaching in ways that have widely changed the nature of the work which writing teachers and students do. With a print journal (*Computers and Composition: An International Journal for Teachers of Writing*), online journals (*Kairos: A Webbed Environment for Teachers of Writing* and *Computers and Composition Online*), an annual conference (Conference on Computers and Writing), and a wealth of single-authored books and edited collections all devoted solely to writing technologies (see Appendix A), new teachers incorporating technology into their teaching for the first time can be overwhelmed by the vastness of the available scholarship. For this collection, we invited experienced scholars and teachers of writing technologies to write for the beginning teacher. We asked them, "Knowing what you know now about teaching with writing technologies, what would you want new teachers to know about these particular issues?" This book arose from our immediate needs ("What do I have the teachers read on Monday?") as program administrators, and those immediate needs revealed to us how seldom scholarship on computers and composition has addressed the beginning teacher lately. Although computers and composition, a field that has been around since the early eighties, has amassed a strong body of information, there are surprisingly few relevant and current resources that can guide instructors who are teaching with computer technologies for the first time. As college and university teachers are increasingly being called upon to teach with writing technologies, the need for such resources is only increasing.

Writing for Teachers Teaching with Technology for the First Time

In addition to addressing the changing technology and being characterized by an increasingly theoretical sophistication, scholarship on technology has developed from calling for technology users to calling for technological critics. The field has channeled an optimism about technology into a critical, accepting stance which now argues that since technologies are an increasingly necessary component of the writer's repertoire, savvy, informed computer and composition teachers and students must be technology *critics* as well as technology *users*. What we advocate is that computer-mediated curricula foster technology citizens, teachers and students who assert their agency, accept their responsibility for their uses of technology, and understand the implications of that use. This double consciousness about technology use is something that current scholarship demands of computer-using composition teachers. Throughout this book, the authors, whether they explicitly say so or not, share a desire that teachers should think critically about technology and should educate their students to be critical users of technology. Critical technological education helps students become better users of technology, thereby harnessing the great potential of writing technologies while at the same time protecting against its considerable potential for harm. The authors in this collection ask us in different ways to be critical users of technology. By suggesting many ways to be critical users of technology, they point to ways in which we need to broaden our field of vision. They ask us to return to the issues we may think we have already solved and to examine them again, knowing what we now know, to see if we really had it right. In this light, although we conceive of this volume as being directed toward writing teachers using writing technologies for the first time, we believe that more experienced and knowledgeable teachers will also find this book helpful and informative.

This is not a how-to book in the traditional sense of the word. Although teachers at all levels of experience might benefit from the theoretical discussions and pedagogical suggestions, the work in this book should not be considered as merely a practical guide. In his book *Thinking Through Theory: Vygotskian Perspectives on the Teaching of Writing*, James Zebroski asserts the theoretical nature of all teaching practices:

> Theory is not the opposite of practice; theory is not even a supplement to practice. Theory is practice, a practice of a particular kind, and practice is always theoretical. The question then is not whether we have a theory of composition, that is, a view, or better, a vision of our selves and our activity, but whether we are going to be conscious of our theory. (15)

Zebroski's point is that any teaching practice we might consider comes with a set of beliefs and assumptions. For example, if we have students work on exercises of grammar, usage, and mechanics outside of their writing, we're assuming that language use can be learned outside of a communicative context. Or, if we break our classes into groups so that students can respond to each other's writing, then we're assuming that effective writing and its learning require a social dimension within which students need to read, write, and respond to each other. Failure to examine our beliefs and assumptions about teaching can lead to what George Hillocks calls teaching as a "protected activity":

> If students do not learn much even when proper teaching has taken place, it is not surprising because they are weak and cannot be expected to learn. The teaching has not failed; the students have. Therefore there is no reason to change the method of teaching. Teaching writing becomes a protected activity. (28)

Teachers have beliefs and assumptions about technology, and their impulse to use it in a specific way contains particular beliefs and assumptions about technology itself. Remaining critically reflective of our assumptions and beliefs about technology is especially important since they form a pervasive cultural trope that has a strong affect on our thinking and on the culture in which we live and work. Technology can be very seductive. But for a teacher to adopt technologies on their own strength rather than on their appropriate fit with his or her pedagogical principles is to let technology be too powerful an influence. Seymour Papert coined the term *technocentric* to describe beliefs and assumptions about computers in which they and their use exist outside of any relevant context. In a technocentric approach, computers in the classroom are value-free tools that focus on the technology itself and the ability of each new technological innovation to correct problems and create new possibilities. Gail Hawisher uses the term *technocentrism* to describe computers and composition's initial optimism for all things technological in the writing classroom.

Examining our assumptions and beliefs about teaching, language, literacy, and technology helps us guard against practices based upon beliefs and assumptions that are irrelevant to or in conflict with what we currently know about the teaching of writing. But the process of critical examination also reminds us to connect all classroom practices, including the use of computers, to relevant and defensible instructional goals. Technology for its own sake is dangerous because it can detract attention and energy from other things that need to be accomplished in the class. A notion of pedagogical practice grounded in the theory, reflection, and inquiry that drive our practices is an important component of this volume. Teachers are never urged to implement one practice or another; instead, they are asked to consider various options within the framework of their instructional goals and existing pedagogical practice and theory. In this way, they are invited to reflect on and to take part in a continuing conversation with others about theory, practice, computers, and the teaching of writing.

The Chapters

While the question guiding this collection—How can and should writing teachers effectively incorporate writing technologies into their curriculum?—

was also addressed by the initial research in computers and composition, the answers arrived at here are very contemporary and benefit richly from the practical, theoretical, and material perspectives of the intervening twenty years. Although this collection is designed for teachers making the initial transition into a technology-rich writing pedagogy, the chapters should be vitalizing and relevant to experienced teachers as well. The authors provide detailed explorations of theories and practices that can prompt readers at all levels to new thinking about their teaching.

The first section, "Writing Technologies for Composition Pedagogies," provides an overview of technology in the writing classroom and introduces the book. Whereas such a section is a traditional opener, the essays comprising the chapters themselves are less about prevailing issues and trends in computers and composition and more about relationships among teachers, students, and technology in the computer writing classroom. Dickie Selfe's essay, "Techno-pedagogical Explorations: Toward Sustainable Technology-Rich Instruction," is a playful, experimental, yet serious look at the ways in which technology impacts literacy and its teaching. Selfe introduces important concepts about computer-mediated communication and its use in the classroom. In addition, he generates a wealth of enthusiasm about teaching writing with technology, providing several bulleted lists, reminders, and suggestions. His essay moves quickly from one issue to another, providing warnings about common pitfalls in the use of particular computer applications in classroom situations. At the end of his essay, he refuses to conclude, reminding us that "there is no way to conclude this process. It's experimental; it changes; there are guidelines but few rules. . . ." In the second essay, "Technology as Teacher," Janet Carey Eldred and Lisa Toner consider a spectrum of situations in which computers can be integrated into instruction—technology-rich campuses (where physical access is high and teaching involves technologies), technology-bound campuses (where the technological infrastructure is present but instructional use is limited), and ill-equipped campuses (campuses without many technological resources or with a haphazard institutional approach to integrating them into institutional life as a whole). Given this range of possibilities, Eldred and Toner hesitate to provide algorithms for teaching with technology; instead, they model a process of decision making about technology and provide teachers with questions to ask themselves about where, when, and in what form technology might enter their pedagogies. Like the other writers featured in this section, Christine Tulley and Kristine Blair, authors of the third essay," Ewriting Spaces as Safe, Gender-Fair Havens," consider computer-mediated classrooms broadly, offering teachers some overarching guiding principles. Concerned about the extent to which students' nondominant subject positions (vis-à-vis race, class, gender, age, and sexual orientation) may have impacted their access and consequently their attitude toward computers both inside and outside the classroom, Tulley and Blair sketch out an inclusive, supportive pedagogy for technology classrooms. By focusing specifically on research that suggests that female students are disadvantaged in computer-enriched classrooms, the authors consider strategies for building more inclusive classrooms for all students. They skillfully weave together feminist pedagogical theories and computer-mediated classroom possibilities, offering caveats as well as suggestions for practice. As they conclude, the feminist pedagogical theories which inform their computer-mediated pedagogies contribute to creating constructive and productive spaces for all students—male and female alike.

Section Two, "Learning to Teach with Technology," provides a more contextualized picture of what it's like to teach writing in a computer classroom. In all three chapters, teachers examine their existing pedagogies, make changes, and suggest lessons for all teachers. In this way, these writings provide not only a clearer picture of computer-mediated pedagogies in practice but also a model of critical reflective practice—a process that can benefit any pedagogical theory and practice. In "Fools Rush In," Scott Lloyd DeWitt and Marcia Dickson relate their experiences as teachers of a shared curriculum that they developed and taught in separate classes. They tell of the lessons they learned through failure and success, revealing the dialectical relationship between theory and practice and offering specific pedagogical theories and strategies as models. DeWitt and Dickson argue and demonstrate convincingly that theory must always inform practice but that, especially in computer-mediated spaces, practices can also impact our existing theories of how people learn and write. Ultimately, their essay is a story of teachers learning with technology as they teach their students. Nicholas Mauriello and Gian S. Pagnucci, in "Balancing Acts," tell three stories of their first experiences integrating technology into their classrooms, extrapolating some guidelines for new teachers, who can thereby reap the benefits of using technology but not have to make the same mistakes that the authors made. The essay illustrates Mauriello and Pagnucci's point about the power and importance of telling stories about literacy and its teaching. They also demonstrate the ongoing process of utilizing technology in the writing classroom. In "But I'm *Just* White; Or, How 'Other' Pedagogies Can Benefit All Students," Samantha Blackmon describes a process of critical, reflective practice in which she surveyed students about technology and found that some were concerned about the lack of representation and the misrepresentation of African Americans on the Web. In response, Blackmon has created a more inclusive and reflexive pedagogy which benefits students of all identity positions (African American, Asian, Muslim, female, male, and "just" white, as a white student describes himself). Blackmon tells us that her experience illustrates that what's important is not the particular skills or activities in which students engage but rather "the practice of thinking critically about technology, its uses (and limits) in high education, and what all of this means for and to students of different and differing discourse communities." Reading about these authors' experiences and observing the authors question their own assumptions that led to the problems that they encountered can provide the new teacher not only with ways to avoid similar problems but also with a methodology for developing and sustaining effective writing pedagogy in the composition classroom.

The third section, "Teaching Beyond Physical Boundaries," addresses a cluster of important issues since technology has always been regarded by some as a way to offer more efficient and cheaper products to the consumer public. In higher education, the application of technology to distance learning has been considered a way to maximize instructional output and to minimize expenses since one plugged-in teacher can reach a multitude of students who don't even have to be on campus. Of course, this kind of instructional model poses some problems for a profession that values context, student-teacher interaction, and the personal, relevant nature of literacy learning. Kathleen Blake Yancey's essay, "The Pleasures of Digital Discussions," focuses not on distance learning per se but on expanding the classroom and the learning environment in ways that connect teachers and students and promote literate practices in an academic environment. As Yancey discusses different electronic forums, outlining their strengths and weaknesses and providing examples of their use through stories and anecdote, she notes that electronic discussions can be used to do things that we already do, like conduct office hours and respond to student papers, and they can also allow us to do new things, like bringing outside speakers into the classroom. Throughout her discussion, Yancey reminds us that incorporating new technologies into the classroom is both exciting and frustrating. Her opening epigram sums up not only her approach but also the eventual influence of technology in all of our classrooms: "It's not a question of whether you'll use technology to help students learn. It's a question of what kind of technology you will include—and when." Stuart Blythe, in "Meeting the Paradox of Computer-mediated Communication in Writing Instruction," turns his focus to why and how computer-mediated communication (CMC) can be included in writing instruction. While offering very practical advice on integrating communication via electronic networks, Blythe also theorizes those uses for new teachers and destabilizes overly optimistic myths about CMC which can set up unrealistic expectations. After reviewing the scholarship on CMC, Blythe rescues it from the optimism principles to guide the new teacher in what CMC can reasonably be expected to do for writing curricula, writers, and teachers. He also provides first-time users with very helpful suggestions for CMC activities and caveats for integrating those activities into one's practice. Throughout, Blythe demonstrates that theory and practice must be in touch with one another if technology is to be used successfully. Next, Gail Hawisher and Cynthia L. Selfe focus their essay, "Teaching Writing at a Distance," on the experiences of women both as teachers and as learners in a distance education environment. They note that the problems encountered earlier by women in computer-mediated environments such as listservs still persist today for women entering the distance-learning environment. Hawisher and Selfe not only highlight women's experiences but also provide a venue in which women teaching in distance learning environments can voice their concerns, frustrations, and commitments regarding their students and teaching. New teachers will profit from the way in which the authors contextualize women's issues in technology-rich educational environments both historically and in terms of the potentials and pitfalls of using technology to teach. Although this essay focuses on women's experiences, it nevertheless offers many important guidelines for both men and women.

Section Four, "Teaching and Learning New Media," introduces new kinds of texts and textual concerns for teachers and students in computer-mediated teaching environments. Although most people in our culture have some awareness of and perhaps even some ability for surfing the World Wide Web, instructors will quickly realize that utilizing the Web to teach academic literacy is a complicated task. Similarly, computer technologies give students great control of an array of printing and publishing options. They can choose font style and sizes and can incorporate pictures and other media into their texts. However, just as we have been teaching students that traditional text forms require a certain rhetorical knowledge about what works well for specific purposes and audiences, we need to introduce them to the principles of visual rhetoric so that they can learn to implement effectively visual elements available through writing technologies into their writing. Sibylle Gruber, in "The Language of Web Texts," argues that although computer technologies such as the Web can be used to teach the rhetorical principles of purpose and audience analysis, teachers must help students learn to read the Web critically (in terms of content and design). Grounding her discussion in a sequence of assignments, Gruber demonstrates not only pedagogical interactions with the Web but also processes for preparing students to be critical Web users. In "Teaching with the World Wide Web," Carolyn Handa provides teachers new to using writing technologies with an important resource for utilizing and controlling such a large and potentially powerful resource as the Web. She reminds us early and often that we must use the Web as we would any technology in the service of teaching students academic literacy. Handa introduces new teachers to ways of incorporating the Web into their pedagogies—for displaying course information and connecting students and teachers, for involving students in collaborative and individual projects, for having students compile and post their work as web folios, and for using the Web as a research guide. Handa's insistence on the pedagogically sound use of this powerful source of technology and her inclusion of many relevant examples will well serve the needs of teachers.

In "With Eyes That Think, and Compose, and Think," Anne Wysocki challenges readers—and teachers of writing—to reexamine (or perhaps, examine for the first time) their assumptions about the way academic pages look. By answering questions readers might have—What is visual rhetoric? Why should we consider visual rhetoric when teaching with computers? What does visual rhetoric look like in writing classes?—she guides teachers to an understanding of how they can teach and work with visual rhetoric in their writing classes. Ultimately, she argues that learning to analyze and compose rhetorically effective communication requires attending not only to the meaning of the words but also to their visual components. Mary Hocks, in "Teaching and Learning Visual Rhetoric," argues that teachers encountering new media need to develop an understanding of visual literacy if they are to teach their students how to negotiate these new spaces as writers and readers. Being more than new texts to be decoded in classroom discussion, new media images present new challenges for students and instructors (as teachers and as users) developing critically, rhetorically sophisticated literacy. Through a series of assignments and her students' creation of new media forms, Hocks provides a map of this new terrain for new teachers as well as some suggestions for moving into it.

The final section, "Assigning and Assessing Student Writing," is one of the most crucial sections of the book. As Richard Miller has reminded us, "learning how to solicit, read and respond" to student writing is one of the most important and difficult components of teaching writing. As the summaries of many of the other essays in this book illustrate, finding ways to use technology in the service of teaching writing means making sure that the pedagogical purposes control the way we use technology. This is no more true than in assigning and assessing student writing. In this light, the three essays in this section not only make an important contribution to the new teacher's understanding of the best ways to use technology to teach but also provide a fitting conclusion to the volume.

In "Variations on a Theme," Karla Kitalong, Tracy Bridgeford, Michael Moore, and Dickie Selfe describe using technology narratives in the writing classroom. Just as writing literacy autobiographies can help students see reading and writing and themselves as readers and writers in new ways, so can producing technology narratives help students and teachers unpack unarticulated assumptions about technology. This kind of an assignment can serve as a model for teachers less experienced with technology who are trying to find an appropriate place for technology in their teaching. Such an assignment also helps students to understand the pervasiveness of technology in their lives and the relationship of technology to their work as students. Kitalong, Bridgeford, Moore, and Selfe illustrate the many ways such an assignment can be used, providing teachers with an abundant resource for creating assignments suitable for their individual institutions and students. Next, Chris M. Anson's essay on technology and student writing, "Responding to and Assessing Student Writing," resembles the good-news/bad-news routine. While emphatically illustrating that computer software cannot respond in any meaningful way to student writing, he does demonstrate many ways in which technology can enrich the way teachers respond to student writing. Such an introduction to technology and ways to respond to student writing should provide teachers with an important resource for choosing and experimenting with methods of using technology to respond to their students. Many of the uses of technology that Anson advocates (such as embedded commentary, online response, and macros) should suggest to teachers the many opportunities technology provides for enriching the kinds of response best able to facilitate their students' learning. In the final essay, "Evaluating Academic Hypertexts," Charles Moran and Ann Herrington focus on student hypertexts. Drawing on their own experience as new hypertext evaluators, they explore the process they experienced trying to read different kinds of texts in new ways. They structure their essay around the reading of two papers used in a scholarly article and available online—one a traditional research paper and the other a hypertext presentation posted on the Web. From this reading they confront the problem of how to evaluate both traditional and web-based student work. In extrapolating criteria for evaluation, Moran and Herrington also develop useful procedures for those inexperienced with reading and evaluating hypertexts. By describing the process of their evaluations and comparisons, they have created a useful tool and documented a process for the daunting task we all face when allowing web-based and hypertextual student assignments.

Having approached the design and editing of this volume with a strong sense of its necessity for writing teachers new to a computer environment and for the people (like us) who are supposed to prepare these teachers, we have learned much from these essays and from working with these contributors. This volume has grown well beyond our initial intent and does much more than merely introducing writing technologies to new teachers. This volume has taken us back to our roots and commitments to teaching and teacher preparation. We hope that it can help others beyond the target audience to do the same.

Acknowledgments

Of course, we'd like to begin by acknowledging the intellectual energy, hard work, and willing collegiality of the contributors. We had already learned so much from them before we began the book, and we continue to turn to them for lessons. We feel honored to have been trusted with their texts. As importantly, we must thank Suzanne Phelps Weir, of Houghton Mifflin Company, for her steady support and encouragement. This project came to life during a great dinner conversation with Suzanne; her enthusiasm and intellectual curiosity contributed greatly to the shape of the project, beginning with that initial conversation and continuing throughout its progress. Working with her has been one of the sustaining pleasures of this endeavor.

And finally, we would like to dedicate our work on this volume to our mothers—Mary Huot and Sherry Sakowitz—who encouraged us from a young age to be learners. A great deal of who we are as teachers is a result of their theories and practices. Although it isn't the pulp fiction novel they both want us to write (the kind of beach reading which they argue could make us rich), we hope they're pleased.

Notes

These articles are all ones which take an introductory posture in discussing some aspect of teaching writing with technology in higher education. It is not meant to be an exhaustive list but rather a suggestive one.

Works Cited

Barker, Thomas, and Fred Kemp. "Network Theory: A Postmodern Pedagogy for the Writing Classroom." *Computers and Community: Teaching Composition in the Twenty-first Century.* Ed. Carolyn Handa. Portsmouth, NH: Boynton/Cook, 1990. 1–27.

Carbone, Nick. "Trying to Create a Community: A First-Day Lesson Plan." *Computers and Composition* 10 (1993): 81–88.

Eldred, Janet. "Pedagogy in the Computer-Networked Classroom." *Computers and Composition* 8 (1991): 47–61.

Hawisher, Gail E. "Electronic Meetings of the Minds: Research, Electronic Conferences, and Composition Studies." *Re-imagining Computers and Composition: Teaching and Research in the Virtual Age.* Ed. Gail E. Hawisher and Paul LeBlanc. Portsmouth, NH: Boynton/Cook–Heinemann, 1992. 81–101.

Hawisher, Gail E., Paul LeBlanc, Charles Moran, and Cynthia L. Selfe. *Computers and the Teaching of Writing in American Higher Education, 1979–1994: A History.* Norwood, NJ: Ablex, 1996.

Hillocks, George. *Teaching Writing as Reflective Practice.* New York: Teachers College P, 1995.

Miller, Richard. "Composing English Studies: Toward a Social History of the Discipline." *College Composition and Communication* 45 (1994): 164–79.

Papert, Seymour. "Computer Criticism Versus Technocentric Thinking." *Educational Researcher* 16 (1987): 22–30.

Selfe, Cynthia L. "Preparing English Teachers for the Virtual Age: The Case for Technology Critics." *Re-imagining Computers and Composition: Teaching and Research in the Virtual Age.* Ed. Gail E. Hawisher and Paul LeBlanc. Portsmouth, NH: Boynton/Cook–Heinemann, 1992. 24–42.

Selfe, Cynthia L. "Redefining Literacy: The Multilayered Grammars of Computers." *Critical Perspectives on Computers and Composition Instruction.* Ed. Gail E. Hawisher and Cynthia L. Selfe. New York: Teachers College, 1989. 3–15.

Selfe, Richard. "What Are They Talking About? Computer Terms that English Teachers Might Need to Know." *Re-imagining Computers and Composition: Teaching and Research in the Virtual Age.* Ed. Gail E. Hawisher and Paul LeBlanc. Portsmouth, NH: Boynton/Cook–Heinemann, 1992. 207–18.

Sullivan, Patricia. "Taking Control of the Page: Electronic Writing and Word Publishing." *Evolving Perspectives on Computers and Composition Studies: Questions for the 1990s.* Ed. Gail E. Hawisher and Cynthia L. Selfe. Urbana, IL: NCTE, 1991.

Yagelski, Robert, and Sarah Powley. "Virtual Connections and Real Boundaries: Teaching Writing and Preparing Writing Teachers on the Internet." *Computers and Composition* 13 (1996): 25–36.

Zebroski, James. *Thinking Through Theory: Vygotskian Perspectives on the Teaching of Writing.* Portsmouth, NH: Boynton/Cook, 1994.

Appendix A
Books and Edited Collections on Writing and Technology

Blair, Kristine, and Pamela Takayoshi, eds. *Feminist Cyberscapes: Mapping Gendered Academic Spaces*. Norwood, NJ: Ablex, 1999.

Handa, Carolyn, ed. *Computers and Community: Teaching Composition in the Twenty-first Century*. Portsmouth, NH: Boynton/Cook, 1990.

Harrington, Susanmarie, Michael Day, and Rebecca Rickley, eds. *The Online Writing Classroom*. Cresskill, NJ: Hampton, 2000.

Hawisher, Gail E., and Paul LeBlanc, eds. *Re-imagining Computers and Composition: Teaching and Research in the Virtual Age*. Portsmouth, NH: Boynton/Cook, 1992.

Hawisher, Gail E., and Cynthia L. Selfe, eds. *Critical Perspectives on Computers and Composition Instruction*. New York: Teachers College, 1989.

Hawisher, Gail E., and Cynthia L. Selfe, eds. *Evolving Perspectives on Computers and Composition Studies: Questions for the 1990s*. Urbana, IL: NCTE, 1991.

Hawisher, Gail E., and Cynthia L. Selfe, eds. *Global Literacies and the World Wide Web*. New York: Routledge, 2000.

Hawisher, Gail E., and Cynthia L. Selfe, eds. *Passions, Pedagogies, and Twenty-first Century Technologies*. Logan: Utah State UP, 1999.

Palmquist, Mike, Kate Kiefer, James Hartvigsen, and Barbara Goodlew. *Transitions: Teaching in Computer-Supported and Traditional Classrooms*. Norwood, NJ: Ablex, 1998.

Palmquist, Mike, and Donald E. Zimmerman. *Writing with a Computer*. Reading, MA: Allyn & Bacon, 1998.

Selfe, Cynthia L. *Computer-assisted Instruction in Composition: Create Your Own*. Urbana, IL: NCTE, 1986.

Selfe, Cynthia L. *Creating a Computer-Supported Writing Facility: A Blueprint for Action*. Boston: Houghton Mifflin, 1989.

Selfe, Cynthia L. *Technology and Literacy in the Twenty-first Century: The Importance of Paying Attention*. Carbondale: Southern Illinois UP, 1999.

Selfe, Cynthia L., and Deborah Holdstein, eds. *Computers and Writing: Theory, Research, Practice*. New York: MLA, 1990.

Selfe, Cynthia L., and Susan Hilligoss, eds. *Literacy and Computers: The Complications of Teaching and Learning with Technology*. New York: MLA, 1994.

Selfe, Cynthia L., Dawn Rodrigues, and William R. Oates, eds. *Computers in English and Language Arts: The Challenge of Teacher Education*. Urbana, IL: NCTE, 1989.

SECTION I:
WRITING TECHNOLOGIES FOR COMPOSITION PEDAGOGIES

Techno-Pedagogical Explorations: Toward Sustainable Technology-Rich Instruction

DICKIE SELFE
Michigan Technological University

Those reading this collection are probably considering how they might, appropriately, integrate sustainable[1] technologies into their pedagogy. Perhaps you've been convinced by Cynthia Selfe's warnings about the consequences of *not* paying attention to technology and the need to develop critical technological literacies for the twenty-first century (cf., Selfe, 1999)? Or maybe you've been arm wrestled into taking on a hybrid (partially online and partially face-to-face) course or a class taught at a distance (cf., Selfe et al., 2001). Perhaps you've read or seen exciting applications of communication technologies in workshops or other classes and want to experiment yourself.[2] Perhaps communication technologies just seem like an inevitable, "natural" part of the modern landscape, and you can't imagine *not* enacting that part of the culture in your class. (Many people apply words like *overdetermination* [cf., Feenberg] and *ideology* [cf., Eagleton] to this sort of observation. Eagleton and Feenberg provide useful theoretical approaches to these concepts.) Whatever interests teachers bring to this task, I have found the following set of reminders of great use to the faculty, staff, and graduate students that I've worked with over the years. Indeed, I have to reconsider them myself each year, each term, each time I teach with technology.

- All technology-rich (TR) pedagogy is experimental.
- Develop locally sustainable teaching practices. Develop locally sustainable teaching practices. Develop locally sustainable teaching practices.
- Don't let the technologies themselves drive your pedagogy.
- Get to know your students, their technological attitudes and abilities, and their expectations for technology-rich instruction.
- Sequence assignments.

- Assess what you do as you go along.
- Don't take yourself and your efforts too seriously.
- For each TR experiment, use the PAR system (preparation, activity, reflection).
- Add a "critical component" to each lesson.
- Network (in the interpersonal sense) with those around you.
- Talk to great teachers from all disciplines and collaborate with them.
- Recruit students as TAs for the next round of TWT (teaching with technology).
- Share your insights with other scholars/teachers.
- Help develop a culture of support for TWT at your institution.

Though these "reminders" can be read in any order, they do tend to build on each other. To make them more useful, wherever appropriate I've included, with the short justification for each claim, several supplemental items:

- a techno-pedagogical exploration (an overview of a technology-rich lesson)
- a short description of the technology itself
- some additional characteristics of the technology being considered
- a warning about the technology itself or the activity that I'm proposing

All Technology-Rich Pedagogy Is Experimental

How can this be? English studies scholars/teachers have been at this since the early 1980s! The fact is that the interface or interfaces that we use, students' lives, access levels, the underlying networks, people's placements on the technological learning curve, the material conditions that surround the class and students, the curriculum, and everyone's expectations are all unstable and change term by term, sometimes even class session by class session. I have to remind myself of this fact every day and confront students with the experimental nature of teaching with technology (TWT). I do this in order to engage them in the experiment. As a teacher, that's part of my responsibility, along with the need to attend to students' techno-pedagogical experiences as carefully (though perhaps not as often) as I do their literacy needs. After all, the two (literacy and technology) are intimately connected (cf., C. Selfe).

Some of these strategies (that I've used in the past) help control these instabilities, and some use them to the class's advantage. This first exploration, on web-based threaded discussions, also illustrates how I try to engage students in the experimental nature of technology use.

Techno-Pedagogical Exploration: Generating Web-based Threaded Discussions

Even the most stable and taken-for-granted application of technology in a class is experimental. Web-based threaded discussions are a good example.

They are based on the old bulletin-board systems that accompanied the earliest networked computers into the classroom. But even these relatively long-lived applications are unstable in the senses previously mentioned, so with students, I frame their use in our class as experimental: "Together we will experiment with online discussions in order to use the transcripts of those discussions in subsequent assignments or in class activities."

First, however, here's a brief description of threaded discussions. They are considered *pull* technologies (as opposed to *push* technologies, such as email) that try to "pull" the participant into the discussion. In other words, you have to go somewhere (in this case through a web browser) to get to the conversation; it doesn't necessarily come to you. After the teacher sets up the discussion forum or topic, participants (those in the class and invited guests) type in a URL (universal resource location or web address), log on to the system, select the appropriate discussion topic or forum, then read and respond to the prompt or to other participants' comments. Different versions of the World Wide Web-based threaded discussion systems can be found in almost all course-management packages (certainly in WebCT and BlackBoard). There are also free and commercial stand-alone systems available that your network administrator might want to install. Several useful attributes of threaded discussions include the fact that they are immediately archived and remain threaded or indented relative to one another. (For an example of what they look like, go to <http://skipper.hu.mtu.edu/~rselfe>, log in as a guest, and then click on one of the workshop or course discussions there.) These discussions also remain available to students and teachers for further study and use without involving any extra work. An additional characteristic is that threaded discussion systems often let you and students attach documents (e.g., Microsoft Word, PowerPoint, web or HTML pages, or image files) to a message. This is one way of allowing your students to "hand in" materials remotely from any web browser. Teachers can also distribute documents this way.

The fact that the discussions are archived and that students and teachers can usually visit them from any browser on or off campus at any time of day is the basis for most of my explorations with these systems. These are often called *asynchronous* discussions, discussions not held in real time. Like most teachers, I set up discussion prompts or require student discussion leaders to do so and give grades based on participation (honest attempts to engage with the material). Because I want these discussions to be discursive and interactive, not prepared drafted documents, I usually encourage one-time posts that promote language fluency, and I avoid grading the surface level aspects of student writing. (However, you could easily do the opposite: ask students to go through several drafts before posting responses. But if you do this, be prepared to provide more time for the "discussion" to unfold.) I often structure the discussion by noting who is responsible for what portions of the conversation: Group One provides the initial posts, Group Two is responsible for responses to those posts, and Group Three evaluates the content of the initial posts and responses (with extra credit given to those who jump into the discussion). The groups then rotate responsibilities as the term progresses.

So what's exploratory about this? How do we engage students in this exploration? My goal is to build the discussions into the projects or purposes of the class, so I tell students about my expectations and remind them of those goals each time we use the technology. For instance, I often tell the class that I expect the discussions to help us better understand each other's reactions to a novel that we're reading (not just my own and those of a few vocal students). Or I explain that we should expect these discussions to help us better understand some primary material we are examining. For instance, frequently these days, I have students read their classmates' own Technology Autobiographies (TA) (see the Kitalong et al. essay in this collection) and expect them to make observations about material that will be useful to current or future classes. In both cases, I explain to them that we are creating a "knowledge base" (our own little database of ideas and observations) that I hope will be useful as they write papers later in the class. Then, at the end of the term, as *I* evaluate their participation, I have *them* evaluate how well my techno-pedagogy worked. Did we actually create a knowledge base? Was it really useful as a resource for future papers or reports? How did the technology work? How could we improve the process we used?

However, heed this warning: Never depend entirely on a system like this one without frequently backing up the conversations you plan on using or grading. Either make sure that the systems administrator is backing them up daily or do so yourself by printing them out or copying them onto another medium such as a floppy disk, a zip disk, or your local hard drive. Remember also that on many systems a class's conversations are wiped out each term to make room on servers for subsequent class discussions. Be sure to find out when this will happen and how you can back up your discussions if you need to keep them.

Commit Yourself to Developing Locally Sustainable Teaching Practices

In order to sustain your own interest and commitment, imagine practical pedagogical objectives that you believe a communication technology (or technologies) might help you accomplish, one that would be difficult to accomplish in your traditional class (however you define *traditional*). Then apply a structured use of the technology to that objective, watch how the community of students reacts to your approach, and let them help you redesign the approach to better accomplish the objective the next time. Let students in on your objectives, and explain them over and over during the term. This is experimental work; students aren't used to teachers being so forthright with them, and, in my experience, they won't "get it" unless you keep reframing it for them as the term progresses.

Techno-Pedagogical Exploration: Publishing Student Work

Do you want your students to consider and write to real audiences? Do you want them to take responsibility for their own work? Do you want to connect your students with people in other parts of the country or world? For many teachers the answer is "Yes." These are often the kinds of objectives teachers use to justify the publishing of student work and, to that end, the use of communication technologies. For years teachers have been publishing print versions of their students' work, but the process was expensive and the copies not often distributed very widely. All of the objectives previously listed, though, are common and valuable in composition classes, and they can all be implemented through electronic publishing inexpensively and quickly and distributed widely if students prepare materials to be published on the Internet.[3] There are, of course, many digital media to choose from: text-only systems like threaded discussions and email as well as multimedia environments like web pages and Adobe Acrobat PDF documents. Choose a medium in which you are comfortable, to which students have easy access, and which is stable and reliable at your institution. Make that medium your platform of choice for the course. Such sustainable teaching practices are important because the exploratory nature of all technology-rich instruction requires us to invest in these practices, refining them over time.

I begin thinking about student publishing efforts by first imagining a general topic for the class and then immediately constructing audiences who might be interested in reading the student writing that would result. These days I do not require publishing or promise that all students will be published. Instead, I set up review boards (made up of former students, teachers, professionals, or students voted on by the class) to choose which material is suitable for publication. I often give students credit or extra credit for being involved in the production phase of publishing as early-content editors, layout designers, proofreaders, graphic and image designers, and usability testers. If I have time, I try to have prospective audiences read and respond to drafts so that students can hear from audience members before final publishing decisions are made. But the main criterion for evaluating this technology-rich effort is whether or not it is sustainable—from my perspective (work load, expertise, access), from the students' perspective (work load, learning curve for publishing technologies, access), *and* from the recruited audience's perspective (work load, usable/interesting final products, and access).

Note these warnings: There are substantial intellectual property (IP) issues involved in publishing student work. IP issues are important these days and may well comprise part of the instruction in your class. Make sure you check with other teachers and administrators about the kinds of permission necessary for publishing. You can get around permissions to some extent by publishing on password-protected sites (like WebCT and Blackboard) and giving out the password to a limited number of readers. But it's best to get permissions anyway. Realize, also, that self-publishing places the students and teacher in a "marketing" position. By that I mean that you have to market or establish an audience for student compositions. Just putting work on the Internet is *not* going to ensure a readership. If you start planning by imagining and then actually contacting sympathetic readers—teachers at your institution, at other institutions, and in other countries—or by requesting help from former students, from professionals whom you know, or from community groups, you will have already done your part to generate an audience for your students' publications.

Commit yourself to developing locally sustainable teaching practices. Yes, doing so *is* important :-). Really, it's as important as everything else combined.

Don't Let the Technologies Themselves Drive Your Pedagogy

A negative corollary: Don't simply engage in a technology exploration because you have heard of or seen interesting things happen in other teachers' classes unless you and the students enter that digital space together, explicitly as explorers. Early adopters of technologies have usually developed sustainable pedagogies over a number of years. They (myself included) are also notorious for telling only half the story in descriptions of their and their students' experiences; these often include only a few of their and their students' motivations, a smattering of details about the material conditions under which they work, and a couple of the steps toward success (when there are actually about twenty, some of which they may not be able to articulate!). This is why online and local mentoring is so important and another reason why those new to technology-rich instruction find the process so experimental. However, over the years you are quite likely see demonstrations of, hear about, or have new technologies that seem to have pedagogical promise imposed on you.

Get to Know Your Students and Their Technological Attitudes, Abilities, and Expectations

Techno-Pedagogical Exploration: Student-Led Web Development

The example of publishing student work has provided me with multiple opportunities to learn new web techniques from advanced students in my classes. I rarely hold a class these days without having students write a technology autobiography (see the Kitalong et al. essay in this volume for more details) early in the term. I find, consistently, that some students enter the course with what I would call advanced literacy skills related to web development. These students' skills and access to advanced software and hardware allow them to manipulate and incorporate images, animations, audio clips, and video clips and to place them artfully onto web pages. Or these students may have programming skills that enable them to create interactive surveys through which the class might gather information related to their research from online visitors. As long as I remain flexible enough and open to valuing my students' new literacy skills, and I start early enough, there is no reason why, together, we can't explore and assess these new technologies critically.

I usually require that these technically advanced students not only *produce* materials, interfaces, or media for the class but also demonstrate how they created these products for the class and show us where other students (and I!) can go to acquire the skills that they possess. As a group, we spend time analyzing the rhetorical effectiveness of their web development. Thus, students can become experts in the class; we all apply rhetorical skills to the end result, and most of us learn a bit about next-generation web tools. I often try to stay in touch with students who seem to have an interest in new media and demonstrate some skill in working with others. They are likely recruits, consultants, or assistants for my future technology-rich classes.

Techno-Pedagogical Exploration: Composing in Many Media

Try letting your students "compose" in many media, at least as an extra-credit exercise. They often have access to their own systems such as web-page editors, animation programs, image manipulation software, and video-editing programs. But don't stop with flexible assignments. If some students are getting credit for composing in systems that other students can't afford or cannot access, require a demonstration of or an introduction to the media that these students are using. Have them provide the names and sites of freeware or for-profit vendors so that the rest of the class can benefit from these media students' expertise. Be forewarned, however: Access issues usually drive the logistics of these media explorations—the composing students' access, your access (for grading purposes), your in-class access, and, of course, your other students' access. You'll find, however, that with encouragement students can be amazingly and even legally resourceful.

Sequence Assignments

One-time activities involving technologies are almost never of great value in and of themselves. That's why workshops that give teachers one-time experiences can really never match or be highly predictive of what actually goes on in classes over time. The systematic use of a technology over time is an experiment in and of itself. I keep reminding myself that the technology experience of my students has to be part of an ongoing set of events that feed into each other.

Techno-Pedagogical Exploration: Synchronous Discussions (Online Chatting)

Online chat systems have been around for a long time as well, though they are obviously an acquired taste. Many of my recent students have had a good deal of experience with systems like AOL's Instant Messenger, through which they communicate with friends and parents locally as well as at a distance. If you press students for the rules of engagement on these systems, they tend to have worked out very sophisticated (though often unstated) guidelines: They only use certain chat spaces, only talk to X number of people at a time, only give out their ID to folks with whom they want to stay in contact, and so on. I learned from these students that classroom chat exercises need their own sets of guidelines or etiquette, and I apply these when evaluating and having students evaluate the transcripts from chat sessions. Most online class-management tools include chat areas (WebCT and Blackboard), though my students have consistently rated these as being much worse than most other types of systems such as AOL's Instant Messenger and the many educational MOOs currently being established at universities. (Don't ask about that name—it takes too long to explain—but do visit and explore these interesting online environments.)

In one of my favorite explorations—if I have access to a lab of networked computers with recent web browsers installed—I have students watch a movie that's of some relevance to the class. Before starting the show, I have them log into a chat system and join a small group in a specific chat room set up for the class. I turn on the recorder in that room so we will have a record of their conversation. Usually, I have prepared a note describing what we have already agreed to in class: "During this showing of *The Matrix*, your group's job is to attend carefully to X as the film unfolds. Later you will review the transcript of the conversation and write a report about your group's observations and present it to the class by next Friday." After all students are in their virtual places, I begin the film and let them chat away as they watch it. What results seems a bit like being in a theater and being able to hear people's thoughts about a movie as progresses. It is difficult for me to keep up with the film and the conversation threads in real time. For most students, however, this seems to be much less of a concern. They watch the film (it is best to choose one that students have already seen), make observations, talk about others' perceptions, and relate personal experiences—all simultaneously. In essence, they are exploring a media experience that is largely beyond their teacher's ability. After the film is over, educational MOOs allow the teacher to email the transcripts within seconds to the class groups. In that way they can then complete the rest of the assignment by the next period.

An additional characteristic of most chat systems is that, like web-based threaded discussion systems and email lists, they allow you to invite guests into your class who would normally not be able to attend. I frequently invite experts or authors of the readings I am using to join classes online. It's a short-term commitment with low overhead in terms of preparation. You'll be surprised at who will come. But you have to ask them!

Warning: Become acquainted with whichever chat system you will be using well before experimenting with it in class. The comfort level for chat systems is only attained with time and useful practice. Most teachers start by meeting online with trusted colleagues and then joining real-time professional conversations, where they can ask questions of experienced teachers who have taught with these systems for years. Also, get to know the ins and outs of your students' access to these systems. If you set up a virtual class where students log in from home, some of their machines might not connect, so you should have practice sessions before big "events" and be ready with a backup plan if the system isn't working or isn't working well (i.e., have those students who are experiencing difficulty come into a lab setting for the session).

Assess What You Do as You Go Along.

Have some way of assessing technically mediated assignments as well as students' written compositions incrementally over the term. When *you* assess student compositions, have *your students* assess the technology-rich activities that led up to their final draft. But there are other ways of creating a dialogue between students and teachers if you have access to technologies such as email-list software. Most institutions provide email accounts for students and faculty these days, and some provide email-list services as well.[4] These "lists," often set up to encourage information exchanges between students and teachers, can be used in a number of ways that seem appropriate to the learning that we all hope goes on in the classroom.

Email-list software on a campus server, which is usually serviced by a central computing department, provides ways for designated individuals to set up lists. The first job of the teacher is to find the person on campus who is in charge of setting up lists or to learn the automated procedure for this process at her institution. (This last comment, of course, is true of all the systems mentioned in this volume.) Teachers and/or students create a name appropriate for the purpose of the list discussion (for example, *techno-assess@genericU .edu* or *Eng101.22@genericU.edu*) and submit that name and all the email addresses of the individuals who will be participating to the person in charge. Many institutions have this system automated with the registrar's office so that teachers can go to a web page, fill out a form, and submit it. All students registered for that course are then automatically subscribed to the email list. I often set up several lists for every class with different purposes for each. The Eng101.22 list might be an informational one for section 22 of a first-year class that is intended mainly to provide logistical information about the class: "We'll meet in the lab this Thursday. Don't forget to bring your draft of . . ." or "Dr. Selfe, I can't get the class web site to come up on my computer."

Techno-Pedagogical Exploration: Email-List Assessment, a Form of Dissensus

One way to assess any aspect of a class during the term, including techno-pedagogical activities, is to set up an email list like the one called *techno-assess@genericU.edu.* As opposed to the very structured way in which I set up the web-based threaded discussions discussed earlier, teachers can just as easily provide students with a forum for holding open discussions about the technology components used in the class. Teachers can choose not to be involved at all (collect mail unread throughout the term until after grades are in), or they can be readers of student comments or active participants in the discussions. Open discussions are interesting and often quite blunt. I try to warn teachers new to these technologies that if they ask students to comment honestly, they should expect them to do just that. We aren't always going to like what students have to say. I have gathered some evidence from many previous list discussions that indicates that this environment is *not* well suited to "coming to consensus." Instead, email lists often promote dissensual conversations containing many issues that remain unresolved. Students need to be made aware of this situation as well. That's why I suggest using email lists along with more anonymous methods of assessment. In this case I might ask students to discuss the pros and cons of a particular activity on the list and then to submit paper copies of their final comments to me individually after the conversation has run its course.

Email lists can be set up so that "replies" either go to the list (promoting open discussion) or to the person who wrote the initial post (promoting more individual exchanges off the list). I suggest having replies go to the list if you want to promote discussions. This is best if you use email lists to invite experts or other out-of-class participants to join your discussions. Other potential "outside" contributors are students who participated in similar events in your previous classes. As I said before, you simply have to keep track of these folks and ask them to help. Many will.

I rarely encourage open discussions in chat systems or on email lists unless the class has developed a netiquette document that outlines the kinds of "rhetorical moves" that are appropriate on the list.

Don't Take Yourself and Your Efforts Too Seriously

Don't take yourself and your efforts too seriously. Have fun and let your students have fun. The chat exploration previously described is fun for most (though not *all*) students. But teachers have to have fun as well! Most of us feel guilty unless it's productive fun, so I suggest you set up something similar to our TWIT (Teaching with Information Technologies) sessions.

Techno-Pedagogical Exploration: TWIT-Like Sessions

First, set up a name for your group that invites play. Make the explorations informative and fun and don't require much preparation by the presenters. Have food and establish an informal, regular meeting time. (For years, we've held brown bag lunches at noon on Fridays.) Tap "experts" who have already used some system (email, word-processing response tools, the World Wide Web, and so on) and after a very short presentation, have people use the system and play with it, exploring one thing and then another, learning from those around them. If someone has the energy, have that person send out a short message describing what you all have learned during the session for others who weren't able to come, thus sowing the seeds for your next session.

Playful engagement is one of the primary survival skills for those trying to integrate communication technologies appropriately into their classes. However, playful activities don't often convince administrators that important work is getting done, and you may be blessed with a "serious" administrator. Nevertheless, at these informal meetings you should have a good time and then send out summaries of the event that focus on the actual work accomplished. The fun part will be spread by word of mouth soon enough.

Use the PAR System: Preparation/Activity/Reflection

Each time you engage in digital explorations, use the PAR system: preparation, activity, reflection. It can be tedious to think through the following questions before implementing any one technology-rich activity. But this method helps you structure the planning of a technology-rich activity, and the questions quickly become second nature, a part of your normal teaching procedure if they aren't already. Many teachers experienced with technologies would argue that you can overplan these activities and thereby lose the spontaneity and value of the collaboration that might occur. I believe, however, that teachers new to any strange medium are uncertain about the value of the activities and therefore need to take a more structured approach to these online events. What follows is simply a list of questions to ask yourself as you prepare for an activity, as you engage in that activity, and as you reflect on or use the materials that resulted from the event(s).

Preparation

- Is it clear to you and to others what is motivating the technology-rich event or activity?
- Have the likely outcomes of the online event been explained to everyone?
- Do all participants have access to the necessary, working technology/ technologies?
- Have you clarified where and when the event will occur (in some cases, include time zones!)?
- Have you checked with the technicians responsible for the system that you will use and asked them or a support person to be available in case of emergencies?
- Do you have all the necessary documentation ready?
- If necessary, have you conducted practice or training sessions with the participants ahead of time?
- Do you have a backup plan if the system or activity is not working?
- Do participants know the etiquette guidelines you would like them to follow when conversing online?
- If appropriate, have you sent out reminders to distant participants reminding them where, when, and why you will be meeting?
- Have you actually run through all of the activities that you will be asking others to engage in?

Activity (Ask during the activity)

- Is your backup plan ready to be implemented?
- Have you decided how or whether *you* will be participating and in what capacity?
- Do you have a method of "capturing" the session or session outcomes for the reflective events to follow? (If nothing else, have people freewrite on a piece of paper about the important moments, issues, or problems that come up immediately after the activity or event.)
- Are the support persons who will help participants navigate and use the technologies present?
- Do you have the email addresses or phone numbers of distant participants, if appropriate, in case there are technical problems during the online event?

Reflection

- How can you use the conversation or materials that resulted from the event?
- How can your students use the conversation?
- Can the conversation be useful to visitors? If so, how can you make it available to them in a form that they can actually use?
- If you have had an online conversation, have you asked the students to pick out the gems and clinkers of the conversation? (*Gems* are the valuable ideas that surface. *Clinkers* are the half-baked ideas that need to be developed in more detail.)
- Do you have some way of assessing whether the outcomes you expected were met or whether other unexpected outcomes resulted (for better or worse)?
- What revisions to the event/activity can you imagine? Write these down immediately!

Add a "Critical Component" to Each Lesson Wherever Possible

English studies professionals generally do *not* want students to become habitual users and consumers of communication technologies per se. We do, however, introduce more students to these technologies than almost any other discipline and are therefore implicated in the technological additions that seem to be sprouting up around us. My "small potent gesture" (C. Selfe, 1999) in response to this trend is to encourage students to be critical, thoughtful users of these systems. I try to indicate the seriousness of my intent by building into almost every use of technology some reflective or critical component. Even the most ubiquitous communication technologies are ripe for critical analysis. The following are a few examples.

Technology	Critical Component(s)
Email	Talk about quoting with permission, privacy issues, overreliance, or avoiding face-to-face interactions.
Word processing	Talk about the ease of copying/nonattribution, appropriate uses of spell or grammar checkers, commenting, and use of other tools.
Web pages	Talk about intellectual property and plagiarism or the credibility of source materials.
Scanning	Talk about copyright and fair use doctrines.
Synchronous environments (chatting)	Talk about civil exchanges, online communities, or the value and dangers of adopting an alternative online persona.

Network with Those Around You: Some Final Strategies Toward Sustainable Technology-Rich Instruction.

Techno-Pedagogical Exploration: Formal and Informal Communication Across the Curriculum (CAC) Events

Some of the most interesting and productive idea-sharing sessions that I've attended have included people from a number of other disciplines who are also interested in communication activities. At Clemson University, for example, there is a formal Communication Across the Curriculum program. In their CAC alumni session (Spring 2001), I heard about some amazingly productive service-learning approaches that involved faculty in the architecture and English departments and elementary school students and teachers (Sustainable School Yard projects). Those at institutions without formal CAC programs can draw people from around the institution by suggesting, holding, or attending informal communication technology sessions. How do you use effective class web pages? How can you "publish" student work? How do you use threaded discussions in class? The technology is the hook, but the conversation should quickly turn to talk of pedagogy. Consider using the TWIT meetings previously described to attract faculty and staff from across campus.

- **Talk to great teachers, get to know them, and then collaborate.**

  Read about, talk to, and listen carefully to people who seem to be excellent teachers—not just those who teach with technology, but anyone (in any discipline!) who seems to engage in interesting, productive teaching activities.

Collaborate locally if possible with teachers who have similar classes with similar objectives or with teachers who have complementary course objectives (several such collaborations are detailed in the 1999 NCTE collection *Electronic Communication Across the Curriculum*). But also consider working with folks from a distance, even short distances. (Cross-town rivalries, for instance, are motivational and give students a reason to communicate with each other.) Going to regional and national conferences and connecting with people gives you a chance to meet new folks and an excuse (which I always need) to go up and talk to presenters after a session. Once you get to know each other, imagine technology-mediated, cross-class, cross-institution units that will support both of your classes' objectives.

- **Share your insights.**

  Every time you conduct a techno-pedagogical exploration, whether it works or not, share your insights (formally, in presentations or publications, or informally, in hallway conversations or over email lists like TechRhet) with a community of scholars/teachers. We are all experimenting, all flailing about here in this changing educational world.

- **Finally, help develop a culture of support for teaching with technology at your institution.**[5] Try to invest a little time in one of the following areas or efforts. Over time, if enough people at your institution do so, the culture supporting your work with technology-rich instruction will change around you.

  - Start a Student Technology Assistant program for which students are recruited, trained, and paid to provide desk-side support for teachers using communication technologies.

  - Set up or lobby for faculty/staff technology experiences.

    - Weekly meetings: informal, self-determining, alternating between hands-on work and discussions of theory and classroom practice, with weekly meeting notes disseminated throughout the department or college
    - Term-by-term, multiple-day workshops: Survey faculty, develop topics for workshops, provide hands-on demonstrations with plenty of support, schedule project work time
    - Paid or supported attendance at an intensive one- or two-week workshop

  - Become involved at an institutional level.

    - Lobby for representation on technology committees.
    - Attend to institutional initiatives that might include things like a student lab fee task force, security/privacy initiatives, distance education efforts, World Wide Web policies on the teaching and ownership of online materials.

- Apply for local grants.

- Work with others to create and maintain effective, technology-rich teaching and learning environments that provide adequate, safe student access to appropriate technologies, provide instructors who want to develop innovative teaching practices with a place to do so, and provide all interested teachers with access to digital literacy environments.

You can't do it all, but neither can any one other person in your department or institution.

A Conclusion?

There is no way to conclude this process. It's experimental; it changes; there are guidelines but few rules; there are many people who will continue to try to figure out where technology-rich and online systems are taking our first-year classes, pedagogies, and curricula. If we connect with trusted others and take slow, sustainable, reasoned steps into the swirling waters of technology-rich instruction, few will be swept away. See you in the shallow eddies.

Notes

[1] The word *sustainable* has a wealth of meaning for me (R. Selfe, 1998). In short, we want locally sustainable technologies because we can't afford to invest time and money in instructional systems that will change overnight; successful teachers explore technology-rich pedagogy over a long period of time, and because these efforts should be tied intimately to changes in our understandings of literacy and learning, neither of which are stable (see the section "All Technology-Rich Pedagogy Is Experimental" for more justification of sustainability).

[2] Cynthia Selfe and I have been running one- and two-week summer institutes for over fifteen years. If you would like to see information about them, point your browsers to <http://www.hu.mtu.edu/CIWIC> and <http://www.hu.mtu.edu/ECAC>.

[3] For descriptions of wide-ranging approaches and issues related to online publishing, see John Barber and Dene Grigar's collection.

[4] Off-campus, free services are also available. I use Yahoomail.com to set up email lists. Yahoo! provides automatic archives of email conversations as well.

[5] For a more complete description of radically different strategies for creating a supportive community at your institution, take a look at Coffield et al. (285–318) and Kemp (267–284) in *The On-line Writing Classroom*, ed. R. Rickly, S. Harrington, and M. Day (Mountain View, CA: Hampton Press, 2000).

Works Cited

Barber, John, and Dene Grigar, eds. *New Words, New Worlds: Exploring Pathways for Writing about and in Electronic Environments.* Mountain View, CA: Hampton, 2001.

Coffield, Kate, Joe Essid, Jane Lasarenko, Linda Record, Dickie Selfe, and Hugh Stilley. "Surveying the Electronic Landscape: A Guide to Forming a Supportive Teaching Community." *The On-line Writing Classroom.* Ed. R. Rickly, S. Harrington, and M. Day. Mountain View, CA: Hampton, 2000. 285–318.

DeVoss, Danielle, Dawn Hayden, Cynthia Selfe, and Dickie Selfe. "Distance Education: Sites of Political Agency." *Moving a Mountain.* Ed. E. E. Schell and P. L. Stock. Urbana, IL: NCTE, 2001. 261–86.

Eagleton, Terry. *Ideology: An Introduction.* London: Verso, 1991.

Feenberg, Andrew. *Critical Theory of Technology.* New York: Oxford UP, 1991.

Kemp, Fred. "Surviving in English Departments: The Stealth Computer-based Writing Program." *The On-line Writing Classroom.* Ed. R. Rickly, S. Harrington, and M. Day. Mountain View, CA: Hampton, 2000. 267–84.

Reiss, Donna, Richard Selfe, and Art Young, eds. *Electronic Communication Across the Curriculum.* Urbana, IL: NCTE, 1998.

Selfe, Cynthia L. *Technology and Literacy in the Twenty-first Century: The Importance of Paying Attention.* Carbondale: Southern Illinois UP, 1999.

Technology as Teacher: Augmenting (Transforming) Writing Instruction

JANET CAREY ELDRED AND LISA TONER
University of Kentucky

> The usual metaphor for everyday software is the tool, but that doesn't seem to be right here. PowerPoint[1] is more like a suit of clothes, or a car, or plastic surgery. You take it out with you. You are judged by it—you insist on being judged by it. . . . But PowerPoint also has a private, interior influence. It edits ideas. It [carries with it] an oddly pedantic, prescriptive opinion—about the way we should think. (Parker, 76)

Computers as teachers—it's an image many of us resist. It conjures visions of a human work force replaced by robotic figures, an Orwellian nightmare of technological surveillance, canned instruction, and thought control—the Stepford teachers. But as Ian Parker hypothesizes in a piece written for the *New Yorker*, computers—or more specifically, computer software programs—are "oddly pedantic"; we learn from them overtly through software designed to teach a certain skill (such as where to put a comma to avoid the dreaded "splice") and intrinsically through use and mere proximity, in word processing or checking out recipes on the Net. In this sense, computers do indeed "teach," and we do indeed learn from them. As we eagerly embrace this technology and the possibilities it offers for enhancing writing instruction, we must become aware of how computer technology does not simply augment traditional teaching strategies—supporting and making these more student-driven and hands-on. In fact, computer technology "augments" traditional teaching strategies in only the weakest sense of providing "support." No matter how traditional, low-tech, and paper-driven a classroom is, computers have transformed and will continue to transform writing instruction. The widespread ownership and use of personal computers inside and outside of the writing classroom have changed not only the ways in which we compose essays and conduct research, even the very ideas about writing that teachers and students hold, but also, as Peter Mortensen's recent work reveals, our complicity in the sometimes harmful managerial practices and environmental consequences of manufacturing hard drives, paper suitable for laser and ink jet printers, and fiber optic networks.[2] Someone somewhere produces these goods, Mortensen reminds us, and the local community and environment are affected by that production. As Myron Tuman argued in 1996, digital literacy "is likely to entail a radical reworking of all the most basic terms and practices of our print-based society." Some would argue it now *has*. Writing teachers integrating pedagogy and technology are pivotal agents in these changes.

Moreover, as Cynthia Selfe's analysis of President Clinton's 1996 Technology Literary Challenge details,[3] the serious social inequities related to computer use—known to many as the "digital divide"—continue to widen. Yet Selfe doesn't advocate our avoidance of technology, our casting out of the unclean. Rather, her thesis is this: Whether or not we teach with computers— or even use computers—we're complicit with the digital technologies that have changed our world, not always for the best, and that thus demand our critical attention, our engagement. She maintains that "we have come to understand technology as 'just another instructional tool' that we choose either to use or to ignore. Working from this context, we divide ourselves into two *meaningless* camps: those who use computers to teach classes and those who don't. Both groups feel virtuous about their choices, and both manage to lose sight of the real issue: how to use technology, or relate to it, in ways that are productive and meaningful" (144). Selfe urges writing teachers to commit to "paying attention" to the manifold meanings and consequences of cultural literacy in a digital society. In more recent presentations, Selfe underscores the fact that students—both traditional and nontraditional—are coming to our classrooms having been changed by new digital technologies.[4] She argues that "teachers who are educated in and committed to print culture" might be less receptive—even suspicious of—new digital literacies that students bring to the chalkboards and desktops of even the most print-bound of writing classrooms. To be effective teachers of writing at the turn of the twenty-first century, she counsels, we need to make ourselves receptive to and critical of the ways in which new digital literacies can further self-awareness and self-presentation, extend social and civic platforms, and, of course, facilitate engaged learning. To ignore technology, Selfe contends, is to ignore our students' backgrounds, experiences, and knowledges and to undermine our best pedagogical intentions. Worse, she points out, failing to engage digital literacies positions us to be victims of, rather than voices in, policy decisions that affect the ways we can do our jobs.

Selfe's argument lends urgency to the project of teaching new literacies responsibly and challenges even those writing teachers on campuses far from the cutting-edge of technology use. Whereas other authors in this volume detail how to use technology to teach emerging literacies such as web pages and multimedia presentations, in this chapter we explain how new technologies can be integrated at various phases of the writing process without requiring teachers to have access to the latest technology or a wired classroom. In other words, this chapter assumes, especially in its organization, a context of production of the kinds of traditional nonfiction compositions written in college classrooms at the vast majority of institutions in the United States, from two-year and liberal arts colleges to regional campuses and Research I institutions. The traditional—print-based—way of mapping institutions of higher learning is by degrees granted. Yet in terms of the possibilities for teaching writing with technology, we might map this landscape differently. *Technology-rich campuses* provide faculty access to the newest technology so that they are easily able, and often expected, to teach and research with multimedia. However, many colleges and universities are what we call *technology bound*. At such institutions, practice falls short of established, often quite lofty, goals. Although all students at a technology-bound campus may have access, say, to minimal technology such as word processing, email, and web browsing, teacher development and equipment allocations lag so that an infrastructure is present, but instructional use is hampered. Such institutions are therefore "bound" in both the progressive and the restrictive senses of the word: They are determined to use technology yet restrained by material and human resources. Finally, some institutions are simply *ill-equipped* to engage new digital literacies. At these campuses, technology is often seen as the new kid on the block, unwelcome in a firmly established neighborhood. Teachers at these campuses face many woes associated with not "paying attention": Availability and access are greatly varied so that some students have access to basic software and some do not. Computer equipment is dated, haphazardly networked, and in various states of repair. Students with means bring their own hardware. Those without do without. On these campuses, writing teachers struggle to find a "happy" medium that accommodates and challenges both groups of students.

Overall, then, when we consider our institutions nationwide, it's difficult to make a universal list of "Top Ten" recommendations for teachers who wish to integrate technology into their writing classrooms. As we've suggested, the settings for using computers to enhance writing instruction are far from standard. The widening gap between technologically rich and ill-equipped campuses presents challenges for writing teachers as well as for writing program directors at both kinds of campuses who seek to develop innovative pedagogies sensitive to the changing demands of students, institutions, and society.[5] Institutional settings exert strong influences not only on how instructors use technology in the classroom but also on how they envision the relationship between teaching and technology. At technology-rich institutions, writing teachers must develop "emerging" digital literacies that explore all that the technology has to offer. In contrast, at technology-bound institutions, where technology use is an explicit administrative goal but where release time and instructional support are less forthcoming, instructors might choose to use the most convenient, accessible, and available resources to fulfill administrators' expectations without researching other options and dreaming the possible. For teachers with a four-four or five-five course load, grant writing and designing pilot projects get relegated to the mythical "back burner" of summer projects or are completely displaced by the exigency of what "works" simply and easily. To operate in this manner, unfortunately, ignores the fact that technology never merely augments teaching practices: It transforms them.[6] As Chris Anson points out, even writing teachers who incorporate email as a convenient concession to technology-bound institutional objectives discover that this technology use changes the relationship between student and teacher. In the best cases, email exchanges enable a student to view writing instruction as a personally, intellectually, and culturally meaningful action; in the worst cases, the student regards such activities as a colossal exercise in "busy work" akin to—but much less interesting than—visiting with hometown friends in chat rooms and surfing the Web for MP3s. Whether an instructor adapts discussion to the peculiarities of electronic communication or simply plunks use of email and online discussion into an expanding pool of assignments, use of technology in teaching writing sooner or later begs teachers to examine their pedagogical assumptions.

What can be done with computers in traditional, print-focused writing classrooms? How can it be done—and done well? Fortunately, there's been a great deal of experimental digital pedagogy, and, as a result, there's a large (and growing) body of work that addresses these questions.

Beginnings: Reading, Discussion, Prewriting, Heuristics, Researching

We begin here where writing classes start: locating writing topics. Although some teachers advocate that students' compositions should comprise the course's only text, many writing teachers rely upon readings collected in marketed, printed anthologies or, alternatively, custom-published photocopied material to generate issues for students' essays. The World Wide Web offers many options for conducting a reading-based course for which students never purchase a page through a publishing house. Electronic versions of texts provide many options for supplanting or supplementing course readings. Reading a classic text such as Thoreau's "Civil Disobedience"? Students can search the archives of the Thoreau Institute.[7] Send the student to a URL, provide her with a link—or have her discover or create her own—and *voila!* the course text appears seemingly free of cost, flexible, and open-ended.[8] Reading about the debate over affirmative action for a course in argument? A quick search will produce position statements and other resources that can be used to discuss not only the issue but also the source and quality of arguments and contexts of publication and distribution. Or if essays, poetry, short fiction, or creative nonfiction better suit your course, educational web sites associated with literary journals provide another option.[9] Interactive novels and short stories might serve as the basis for an entire course, and rhetorical analysis of Web sites can teach audience analysis and adaptation.[10] Even for instructors of first-year classes whose texts are selected for them by others, "companion web sites" provide a wealth of additional materials and resources.

For either group of teachers, certain questions should guide the decision to "go digital": Is electronic availability the best criterion for selecting texts? What do we lose when we exclude materials found only in archives or print? Will students be likely to want a portable, hard copy of the text, and how much will printing pages at campus labs cost students? To what extent has the Internet, that vast conglomeration of personal, institutional, and marketing choices, become the teacher, selecting for us the content for our discussions? Parker relates the example of a Stanford professor who changed his course texts because one book could not be neatly "bulleted" into key points for a PowerPoint-enhanced lecture: "I hate to admit this," he tells Parker, "but I actually removed a book from my syllabus last year because I couldn't figure out how to PowerPoint it. It's a lovely book . . . but it's very discursive; the charm of it is the throwaways. When I read this book, I thought, My head's filled with ideas, and now I've got to write out exactly what those ideas are, and—they're not neat" (Parker, 87).

Further, the seminar-type discussion or its cousin, the question-and-answer adaptation of Socratic dialogue, can be conducted electronically— entirely (a class never meets face to face) or partially (some discussions take place online, others in traditional classroom settings). Electronic discussions take several forms: listservs (users read messages which arrive with their email), bulletin boards (users navigate at their convenience to some shared electronic space to post or read messages), or chats (users from various locations log on at the same time to exchange what one commercial online service provider calls "instant messages").[11] All of these forms can result in an electronic "paper trail" or record. Electronic discussions in both educational and workplace settings have attracted a great deal of speculative, critical, and empirical research (Eldred and Hawisher). Generally, this practice has many potential benefits: more participation by generally reserved students, the decentering of teacher authority, and egalitarian changes in social dynamics informed by temperament, gender, class, nationality, and race.[12] However, teachers should prepare for some problems to arise, such as a disturbing lack of focus or depth (chat formats especially tend to encourage short and off-topic responses), "flaming" or verbal bullying, and "venting" or hostile and hateful remarks.[13] In addition, many comments on lists or bulletin boards go without reply, or even acknowledgment, raising the question: If a remark appears in a chat session, and everyone skims it without responding, what kind of "dialogue" has really taken place? Writing teachers need to observe whether particular students' comments are repeatedly ignored or if a student's participation consists entirely of one-line affirmations of others' ideas, such as "Sandy makes a good point" or "I agree with Bob." Requiring students to respond to at least two other writers per week, to compose replies of a given word-count range (e.g., 50–150 words), and to post one thought question for the class during the semester are ways of helping students negotiate the peculiar context of online discussions with classmates whom they might actually see in class every day. In addition, teachers can establish "netiquette" rules for discussion, such as "avoid sarcasm and jokes" and "disagree by acknowledging one good point made by the other person," and can also maintain a right to revoke privileges in order to facilitate on-task, respectful discussion.

Discussion is one way of facilitating ideas, but writing classrooms also turn to other, more classical forms called *heuristics*. (A heuristic is a set process or method used to solve a problem or explore an idea. It allows writers to approach an unknown topic through known strategies.) Given the centrality of heuristics in classical rhetoric (and the frequency with which classical strategies are adapted for contemporary composition classes), it's not surprising that teachers have experimented with electronic heuristics. The best-known of these, Daedalus, a software program designed for use in the composition classroom, adapted classical heuristics as well as the process-writing techniques described by Flower and Hayes and real-time chat features to prompt ideas in order to help writers generate content.[14]

Generating Ideas for Research

Some of the pillars, then, of humanities teaching have been affected by technology: what texts we teach, how we discuss them, and how we generate ideas. But one of the most obvious ways that technology is changing the way we teach composition is the hodge-podge of academic and nonacademic information available through the World Wide Web.[15] Teachers who used to meet with students in the library for a class period or two to help them manipulate bound indexes and locate texts in the library's holdings can now meet them in computer labs. Whereas in past decades teachers' research expectations had been restricted by their college's limited print holdings, writing teachers can now devise research projects which incorporate students' scouting out a diverse range of sources, including pamphlets from outreach and political organizations, corporations' annual reports, and statistics from government agencies. Writing instructors now need to set aside time to teach students (a) how to evaluate web sources for their "slant" or attitude toward or investment in a topic, (b) how to determine a web site's sponsoring agency from its URL and other clues, and (c) how to obtain quality information through subscription services such as InfoTrac and Academic Universe (to which libraries can subscribe) and publicly available search engines like Yahoo! and Metacrawler. Whether in digital or traditional classrooms, teachers can ask certain questions when designing a research project: How and when will students learn to read between the lines of online as well as print arguments to infer contexts of production often obscured in the syntax of URLs? How can students learn to scrutinize search results to sift through an overwhelming number of sources and distinguish among discourse genres, including research articles, personal musings, slanted news, and infomercials?

Unfortunately, the World Wide Web also augments a long-standing problem in writing studies: plagiarism, here defined to mean either the purchasing of papers or the "pasting" of whole texts or large chunks of text.[16] Because whole texts are so easily accessed on the Web, some students, usually in a time crunch, find it difficult to resist the temptation to cut and paste or to download. But if web piracy is easy for students, so usually is its detection. A key-word search on a popular search engine like Google usually brings up the source text; if it doesn't, subscription services can perform searches for instructors.[17]

Drafting

Before the Web changed the way we obtain information, word processing completely transformed the way we compose it. Typewriters are now rarely used, although they are still embraced by those who consider themselves holdouts against encroaching technology (see Wendell Berry's "Why I Won't Buy a Computer") or for filling out forms and perhaps addressing envelopes. Word processing is definitely here to stay; it's now part of the writing class's furniture.

Still, writing instructors need to make sure that the furniture doesn't become too comfortable; they need to explore and cautiously use the drafting potential of word processing computers.[18] Most of us are accustomed to a grinning image of a paper clip or other creature wiggling in the foreground of our computer screens and asking, "Do you need help with this letter?" The templates provided by such help features—often named *wizards*— are useful. For example, since Microsoft Word is available to all students at the University of Kentucky, Eldred frequently tells graduating seniors suddenly panicking about needing a résumé that the software's résumé wizard provides an easy-to-use heuristic. The question becomes, of course, whether such easy advice is always good. When allowing or requiring students to use tools like these, writing teachers need to ask themselves some questions: In what cases should students consult templates for form guides? In what cases should they undertake the rhetorical challenge of discovering their own forms? Once again, instructors would do well to pass along to students Parker's admonition. As invention prompts, templates or form guides are wonderfully suggestive: Has the writer considered *X*? Does *Y* form work better? But as fill-in-the-blank software, they are "oddly pedantic," with that "private interior influence." They "edit ideas" before we can ever formulate them. For Parker, "PowerPoint empowers the provider of simple content," it suggests to writers what they might include and in what order, "but it risks squeezing out the provider of process—that is to say, the rhetorician, the storyteller, the poet, the person whose thought cannot be arranged in the shape of an AutoContent slide" (87). Such software thus squeezes out the very critical and creative values humanities seek to teach, the very heart of composition instruction. Is such "squeezing out" necessary? For writing teachers integrating technology, it becomes crucial to determine how the software drives a particular way of thinking and whether or not the engine can be diverted from the programmed path and encouraged to take alternative mental routes.[19]

Another kind of drafting, drafting by a team of writers, has also been enhanced by word processing technology. Collaborative writing software, originally designed for business use, allows multiple users to make changes to a single working draft and compose a single document at the same time. Computers also facilitate collaboration through the easy and rapid transfer of text, usually through email attachments. Particularly in classrooms composing in multimedia, collaboration becomes crucial as authors work as part of a project team.[20]

Peer and Instructor Reviewing

Reviews of multiple drafts are central to process-writing classrooms, and in this area even the most low-tech classrooms have seen practices change.

Although the collegiate tradition of turning in hard copy does not die easily, electronic mail has crept its way into the process. Minimally, students might email instructors or peers for advice and feedback on papers in progress. In some cases works in progress are attached, looked over, and sent back with email comments—all in the context of a class not designated as a "computer" section.[21] Such practices have developed as a logical extension of email habits—and our grading habits.[22] If it is tempting to copyedit student papers in print form, it is even more irresistible when the text appears electronically on screen, just waiting to be manipulated. The computer technology here seems to make more clearly visible the very troubled grading acts we do with pen and paper. Consider, for example, this description from Norton's *Connect Web* (<www.connectweb.com>): "Teachers read and comment on papers, using free form comments, an online handbook, and predefined remarks. Students read your graded paper in one window and edit their untouched paper in another. All online, anytime." The description certainly allows instructors a glimpse of the software's features, but it also belies the tensions central to grading—the tension between "fixing" problems and encouraging exploration through drafts, the tension between coauthoring through extensive editing and encouraging exploration through probing questions. Somehow deleting and adding words to electronic text feels like authoring in a way that striking phrases and writing in words or phrases do not. The latter practices we can convince ourselves fall into the realm of "suggestion"; it's difficult to accomplish that same rhetorical move with the former—unless, of course, one is using software that records deletions and additions.[23]

Editing with Spell Checkers and Grammar Checkers

Ten years ago, programs like Grammatik that claimed to parse sentences and make them grammatically correct were marketed as separate software packages. Now such software, along with spell-checking dictionaries and thesauruses, are standard features of word processing programs. That such programs are not 100 percent accurate has long been known by linguists or writing teachers who continued in the face of technology's optimists to predict (accurately) that computers would not be able to crunch human speech with the same efficiency with which they crunch numbers. Students, however, are more hopeful—that is, if they make use of the features at all. And here students seem to be not so distinct from professional writers. An editor for whom Janet freelances places a box on the standard contract that reads, "I have used the spell checker to proof this piece." To receive payment, authors are required to check the box. One time, Janet automatically checked the box even though her spell checker was trying to alert her that "Niagra Falls" was repeatedly and incorrectly used throughout the piece. She was humbled by the editor's observation that "Niagra Falls" is a common misspelling of *Niagara Falls* but more humbled by her not-so-gentle warning to make sure pieces are run through the spell checker. Janet's lowest point came when she admitted that she had, in fact, run the spell checker—and ignored its advice. So professional and student writers need to be encouraged to use the spell-checking feature and to pay attention to it. Of course, the standard caveats have to be issued: The spell checker doesn't catch every misspelled word or tell users which "to" to choose. A grammar checker is imprecise and inaccurate, and, although useful, is only vaguely suggestive of revisions. Finally, the parsing of sentences must be done by humans; the rhythms must be felt or heard by humans. And, of course, a thesaurus is merely suggestive. Although it's handy to see a list of alternative words (the thesaurus just produced the word *handy* rather than *useful*), blithely tapping "Insert word" on every word search can result in the same kind of ridiculousness produced with pen, paper, and the printed editions.

Publishing and Grading

Writing instructors have long known the value of publishing student work in some form. Producing student publications by traditional photocopying is both time-consuming and expensive. For classrooms in which student writing is the main event, or for classrooms that depend heavily on samples of student writing, the Web provides relatively fast and inexpensive text distribution. Even though some institutions might still rely on technology that requires knowledge of HTML or FTP, increasingly programs exist that make such knowledge unnecessary—at least insofar as publishing student texts. Microsoft Word has a "Save as HTML" feature, and other software such as Dreamweaver or Frontpage facilitates the composing of web pages that can include images, including photographs, as well as text. Desktop publishing software such as Quark or Adobe's InDesign provides perhaps even better options than standard webpage software does because it is designed to accommodate the long segments of text central to the traditional writing classroom. Janet's upper-division courses in essay writing both begin and end with web anthologies of student work. The class begins by studying essays produced by professionals and by students in previous semesters whose work has been published on the campus's web site. The course ends when students compose their own essays to add to those written and published in previous years. One telling comment—anecdotal evidence, to be sure—suggests that students write differently for the Web than they would for a grade. "Grade this one," the student said as he turned in a paper on time, "but I want to work more on the version I put on the Web. I know I can make it much better." When Janet asked if he wanted more time to work on the graded version, he replied, "No, that draft's OK for a grade."[24]

Hypertext and other web technologies are also fostering new written products. Some instructors have experimented with forms that combine traditional essayist concerns with technological innovation. Students compose personal narratives and family histories that include annotations of people, events, and places as well as photographs, music clips, newspaper articles, and critical commentary referencing historical and sociological research. Such assignments encourage students to consider relationships between visual and linguistic rhetorics and their effects on an audience's understanding of a topic.[25]

Whole Classroom Management

A class web site, listservs, shared drafts—technology adds to the management skills necessary for effective class planning. Some turn to software to manage their courses. With web-based packages such as Blackboard and Course Compass, teachers can create course web sites relatively quickly by using prepackaged templates that organize uploaded files, such as grades, handouts, assignments, and readings. Course materials then reside on a school's or publisher's network server, enabling round-the-clock availability of these materials to students who purchase access codes. However, such "oddly pedantic" packages, or even local area networks, can lend themselves to canned instruction and authoritarian classroom dynamics. Charles Moran observes that otherwise student-centered writing teachers can become autocrats when they become responsible for running computer labs, and he warns that software that allows teachers to control the displays of monitors at any lab workstation (e.g., in the early 1990s, Robotel and CT System III) undermines the best of composition teachers' pedagogical efforts to give authority to their students. Similarly, Janangelo highlights the abuses of teachers who access system information to determine how much time a student has spent online composing drafts, surfing the Internet, and visiting chat rooms or to spy on colleagues' teaching practices by surreptitiously downloading documents stored on a network but meant to be viewed by individual students or a whole class.[26] In a networked classroom, writing teachers and students alike need to become cognizant of potential breaches of privacy and professional ethics.

Pilots, Resources, Planning

There are degrees to which technology can be integrated into the classroom. It's crucial that teachers recognize the range of choices—ethical choices—before them and that they honestly balance what they wish to accomplish, what they are prepared to accomplish, with what resources a university hopes to have, actually has, or has a chance of getting. For any writing course piloting a new technology, an instructor needs to consider the following, listed in order of importance:[27]

- Writing instructors using computers in the classroom need to be committed to teaching new digital literacies. That is, instructors must be in large part persuaded by Selfe's argument that we ignore new literacies at our own—and at our students'—civic peril. Students very easily discern the difference between a course in which technology seems central to the goals of writing and one in which computers seem supplemental, or simply added onto an already very full course. Success depends on instructor commitment.
- Instructors need to determine whether their campus is technology rich, technology bound, or ill-equipped. Is full instructional technology avail-

able on campus, including writing software? If the answer here is "no," the outlook can actually still be positive. Increasingly, textbook companies provide a wide range of instructional software (including whole-class management software) either as part of a textbook adoption or as a paid service. Such services can even include twenty-four-hour, 800 number support. Textbook representatives and colleagues at other institutions who have used the service can help instructors gauge whether it's desirable and possible to adopt such options.

- Instructors need to determine whether sound instructional technology is valued on their campus. If it isn't, it will take (a) desire, (b) energy, and (c) time to begin to change the situation. All are precious resources.[28]
- Instructors will need to negotiate time issues, especially when first teaching with technology. Courses piloting technology take time, two different kinds of time to be exact: professional development time and classroom time. It takes time to imagine how classroom practices should be changed. It takes time for instructors (and later for their students) to learn to use software. It takes time after the fact to evaluate how the technology worked—and to make the necessary adjustments. Will the institution offer course release for a technology pilot? A release from some service obligations? Although it seems foolish, perhaps even unethical, for those training for twenty-first-century teaching to ignore technology because of time restraints, it is frustrating for them to spend time in a place where that time is not valued. It's necessary to balance idealism with practicality. Likewise, technology use makes demands on students' time. Again, one way to assure the failure of a pilot is to "add on" technology rather than integrate it. If an instructor schedules an online discussion outside of class time, she or he must be willing to reduce the amount of out-of-class preparation, cancel part of class, or find some other way to accommodate the additional demands on students' already packed schedules. Web searches for a variety of quality sources, for instance, can take extraordinary amounts of time. The old college rule of thumb, "two hours of outside work for every hour spent in class," is one way of gauging time. Technology use should not add to the total time commitment. Tell students how time is being measured and modified for your digital course.
- Instructors need to envision the kind of classroom they are trying to create. A mostly traditional classroom with a writing lab add-on component requires a much different investment of time, talents, and resources than does a virtual classroom that never meets face to face. Between these two options is a range of combinations: a course that meets equally face to face and virtually, a course that first meets face to face and later virtually, or a course that meets twice a week in a computer lab and once a week in a traditional classroom space. There's no "right" configuration; rather, the decision is deeply rhetorical. Individual instructors must work within institutional contexts to determine what configuration best serves their goals.

Conclusion

> *PowerPoint, which can be found on two hundred and fifty million computers around the world, is software you impose on other people.*
>
> —Ian Parker

Parker's (power) point is well taken. The interfaced design of PowerPoint, with its focus on bullets of information, certainly does hollow out a techno-rut which is made even deeper, perhaps, when it's used for instruction. One can indeed imagine a legion of Stepford teachers, each clicking through presentations that compress complicated, messy rhetorical thought into tidy bits of streamlined, visually pleasing maxims. But caveats about PowerPoint's potential for abuse can be applied, to varying degrees, to all forms of technology—computer and print. We can't escape the Stepford dilemma by retreating into some predigital print nirvana. Computer technology is much too central a feature of twenty-first-century literacy, environment, culture, and economics to pretend that it merely "augments" pedagogy. Electronic literacy has already transformed writing instruction. Software already teaches. It's our job to teach with it—and against it.

Notes

[1] PowerPoint is presentation software based loosely on the idea of a slide show.

[2] For more on technology, literacy, and the environment, see Mortensen. Mortensen's article looks at paper production and is part of a larger project that looks at the reading materials on which literacy depends.

[3] *Technology and Literacy in the Twenty-first Century: The Importance of Paying Attention* (Carbondale: Southern Illinois UP, 1999).

[4] In October 2001, Selfe made this argument before writing program administrators. In her presentation, Selfe used personal narratives to exemplify the varying degrees and kinds of technological literacy students bring to our classrooms.

[5] This division is evidenced by changes in the focus of the Computers and Writing Conference. Gerrard points out that a widening gap is reflected in a "social hierarchy" (279) of interests among attendees of the Computers and Writing Conference, which was initiated in 1982 at the University of Minnesota. She observes that "despite our nonhierarchical ethic [as a discipline], computers and composition has become socially stratified, encompassing teachers newly interested in using computers to teach writing and those at the 'cutting edge' of theory and practice" (288–89). Reynolds and Lewis urge technoenthusiasts to examine "the very material conditions under which student writers labor" (272) and note that "nontraditional" students in particular

have little or no time to avail themselves of university labs, do not necessarily own computers, face demanding family and work as well as school obligations, and might be on the whole "more distant from computer culture than their younger peers" (272). Reynolds and Lewis urge writing teachers and program administrators to begin "inventorying campus facilities and speaking with support staff, as well as surveying students in writing programs about outside access (and inside access in other courses)" (277).

[6] DiMatteo argues that, in contrast to print-based learning and communication, what he terms "medium-emphatic technologies," digital learning and communication, which take place in an "element-emphatic medium" (such as online chats or instant messaging), not only "promote a sense of the ease of communication" but also prevent users from critiquing an exchange. He warns that "the danger of electronic writing is its apparent seamlessness" (17) and suggests that teachers use students' belief in the "apparent seamlessness" of electronic discourse to draw attention to the communicative process itself, specifically how meaning is created through, not attached onto, language (9–16). LeBlanc cautions teachers against whole-heartedly adopting grammar-correcting and editing softwares because these readily undermine teachers' efforts to foster students' learning of a writing process as a means of developing a well-written product (10–11). LeBlanc encourages writing teachers to recognize "that the computer's mere ability to perform a task well gives that performance a kind of validity that flies in the face of our better knowledge," and he recommends that teachers examine software for assumptions about "our ideological question[s] of 'What is good?'" in terms of written products and writing pedagogy (11). In a critique of various perspectives on the benefits of using computers to teach writing, Kemp suggests teachers adopt softwares that help students answer such rhetorical challenges as "How can I make the reader keep reading?" and which teach students to "recognize that words, even after they are written, can be beaten, pounded, and kicked into vastly different shapes and to different effects" (24). Cynthia Selfe asks writing teachers broader questions: "How do we make sure that students and teachers—not technology—occupy the forefront of our educational attention and drive our decision making about literacy issues? How do we prepare students to be literate citizens and effective change makers in a world increasingly dependent on technologically based communication, while retaining humanistic perspectives? Can we use technology to provide students and faculty with the literary environments and literacy communities that help them most . . . ; or will technology serve to distract us from this task?" Ultimately, Selfe asks writing teachers to consider: "Can we use technology to play some role in our educational system and our culture at large . . . or will our use of technology simply exacerbate these ills or mask their effects?" ("Three Voices," 310). Hawisher and Selfe, "The Rhetoric of Technology."

[7] See <www.walden.org>.

[8] Those who focus on print and electronic literacies' impact on the environment would remind us that the costs might be invisible to users but are there nonetheless. See Mortensen.

[9] See, for example, <www.sarabandebooks.org>, which links to a Sarabande in education site, or <http://www.creativenonfiction.org>, which offers educational enrichment, including real-time and chat features.

[10] Moulthrop and Kaplan provide an example of how to use "interactive fiction" in an introductory literature course. See, for instance, Beers; Yoshimura. For a variety of ways of incorporating the World Wide Web into English teaching, see Gruber (*Weaving*). For examples of how to use computers to construct a classroom discourse community, see Howard, Gooch, and Goswami; Galin and Latchaw.

[11] See D. Selfe in this volume. Also Faigley; Hawisher and Moran. For an example of using online asynchronous discussion in a contemporary literature class, see Miller. For ideas on how to use MOOs in teaching, see a collection of essays edited by Haynes and Holmevik.

[12] Kremers explains how online dialogue has helped basic writers participate more fully than in class face-to-face discussion. He suggests that teachers give "guidance that allows students to participate in a dialogue that they feel drawn to as co-equals, as collaborators" and take up their role as "mentor, as someone to ask questions and offer prompts" (36). Teachers can ask themselves several questions to help students participate online effectively: Can I help a student "generalize, reason, or follow a line of thought" further or "pick up on someone else's thought" (38)? Can I use "role-playing scenarios" to jump-start students' creativity (39) or use a printed transcript of an exchange as the basis for an essay assignment (40)? Kremers also suggests that online discussion be "[u]sed as a heuristic tool, a forum for positing and testing and debating conflicting data" in students' readings, research, and experiences or to enhance "brainstorming sessions" (41). O'Brien adds to Kremers's model questions and directives for teachers to help students interact with others' ideas (81–82). Palmquist's case study of electronic discussion reveals that the more students engage in networked exchanges, the better their "academic performance" and their participation in collaborative groups, especially in first-year writing courses aimed at teaching academic argument and research. Bennett and Walsh outline their experience with cross-continental electronic exchanges between two classes of students with markedly different racial demographics who were asked to examine the same text, Zora Neale Hurston's *Their Eyes Were Watching God*. Their discussion provides helpful insight into the complications and benefits of arranging such exchanges. See Diane Thompson.

[13] Holcomb. See also Alexander; Blair; Buckley; Carbone et al.; Castner; Cooper and Selfe; Eldred; George; Holcomb; Johnson-Eilola and Selber; Hartman et al.; Regan; Romano; Sirc; Takayoshi; Taylor; Warshauer.

[14] See Andersen; Schwartz, Fitzpatrick, and Huot; Strickland; and Hodges.

[15] See Tu et al.; Clark; Anstendig; Arnold and Jayne; Burton and Chadwick; Gardner and Newell; Gillette and Videon; Isaksen et al.; Sorapure, Inglesby, and Tatchisin.

16 As difficult as it is to sometimes tell the difference, we want to be careful here to distinguish this kind of intentional piracy from what Rebecca Moore Howard calls "patch writing."

17 Publishers, ever eager to find out what writing instructors really want and need, are offering creative solutions. Here, for example, is a marketing blurb from Prentice-Hall: "Want to end plagiarism in your class? We recently signed an exclusive agreement with Turnitin.com. This online service helps teachers identify and prevent student plagiarism from the Web. Prentice-Hall can waive the site license fee for those college courses where you require a Prentice-Hall English text. To learn more about Turnitin, click here http://www.turnitin.com/new.html. To learn how to set up a Prentice-Hall account with Turnitin, please contact your local Prentice-Hall sales representative or email us at english_service@prenhall.com."

18 For results of how word processing improves student writing, see Markel. See also Kantrov; Sudol; and Tuman, "Campus Word Processing."

19 It is especially important for teachers of introductory-level courses to consider how a software program might constrain and direct students' writing practices. In a study of the influence of using computers to enhance the writing process, Slattery and Kowalski (1998) found that when composing online, first-year college students tended to expand their writing processes whereas upper-level students compressed theirs. See also Wysocki.

20 See Kaufer and Neuwirth; Thompson, "Electronic Bulletin Boards"; Balester, Halasek, and Peterson; Sirc and Reynolds.

21 For a discussion of the ways in which instructors' online commentary changes the nature of teaching and learning, see Hawisher and Moran, "Responding to Writing On-Line." For an examination of the effects on student interaction, see Peckham.

22 See Reynolds and Bonk; Van Der Geest and Remmers; LeBlanc, "How to Get the Works Just Right." See also Anson, "In Our Own Voices."

23 Specific software does exist that tries to simplify or make neater or more technological the process of reviewing and evaluating drafts. Some of this software shares the "oddly pedantic" features of templates: instructors can use predefined marks or drop in links to online handbooks, the digital equivalent of scrawling "6e" in the margin, a grading method still practiced, despite literature that suggests the method's drawbacks. Some programs offer more open-ended comment features by providing rhetorical prompts; others use embedded windows, a notation feature, or voice recordings to insert instructors' comments into a student author's text. For other ideas about using computers to enhance the revising process, see Crafton; Duin; Hill, Wallace, and Haas; Heilker.

24 See Sullivan.

[25] See Tweddle and Moore; DiPardo and DiPardo; Heba. Grading digitally produced documents requires special considerations. See Takayoshi, "The Shape of Electronic Writing." For a discussion of the challenges and benefits of using electronic portfolios, see the special issue on this topic in *Computers and Composition* 13.2(1996).

[26] Moran; Janangelo.

[27] A number of publications provide additional advice to help writing teachers integrate computers into their courses. See Yagelski and Powley; Douglas; Gruber, "Ways We Contribute"; Peyton; Wahlstrom and Selfe.

[28] In "Computers and Compositionists: A View from the Floating Bottom," Lisa Gerrard points out that because implementing computer-assisted instruction takes a lot of time, adjunct and untenured faculty who teach composition can be especially—and, perhaps, wisely—reluctant to adopt it.

Works Cited

Alexander, Jonathan. "Out of the Closet and Into the Network: Sexual Orientation and the Computerized Classroom." *Computers and Composition* 14.2 (1997).

Andersen, Wallis M. "Computerized Invention for Composing: An Update and Review." *Computers and Composition* 9.1 (1991): 25–38.

Anson, Chris M. "Distant Voices: Teaching Writing in a Culture of Technology." *College English* 61 (1999): 261–80.

Anson, Chris M. "In Our Own Voices: Using Recorded Commentary To Respond To Writing." *New Directions for Teaching and Learning* 69 (1997): 105–13.

Anstendig, L., J. Meyer, and M. Driver. "Web Research and Hypermedia: Tools for Engaged Learning." *Journal on Excellence in College Teaching* 9 (1998): 69–91.

Arnold, J. M., and E. A. Jayne. "Dangling by a Slender Thread: The Lessons and Implications of Teaching the World Wide Web to Freshmen." *Journal of Academic Librarianship* 24.1 (1998): 43–52.

Balester, Valerie, Kay Halasek, and Nancy Peterson. "Sharing Authority: Collaborative Teaching in a Computer-Based Writing Course." *Computers and Composition* 9.3 (1992): 25–40.

Beers, T. "Self-representation and the World Wide Web." *Composition Studies/Freshman English News* 26.2 (1998): 13–34.

Berry, Wendell. "Why I Am Not Going to Buy A Computer." *What Are People For?* North Point Press, Farrar, 1990. Rpt. in *Literacies and Technologies.* Ed. Robert P. Yagelski. New York: Longman, 2001. 103–11.

Blair, Kristine L. "Microethnographies of Electronic Discourse Communities: Establishing Exigency for E-Mail in the Professional Writing Classroom." *Computers and Composition* 13.1 (1996).

Buckley, Joanne. "The Invisible Audience and the Disembodied Voice: Online Teaching and the Loss of Body Image." *Computers and Composition* 14.2 (1997).

Burton, V. T., and S. A. Chadwick. "Investigating the Practices of Student Researchers: Patterns of Use and Criteria for Use of Internet and Library Sources." *Computers and Composition* 17 (2000): 309–28.

Carbone, Nick, et al. "Writing Ourselves On-Line." *Computers and Composition* 10.3 (1993): 29–48.

Castner, Joanna. "Virtual Complexities: Exploring Literacy at the Intersections of Computer-Mediated Social Formations." *Computers and Composition* 14.2 (1997).

Clark, Irene. "Information Literacy and the Writing Center." *Computers and Composition* 12.2 (1995): 203–9.

Cooper, Marilyn M., and Cynthia L. Selfe. "Computer Conferences and Learning: Authority, Resistance, and Internally Persuasive Discourse." *College English* 52 (1990): 847–69.

Crafton, Robert E. "Promises, Promises: Computer-Assisted Revision and Basic Writers." *Computers and Composition* 13.3 (1996): 317–26.

DeWitt, Scott L. "The Current Nature of Hypertext Research in Computers and Composition Studies: An Historical Perspective." *Computers and Composition* 13.1 (1996): 69–84.

DiMatteo, Anthony. "Communication, Writing, Learning: An Anti-Instrumentalist View of Network Writing." *Computers and Composition* 8.3 (1991): 5–29.

DiPardo, Anne, and Mike DiPardo. "Towards the Metapersonal Essay: Exploring the Potential of Hypertext in the Composition Class." *Computers and Composition* 7.3 (1990): 7–22.

Douglas, Jane Y. "Technology, Pedagogy, and Context: A Tale of Two Classrooms." *Computers and Composition* 11.3 (1994): 275–82.

Duin, A. "Computer Exercises to Encourage Rethinking and Revision." *Computers and Composition* 4.2 (1987): 66–105.

Eldred, Janet. "Pedagogy in the Computer-Networked Classroom." *Computers and Composition* 8.2 (1991): 47–61.

Eldred, Janet, and Gail Hawisher. "Researching Electronic Networks." *Written Communication* 12 (1995): 330–59.

Faigley, Lester. *Fragments of Rationality: Postmodernity and the Subject of Composition.* Pittsburgh UP: 1993.

Galin, Jeffrey R., and J. Latchaw, eds. *The Dialogic Classroom: Teachers Integrating Computer Technology, Pedagogy, and Research.* Urbana, IL: NCTE, 1998.

Gardner, S. A., H. Benham-Hiltraut, and B. M. Newell. "Oh, What a Tangled Web We've Woven! Helping Students Evaluate Sources." *English Journal* 89 (1999): 39–44.

George, E. Laurie. "Taking Women Professors Seriously: Female Authority in the Computerized Classroom." Spec. issue of *Computers and Composition* 7 (1990): 42–45.

Gerrard, Lisa. "Computers and Compositionists: A View from the Floating Bottom." *Computers and Composition* 8.2 (1991): 5–15.

Gerrard, Lisa. "The Evolution of the Computers and Writing Conference." *Computers and Composition* 12.3 (1995): 279–92.

Gillette, M. A., and C. Videon. "Seeking Quality on the Internet: A Case Study of Composition Students' Works Cited." *Teaching English in the Two-Year College* 26 (1998): 189–94.

Gruber, Sibylle. "Ways We Contribute: Students, Instructors, and Pedagogies in the Computer-Mediated Writing Classroom." *Computers and Composition* 12.1 (1995): 61–78.

Gruber, Sibylle, ed. *Weaving a Virtual Web: Practical Approaches to New Information Technologies.* Urbana, IL: NCTE, 2000.

Hartman, Karen, et al. "Patterns of Social Interaction and Learning to Write: Some Effects of Network Technologies." *Written Communication* 8.1 (1991): 79–113.

Hawisher, Gail E., and Charles Moran. "Electronic Mail and the Writing Instructor." *College English* 55 (1993): 627–43.

Hawisher, Gail E., and Charles Moran. "Responding to Writing On-Line." *New Directions for Teaching and Learning* 69 (1997): 115–25.

Hawisher, Gail E., and Cynthia Selfe. "The Rhetoric of Technology and the Electronic Writing Class." *College Composition and Communication* 42 (1991): 55–65.

Haynes, Cynthia, and Jan R. Holmevik, eds. *High Wired: On the Design, Use, and Theory of Educational MOOs.* Ann Arbor: University of Michigan P, 1998.

Heba, Gary. "HyperRhetoric: Multimedia, Literacy, and the Future of Composition." *Computers and Composition* 14.1 (1997).

Heilker, Paul. "Revision Worship and the Computer as Audience." *Computers and Composition* 9.2 (1992): 59–69.

Hill, Charles A., David L. Wallace, and Christina Haas. "Revising On-line: Computer Technologies and the Revising Process." *Computers and Composition* 9.1 (1991): 83–109.

Hodges, James E. "Electronic Aids in Writing." *Teaching English in the Two-Year College* 20.2 (1993): 132–36.

Holcomb, Christopher. "A Class of Clowns: Spontaneous Joking in Computer-Assisted Discussions." *Computers and Composition* 14.1 (1997).

Howard, Rebecca M. "Plagiarism, Authorships, and the Academic Death Penalty." *College English* 57.7 (1995): 788–806.

Howard, Tharon, C. Benson, R. Gooch, and Dixie Goswami, eds. *Electronic Networks: Crossing Boundaries/Creating Communities*. New York: Heinemann/Boynton, 1999.

Isaksen, J. L., T. Waggoner, N. Christensen, and D. Fallon. "World Wide Web Research Assignments (What Works for Me)." *Teaching English in the Two-Year College* 26 (1998): 196–98.

Janangelo, Joseph. "Technopower and Technopression: Some Abuses of Power and Control in Computer-Assisted Writing Environments." *Computers and Composition* 9.1: 47–64.

Johnson-Eilola, Johndan, and Stuart A. Selber. "Policing Ourselves: Defining the Boundaries of Appropriate Discussion in Online Forums." *Computers and Composition* 13.3 (1996): 209–21.

Kantrov, Ilene. "Keeping Promises and Avoiding Pitfalls: Where Teaching Needs to Augment Word Processing." *Computers and Composition* 8.2 (1991): 63–77.

Kaplan, Nancy. "Something to Imagine: Literature, Composition, and Interactive Fiction." *Computers and Composition* 9.1 (1991): 7–23.

Kaufer, David S., and Chris Neuwirth. "Supporting Online Team Editing: Using Technology to Shape Performance and to Monitor Individual and Group Action." *Computers and Composition* 12.1 (1995): 113–24.

Kemp, Fred. "Who Programmed This? Examining the Instructional Attitudes of Writing-Support Software." *Computers and Composition* 10.1 (1992): 9–24.

Kremers, Marshall. "Sharing Authority on a Synchronous Network: The Case for Riding the Beast." Spec. Issue of *Computers and Composition* 7 (1990): 33–44.

LeBlanc, Paul. "Competing Ideologies in Software Design for Computer-Aided Composition." *Computers and Composition* 7.2 (1990): 8–19.

LeBlanc, Paul. "How to Get the Works Just Right: A Reappraisal of Word Processing and Revision." *Computers and Composition* 5.3 (1988): 29–42.

Markel, Mike. "Behaviors, Attitudes, and Outcomes: A Study of Word Processing and Writing Quality among Experienced Word-Processing Students." *Computers and Composition* 11.1 (1994): 49–58.

Miller, Melinda. "Electronic Conferencing in the Networked Classroom." *College Teaching* 39.4 (1991): 136–39.

Moran, Charles. "The Computer-Writing Room: Authority and Control." *Computers and Composition* 7.2 (1990): 61–69.

Mortensen, Peter. "Reading Material." *Written Communication* 18.4 (2001): 395–439.

O'Brien, Sheila R. "The Medium Facilitates the Messages: Electronic Discourse and Literature Class Dynamics." *Computers and Composition* 11.1 (1994): 79–86.

Palmquist, Michael E. "Network-Supported Interaction in Two Writing Classrooms." *Computers and Composition* 10.4 (1993): 25–57.

Parker, Ian. "Absolute PowerPoint." *New Yorker* 28 May 2001: 76+.

Peckham, Irv. "If It Ain't Broke, Why Fix It? Disruptive and Constructive Computer-Mediated Response Group Practices." *Computers and Composition* 13.3 (1996): 237–339.

Peyton, Joy K. "Technological Innovation Meets Institution: Birth of Creativity or Murder of a Great Idea?" Spec. issue of *Computers and Composition* 7 (1990): 105–22.

Regan, Alison. "'Type Normal Like the Rest of Us': Writing, Power, and Homophobia in the Networked Composition Classroom." *Computers and Writing* 10.4 (1993): 11–23.

Reynolds, Thomas J. "The Changing Topography of Computer Access for Composition Students." *Computers and Composition* 14.2 (1997).

Reynolds, Thomas H., and Curtis J. Bonk. "Facilitating College Writers' Revisions within a Generative-Evaluative Computerized Prompting Framework." *Computers and Composition* 13.1 (1996): 93–108.

Romano, Susan. "The Egalitarianism Narrative: Whose Story? Which Yardstick?" *Computers and Composition* 10.3 (1993): 5–28.

Schwartz, Helen J., Christine Y. Fitzpatrick, and Brian A. Huot. "The Computer Medium in Writing for Discovery." *Computers and Composition* 1.2 (1994): 137–49.

Selfe, Cynthia L. *Technology and Literacy in the Twenty-first Century: The Importance of Paying Attention*. Carbondale: Southern Illinois UP, 1999.

Selfe, Cynthia L. "Three Voices on Literacy, Technology, and Humanistic Perspective." *Computers and Composition* 12.3 (1995).

Selfe, Cynthia L., and Richard J. Selfe Jr. "The Politics of the Interface: Power and Its Exercise in Electronic Contact Zones." *College Composition and Communication* 45 (1994): 480–504.

Sirc, Geoffrey. "The Twin Worlds of Electronic Conferencing." *Computers and Composition* 12.3 (1995): 265–77.

Sirc, Geoffrey, and Tom Reynolds. "The Changing Face of Collaboration in the Networked Classroom." Spec. issue of *Computers and Composition* 7 (1990): 53–70.

Slattery, Patrick J., and Rosemary Kowalski. "On Screen: The Composing Processes of First-Year and Upper-Level College Students." *Computers and Composition* 15.1 (1998): 61–81.

Sorapure, M., P. Inglesby, and G. Tatchisin. "Web Literacy: Challenges and Opportunities for Research in a New Medium." *Computers and Composition* 15 (1998): 409–24.

Strickland, James. "Computers, Invention, and the Power to Change Student Writing." *Computers and Composition* 4.2 (1987): 7–26.

Sudol, Ronald A. "Principles of Generic Word Processing for Students with Independent Access to Computers." *Computers and Composition* 41.3 (1990): 325–31.

Sullivan, Patricia. "Computer-Aided Publishing: Focusing on Documents." *Computers and Composition* 10.1 (1992): 135–49.

Takayoshi, Pamela. "Building New Networks from the Old: Women's Experiences with Electronic Communications." *Computers and Composition* 11.1 (1994): 21–35.

Takayoshi, Pamela. "The Shape of Electronic Writing: Evaluating and Assessing Computer-Assisted Writing Processes and Products." Spec. issue of *Computers and Composition* 13.2 (1996): 245–57.

Taylor, Todd. "The Persistence of Difference in Networked Classrooms: Non-Negotiable Difference and the African-American Student." *Computers and Composition* 14.2 (1997).

Thompson, Diane. "Electronic Bulletin Boards: A Timeless Place for Collaborative Writing Projects." *Computers and Composition* 10.3 (1990): 43–53.

Thompson, Diane. "Interactive Networking: Creating Bridges Between Speech, Writing, and Composition." *Computers and Composition* 5.3 (1988): 17–27.

Tu, Thuy Lin, Debra W. Rush, Alicia H. Hines, and Alondra Nelson. "Communities on the Verge: Intersections and Disjunctures in the New Information Order." *Computers and Composition* 14.2 (1997).

Tuman, Myron. "Campus Word Processing: Seven Design Principles for a New Academic Writing Environment." *Computers and Composition* 10.3 (1993): 49–62.

Tuman, Myron. "Literacy Online." Abstract. *Annual Review of Applied Linguistics* 16 (1996): 26–45.

Tweddle, Sally, and Phil Moore. "English Under Pressure: Back to Basics?" *Computers and Composition* 11.3 (1994): 283–92.

Van Der Geest, Thea, and Tim Remmers. "The Computer as Means of Communication for Peer-Review Groups." *Computers and Composition* 11.3 (1994): 237–50.

Wahlstrom, Billie J., and Cynthia L. Selfe. "A View from the Bridge: English Departments Piloting Among the Shoals of Computer Use." *ADE Bulletin* 109 (Winter 1994): 35–45.

Walsh, Kathleen. "Desperately Seeking Diversity: Going Online to Achieve a Racially Balanced Classroom." *Computers and Composition* 14.2 (1997).

Warshauer, Susan C. "Rethinking Teacher Authority to Counteract Homophobic Prejudice in the Networked Classroom: A Model of Teacher Response and Overview of Classroom Methods." *Computers and Composition* 12.1 (1995): 97–111.

Wysocki, Anne. "Impossibly Distinct: On Form/Content and Word/Image in Two Pieces of Computer-Based Interactive Multimedia." *Computers and Composition* 18.2 (2001).

Yagelski, Robert P., and Sarah Powley. "Virtual Connections and Real Boundaries: Teaching Writing and Preparing Writing Teachers on the Internet." *Computers and Composition* 13.1 (1996): 25–36.

Yoshimura, F. "On the Use of Hypertext to Enhance the Importance of Rhetorical Organization." *Journal of Technical Writing and Communication* 28 (1998): 227–36.

Web sites referenced:

<www.walden.org>

<www.sarabandebooks.org>

<http://www.creativenonfiction.org>

<http://www.turnitin.com/new.html>

Ewriting Spaces as Safe, Gender-Fair Havens: Aligning Political and Pedagogical Possibilities

CHRISTINE TULLEY
University of Findlay

KRISTINE BLAIR
Bowling Green State University

Introduction: Advocating Safe Spaces

In his epilogue to the 1999 *Computers and Composition* special issue on computers, composition, and gender, Hugh Burns outlines five important goals for computer-mediated writing teachers: that our curriculum and our teaching are gender neutral, that our instructional practices are fair across the board, that our networked classrooms are safe havens for individual differences, that our writing curriculum stimulates freedom of expression and values all human discourse, and that students think critically about and critique thoughtfully how technology intensifies the public discourse on gender, ethnicity, class and economic status (168). Although Burns is clearly acknowledging the potential for electronic writing environments to be tools of empowerment, he does not presume that the technology itself is a de facto means to an end. Rather, it is the pedagogy enacted within an electronic writing environment that determines the extent to which it is empowering for students, particularly students whose gender, race, class, age, and sexual orientation may have impacted their access and thus their attitude toward computers both inside and outside the classroom. Such acknowledgment represents a shift from early "rhetorics of technology" (Hawisher and Selfe, 1991) or "egalitarianism narratives" (Romano, 1993) in the field of computers and writing that touted the networked computer as being able to erase discrimination and provide a utopian forum in which students were freed from material conditions that empower some and disenfranchise others.

Yet with respect to gender, Benjamin and Irwin-Devitis (1998) contend that gender bias continues to pervade English classrooms and that "the transition from girl to woman is a treacherous one in which many girls begin to doubt their own feelings and move toward relationships based on cultural stereotypes" (67). For scholars addressing computers and writing, including Lisa Gerrard (1999), one prevailing cultural stereotype is the "male image of computers," whether that image is reinforced by the advertisements in most popular computing magazines, by the sheer numbers of men as opposed to women in the technology-based fields, or by the continuing development of video and computer games—designed by males for a predominantly male audience (Cassell and Jenkins, 1999)—that position men as subjects and women as objects or completely absent from the picture (378–79). These male-dominated visions of technology send powerful messages to male and female students alike, and in many cases, the message that girls have traditionally received is that computers are not for them. As Gerrard and others have noted, "video games are helping male students become adept at computers, while girls are being left behind" (380). Although there are web sites and video games specifically designed by females to create emotionally safe and intellectually supportive spaces for women and girls (Kaplan and Farrell, 1994; Takayoshi, Huot, and Huot, 1999), these espaces continue to be the exception rather than the rule.

The extent to which safe espaces exist for women and girls outside the electronic writing classroom impacts the extent to which safe spaces can exist inside the electronic writing classroom. Indeed, by the time many girls reach high school and college, "boys are the ones who monopolize the spaces in the school's computer room at lunch and before and after school, and they take more computer courses in high school and college" (Sadker and Sadker, 123). But because the Internet is on its way to becoming the workplace of the future, it has become vital for our female students to claim their online space both in their roles as working professionals and in their roles as literate citizens, using these newest technologies of literacy to effect the type of social change Hugh Burns calls for both inside and outside the electronic writing classroom. Moreover, such goals are consistent with a recent study by the American Association of University Women in which a series of focus groups revealed that "while girls show little interest in the inner workings of the computer, they are very interested in the possibilities of using technology to promote human interaction" as opposed to boys' view of the computer as "inherently interesting" (9). As teachers in electronic writing spaces, we must explore ways to move all students beyond knowing how the metal box works to understanding what it can do for all students, regardless of gender and other subjectivities. Thus, our purpose in this chapter is to align political possibility with pedagogical application. To do this, we weave a web of theoretical goals consistent with Burns's list, the recent call for gender equity in technology education by the American Association of University Women, and feminist pedagogical theory. We offer specific instructional initiatives that can allow students to develop technology-based literacies in a supportive and nonthreatening environment. As we shall conclude, such enabling spaces within our own virtual classrooms have the potential to reverse the more negative impact of historically gender-imbalanced espaces within the larger political culture.

Designing Safe Ewriting Spaces

Clearly, as Burns, the AAUW, and others have affirmed an electronic environment can give voice to the disenfranchised, but technology in and of itself is not necessarily empowering. Thus, where does feminist pedagogy intersect with electronic writing environments, and what does this intersection mean for teachers of online writing attempting to design a course situated in feminist or gender-fair pedagogies? According to Eileen Schell, "feminist pedagogy revalues the experience of women students and encourages individual voice and personal growth in the writing classroom" (75). Such pedagogy can be used as a framework to support the goals Hugh Burns outlines, especially since a variety of studies have shown that, under the right circumstances, individual voice and personal growth can be cultivated in electronic writing environments for some students (Blair and Sauer, 2000; Hawisher and Sullivan, 1998). The greater challenge is to extend existing research to develop online environments supportive of all students of varying ethnicities, economic circumstances, sexual orientations, ages, and abilities. Feminist pedagogy offers a foundation for developing an effective writing environment because it endorses revaluing the experience of female students, who have repeatedly been shown to struggle not with the technology itself but with underlying political factors that continue to disenfranchise them. An endorsement of feminist pedagogy can also address difficulties resulting from race, class, and age issues that always intersect with gender-related issues. According to Wendy Hesford (1998) "Feminists should develop writing pedagogies that reflect the experiences and languages of traditionally oppressed groups and simultaneously bear witness to social constructions of whiteness and to the way such constructions shape reader–writer and student–teacher relations" (148).

Though space doesn't permit us room to address these related issues, an underlying feminist framework can be broadened to revalue the experience of *all* students in the computer-aided writing classroom, and it can offer a way for a safe electronic writing environment to thrive. Moving beyond rhetorics of technology and egalitarian narratives present in previous research on computers and composition means not only theorizing goals but actually articulating practicalities involved in designing a computer-mediated writing classroom based on feminist pedagogies. In this chapter, we suggest that teachers interested in incorporating feminist/gender-fair pedagogy into an electronic writing classroom should do the following: redefine *computer literacy*, respect multiple points of entry into the electronic writing environment, collaborate to establish ground rules for communication, establish "friendship groups" or a buddy system as a support network, and recruit technology mentors for students.

Redefining *Computer Literacy*

Before developing an online writing course, teachers need to redefine the term *computer literacy*. The AAUW has pointed out that computer literacy involves much more than the word processing which girls are already skilled at; it involves solving real-life problems with technology (xii). Making such a distinction is important in the electronic writing environment because students typically already possess basic technological skills such as navigating the Internet and sending email, and scholars such as Bolter (1995) and Johnson-Eiola (1997) have demonstrated that hypertextual writing environments demand more complex thought skills. Hypertextual writing often calls for giving serious consideration to issues such as what amount of text to use on the screen and how links between pages function, considerations that don't exist in the traditional writing environment. Yet many early discussions of hypertext (Bolter, 1991; Landow, 1992) focus on issues of usability and consumption of preexisting content by expert authors. As Laura Sullivan (1999) asserts, "Most male theorists see hypertext as a tool through which teachers can bring information to students and have students manipulate and respond to this information in new ways" (29). For Sullivan and other feminist teachers, however, the multilinear nature of hypertext not only allows for the representation of diverse voices but also for multiple, fragmented subjectivities. In the context of the writing classroom, this may manifest itself in online assignments that blend the personal and academic—and the visual, verbal, and aural—in order to enhance opportunities for establishing situated yet fluid knowledges and identities. For female students in particular, the potential for reinventing one's self through hypertext and electronic discourse has its roots in Donna Haraway's (1996) discussion of the gender-neutral cyborg, within which traditional binaries of male/female, body/machine collapse in ways that foster empowerment. Although the extent to which Haraway's manifesto is seen as utopian has been a subject addressed by many technofeminists, practical experimentation with cyborg writing can indeed occur. For example, as a way of enabling students to see the technical and personal power of image editing, we have each had our students experiment with altering their own digitized self-images by using filters and other features of image-editing programs such as Adobe Photoshop. These software applications enable students to change the colors and orientations of their images, "crystallize" themselves (each of the pixels is enlarged to make the image appear to be composed of crystals), or design themselves with three heads by using the cut-and-paste option.

For many women, controlling their own images online represents a form of agency that differs dramatically from their experiences with web sites designed to objectify rather than personify the female image. Some sites that present positive female images show readers how the site writers edit pictures of themselves. On the Grrl.com site, Bonnie Burton shows herself in a variety of poses and then jokingly tells readers that some people think she is vain for posting pictures of herself (Grrl). This contradiction reveals some of the core prejudices women face online. Burton's situation reveals that although the formats may vary, identity seems to be an ever-present issue for female students. In this sense, computer literacy becomes less of a "how" than a "why." The use of hypermedia technologies allows collaboration as well as the establishment and reinvention of personal identity that in the case of women is based on something more than their external image.

However, developing positive images is only part of the equation. In addition to encouraging alternative/feminist forms of communication such as image editing, cultivating the supportive sense of community that feminist pedagogy advocates means exploring how hypertext writing can be feminist. In comparison to print documents that often possess the traditional introduction, body, and conclusion, electronic discourse and hypermedia formats lend themselves well to the open-ended, discursive, and/or unfinished writings that female students appear to prefer (Benjamin and Irwin-DeVitis, 1998; Stygall, 1998; Cleary, 1996). Teachers can design assignments that foster these more experimental, nonlinear features. Eileen Schell notes that feminist pedagogy values the authentic voice often found in nontraditional sources (75). Ultimately, electronic writing environments lend themselves well to nontraditional spaces for genres such as online journals and discussion forums.

Respecting Multiple Points of Entry into the Electronic Writing Environment

In addition to redefining what it means to be computer literate, the AAUW recommends that instructors respect multiple points of entry into the electronic writing environment (xii). Every teaching approach will not work effectively with every student; thus, a variety of approaches is needed to address different learning styles, particularly those that have been identified as feminine by theorists such as Carol Gilligan (1982) and Mary Belenky et al. (1997). It is likely that students will have a range of technological prowess, and students who aren't technologically skilled have the dual task of learning both the technological skill and the content for the class. Permitting extra lab time to navigate thorny technological issues can provide a lifesaver for these students and those who feel uncomfortable in the computer classroom.

Teachers can use part of that extra time to utilize assessment strategies that equalize knowledge among students rather than penalize those with fewer technological skills. One specific assessment option is the use of a student "eportfolio." In her introduction to the recent AAHE collection on eportfolios, coeditor Barbara Cambridge (2001) refers to eportfolios as knowledge builders, citing previous research that defines both the theoretical and practical characteristics of eportfolio assessment: their ability to feature multiple examples of work, to be context rich in providing more descriptive analyses of both process and product, to offer opportunities for selection and self-assessment, and to offer a sense of technological literacy development over time (2). Certainly, an eportfolio approach is similar in its goals to a print-based portfolio approach. In the context of hypertext writing, however, the multilinear, media-rich document design process and the multiple, real-world

Internet audiences both suggest the necessity for continual revision. These phenomena make a portfolio approach not only instructionally viable but also theoretically consistent with student-centered learning and feminist pedagogy, particularly in its encouragement of self-reflection and self-assessment.

Encouraging Collaboration to Establish Ground Rules for Online Communication

In addition to engaging in self-reflection and taking more responsibility for more formalized assignments, students should collaborate on establishing "ground rules" for online communication in the networked environment. Indeed, online communities do not exist by sheer virtue of the technology or by putting a group of people together online. Rather, communities must be nurtured in a way that involves the equal collaboration between teachers and students and the recognition and respect of differences within the group. As many teachers have noted, students new to the online environment will often say things online that they would never say in real-time situations. Before online conversation begins, teachers can spend time discussing what kinds of communication are appropriate in the virtual environment, stressing that maintaining decorum and demonstrating mutual respect are the social and academic responsibilities of the entire class, not only those of the teacher. Wahlstrom (1994) notes co-ed writing forums are often contentious because women and men often approach collaboration and negotiation differently, a finding supported by Gilligan (1990), among others. In fact, "computer-supported writing systems often fail because they don't take into consideration conflict and consensus in group decision making" (Duin as qtd. in Wahlstrom 183) To counteract this problem, teachers can assign roles and responsibilities to students to ensure equal accountability and leadership between genders and to enable collaborative knowledge-making. Offering alternatives to the notion of electronic discourse as yet another space to be mastered is necessary to empower marginalized students who find traditional discourse threatening or exclusive because of its emphasis on linear, and in some cases agonistic, concepts of argumentation and of a singular voice that represents or refutes others. Furthermore, endorsing collaboration rather than competition might ease some of the tension female students may be feeling in the classroom.

Establishing a Buddy System or "Friendship Groups" at the Computer

Taking the concept of collaboration a step further, teachers can establish a buddy system or "friendship groups" at the computer. Sanders (1986) argues that even though the computer lab and computer culture in general have been male dominated and even threatening to women (Miller, 1997; Dibbell, 1993; Van Gelder, 1985), those interested in helping female students navigate technology more comfortably shouldn't be searching for an overarching "villain."

Instead, she notes that factors previously considered relatively minor, such as the absence of girlfriends in the lab, actually make a significant difference. Since female students place preeminent value on peer relationships, it is understandable that the computer lab would seem much more welcoming if other same-sex peers were present. Sanders further contends in "Villain Wanted" (1995) that "by the same token, girls also reported that their girl-friends' lack of interest in computing was far more powerful in discouraging their computer use than any other factor" (154). Our own "Cybergrrl Project," an after-school computer camp in which we taught eleven junior high school girls to create web sites for family and friends, reflects this dilemma (Blair and Sauer, 2000; Sauer, 2001). Three girls who were not part of the established groups that formed during the study failed to complete the project, in part because of a lack of communication with and support from friends. As we noted, these girls came and left each week alone and were also isolated during the actual work time. While the Cybergrrl Project invited them to construct their own visions of what a "girl-friendly" web space might entail, clearly, a safe haven—created and sustained by all participants—is necessary for females to remain and interact in electronic environments.

Buddy systems can also extend beyond the actual classroom. Hawisher and Sullivan found in their study of the listserv women@waytoofast that even after the study ended, women went to the listserv to call for help negotiating harassment situations online. They note, "There was a tremendous feeling of power in the knowledge that support was only an email message away" (195). Students can similarly employ online forums to share difficulties and solutions and thus feel more comfortable in the classroom if they have an intense support network.

Cultivating Mentoring Relationships for Students

Since the AAUW (1996) has found that "nothing is more important to girls' developing sense of self than a mentor," teachers can also cultivate mentoring relationships for students (86). The 2000 AAUW report suggests that teachers follow these steps to strengthen such relationships: secure course release time for mentoring work, give public recognition to mentors, provide resources for legal protection, and offer more than one adult connection to female students (87). Because composition teachers often find themselves in mentoring roles due to the nature of the writing course (i.e., providing personal feedback on papers, holding one-on-one conferences with students), these suggestions can help them negotiate the leap between the traditional classroom and the computer-aided composition class. For instructors who find themselves in the position of teaching students who already have technological skills, Roberta Furger (1998) advocates that female teachers learn additional technical skills right along with the students. Doing this will provide students with female role models who are interested in technology and believe it is important. Many teachers rely on instructional technology specialists at their institutions to perform hands-on demos or to troubleshoot with other technical problems, so mentoring relationships can counter what can become a "white-coat" syndrome, in which technological expertise and authority is invested in the techie specialist, often male. Although the workshop and hands-on elements of the computer classroom do foster an informal mentoring in which students naturally help each other—particularly with evolving skills such as web design and digital imaging—instructors should establish more formalized mentoring contexts as well. For example, instructors might assign minisoftware lessons to individuals or teams of students and require both documentation and demonstration. Allowing students to become the experts and to teach both the instructor and fellow students disrupts the expected balance of power in the computer classroom and enables the disenfranchised, thus realizing the feminist pedagogical tenet of giving voice to those who have no voice. Yet even while enacting such mentoring initiatives, students themselves, both male and female, may have traditional attitudes about who should teach (the teacher) and who knows more about technology (males). These traditional notions create a "mastering"—as opposed to a "mentoring"—phenomenon that may actually reinscribe the very hierarchies teachers are working to dismantle. Given this possibility of student resistance to more decentered approaches, it is equally important to recognize students' differing expectations and to encourage critical discussion among students about how technology intersects and impacts gender, ethnicity, age, sexual orientation, class, and economic status arenas in the classroom. Hawisher and Sullivan argue:

> Electronic networks, neither egalitarian utopias nor sites devoid of power and influence for women, offer women a way into the male-dominated computer culture. But gaining access to this culture means that women must confront issues of gender and power in the construction of their views of e-space. (173)

Confronting these issues guarantees that they will not be overlooked as class projects are completed. Traditionally, female students have had a problematic relationship with technology, encountering problems such as online harassment and prejudice from male colleagues. Understandably, female students come to the writing classroom with a host of (sometimes conflicting) expectations. As Hawisher and Sullivan found in their 1994 study of their woman@waytoofast listserv,

> some women wanted e-spaces to be a supportive community; some wanted them to be sites of scholarly discussion about composition studies; some wanted them to ease the burdens of professional or personal isolation; some wanted public discussions to take on the comforting qualities of personal e-mail; some wanted fun and escape from their day-to-day, overworked lives; some wanted efficient forums for the exchange of professional information. (178)

Clearly participants were looking for varying, often contradictory, levels of support from colleagues and a range of formalities and "appropriate" discussion topics, making it impossible for Hawisher and Sullivan to design a listproc capable of meeting the needs of all women. Indeed, in their subsequent analysis of their own participation as lesbian feminists on the women@ waytoofast list, Joanne Addison and Susan Hilligoss (1999) noted the absence of commentary on what were essentially their initial coming-out narratives on the list. As a result of this experience and other research grounded in a feminist materialist perspective, they conclude that "women-centered lists are not inherently more democratic than other types of lists and we have a responsibility as feminist teachers and researchers to recognize our own antidemocratic practices so that we can move toward transforming them as well as the technology" (29). Within the context of the first-year writing classroom, it is important for teachers to remember that an "add computer and stir" model of technological integration will not guarantee safer, more egalitarian online spaces for our students, particularly those from more diverse backgrounds. Even the best attempts at egalitarianism can lead to expressions of racism, sexism, and homophobia, as composition specialists have noted (Faigley, 1992). Thus, we must experiment with a range of assignment contexts, teaching styles, and communication protocols collaboratively established by teacher and students to better foster safe havens for all students.

Granted, a listproc or other online forum doesn't have to please everyone to function smoothly or to be a challenging learning experience. Electronic environments *do* allow an accessible forum for all participants to post their opinions, and many conflicting opinions about the appropriateness of cutesy Thanksgiving pictures or the value of rehashing the online harassment narratives were voiced in the all-female forum on which Hawisher and Sullivan report. Although female students accustomed to "being nice" might feel uncomfortable with confrontation, such disagreements often "invigorate the discussion" and increase the number of postings on listservs, according to Hawisher and Sullivan (184–85). In fact, Burns argues that an effective online writing curriculum should stimulate freedom of expression and value all human discourse. Recognizing and acknowledging differences reinforces critical thought about technology's relationship to writing. Negotiation should be the order of the day if all voices are valued.

Conclusion: Paying Attention to Pedagogy

Realizing an electronic writing classroom informed by feminist pedagogy is possible when the previously discussed strategies are enacted, and such strategies can pave the way for the effective online writing classrooms Burns and others envision. Basing a computer-mediated writing classroom on feminist pedagogy invites female students in particular to actively claim espace as a safe haven. Hawisher and Sullivan argue that doing this is necessary, saying,

> We agree that feminists must harness the new technologies to serve their own just political and social goals. Though women do not always know how to harness e-spaces as sites for feminist power, it is our contention that women's participation in e-space will necessitate a rethinking of public and private space. (195)

By encouraging safe havens within the electronic writing classrooms, teachers provide both male and female students with an opportunity to develop a technological literacy that extends beyond mere technical skill to higher-level thinking capacities, including a more critical understanding of how the visual, verbal, and aural features of eliteracy can be used to sometimes reinforce, and sometimes transform, cultural norms. Indeed, as Selfe (1999) insists, a critical technological literacy requires that both teachers and students "pay attention" to the ways in which technological access and ability are mediated by the cultural and materialist constructions of gender, race, class, age, and sexual orientation. As we have suggested, the fact that students can write in (assumed) private, online spaces in a networked classroom doesn't guarantee that such spaces are safe. The amount and type of interaction the student has with peers in the class, the pedagogical motivations behind how either the lab or the virtual environment is designed, the types of projects assigned, and the extent of instructor and peer guidance all contribute to constructing a nonthreatening space for both female and male students. Ultimately, the feminist theoretical and pedagogical principles woven throughout this chapter can help to better realize the technological literacy and gender-equity goals for which Hugh Burns, the AAUW, and countless others have called.

Works Cited

Addison, J., and S. Hilligoss. "Technological Fronts: Lesbian Lives 'on the Line.'" *Feminist Cyberscapes: Mapping Gendered Academic Spaces.* Ed. K. Blair and P. Takayoshi. Stamford, CT: Ablex. 21–40.

American Association of University Women Educational Foundation. *Girls in the Middle: Working to Succeed in School.* New York: AAUW, 1996.

———. *Tech Savvy: Educating Girls in the New Computer Age.* New York: AAUW, 2000.

Belenky, M. F., B. M. Clinchy, N. R. Goldberger, and J. M. Tarule. *Women's Ways of Knowing: The Development of Self, Voice, and Mind.* 10th ed. New York: Basic Books, 1997.

Benjamin, B., and L. Irwin-DeVitis. "Censoring Girls' Choices: Continued Gender Bias in English Language Arts Classrooms." *English Journal* 87 (1998): 64–71.

Blair, K., and C. Sauer. "Re-imaging a Feminine Self Online: Studying the Literate Practices of Cybergrrls." Paper presented at the Conference on College Composition and Communication, Minneapolis, MN. 2000.

Bolter, J. *Writing Space: The Computer, Hypertext, and the History of Writing.* Hillsdale, NJ: Erlbaum, 1991.

Burns, H. "The Writers We Happen to Teach: An Epilogue." *Computers and Composition* 16 (1999): 167–69.

Cambridge, B. L., S. Kahn, D. P. Tompkins, and K. B. Yancey. *Electronic Portfolios: Emerging Practices in Student, Faculty, and Institutional Learning*. Washington, DC: AAHE, 2001.

Cassell, J., and H. Jenkins, eds. *From Barbie to Mortal Kombat: Gender and Computer Games*. Cambridge, MA: MIT, 1998.

Cleary, L. M. "I Think I Know What My Teachers Want Now: Gender and Writing Motivation." *English Journal* 85 (1996): 50–57.

Dibbell, J. *A Rape in Cyberspace*. Online. 10 April 1999. Original work published in 1993.

Faigley, L. *Fragments of Rationality: Postmodernity and the Subject of Composition*. Pittsburgh: University of Pittsburgh P, 1992.

Furger, R. *Does Jane Compute? Preserving Our Daughters' Place in the Cyber Revolution*. New York: Warner, 1998.

Gerrard, L. "Feminist Research in Computers and Composition." Ed. K. Blair and P. Takayoshi. *Feminist Cyberscapes: Mapping Gendered Academic Spaces*. Stamford, CT: Ablex, 1999. 377–400.

Gilligan, C. *In a Different Voice: Psychological Theory and Women's Development*. Cambridge, MA: Harvard University P, 1982.

Gilligan, C., N. P. Lyons, and T. Hanmer, eds. *Making Connections: The Relational Worlds of Adolescent Girls at Emma Willard School*. Cambridge, MA: Harvard University P, 1990.

Grrl. 5 July 2001 <http://www.grrl.com>.

Haraway, D. "A Cyborg Manifesto." *CyberReader*. Ed. V. J. Vitanza. Boston: Allyn & Bacon, 1996. 191–233.

Hawisher, G., and C. L. Selfe. "The Rhetoric of Technology and the Electronic Writing Classroom." *College Composition and Communication* 42 (1991): 55–65.

Hawisher, G. E., and P. Sullivan. "Women on the Networks: Searching for E-spaces of Their Own." *Feminism and Composition Studies: In Other Words*. Ed. S. C. Jarratt and L. Worsham. New York: MLA, 1998. 172–97.

Hesford, W. "'Ye Are Witnesses': Pedagogy and the Politics of Identity." *Feminism and Composition Studies: In Other Words*. Ed. S. C. Jarratt and L. Worsham. New York: MLA, 1998. 132–52.

Johnson-Eilola, J. *Nostalgic Angels: Rearticulating Hypertext Writing*. Norwood, NJ: Ablex, 1997.

Kaplan, N., and E. Farrell. "Weavers of Webs: A Portrait of Young Women on the Net." *The Arachnet Electronic Journal on Virtual Culture* 2.3 (1994).

Landow, G. *Hypertext: The Convergence of Contemporary Critical Theory and Technology*. Baltimore: Johns Hopkins UP, 1992.

Miller, L. "Women and Children First: Gender and the Settling of the Electronic Frontier." *Resisting the Virtual Life: The Culture and Politics of Information*. Ed. J. Brook and I. A. Boal. San Francisco: City Lights, 1995.

Romano, S. "The Egalitarianism Narrative: Whose Story? Whose Yard-stick?" *Computers and Composition* 10 (1993): 5–28.

Sadker, M., and D. Sadker. *Failing at Fairness: How Our Schools Cheat Girls.* New York: Simon, 1994.

Sanders, J. "Closing the Computer Gender Gap." *The Education Digest* 52 (1986). 20–23.

Sanders, J. "Girls and Technology: Villain Wanted." *Teaching the Majority: Breaking the Gender Barrier in Science, Mathematics, and Engineering.* Ed. S. V. Rosser. New York: Teachers College P, 1995. 147–59.

Sauer, C. "Removing the Mask of Silence: Counteracting Gender Bias in the Junior High Language Arts Classroom Using Cybergrrls." Bowling Green, OH: Bowling Green State University, 2001.

Selfe, C. *Technology and Literacy in the Twenty-first Century: The Importance of Paying Attention.* Carbondale: Southern Illinois UP, 1999.

Stabile, C. A. *Feminism and the Technological Fix.* New York: St. Martin's, 1994.

Stygall, Gail. "Women and Language in the Collaborative Writing Classroom." *Feminism and Composition Studies: In Other Words.* Ed. S. C. Jarratt and L. Worsham. New York: MLA, 1998. 252–75.

Sullivan, L. "Wired Women Writing: Towards a Feminist Theorization of Hypertext." *Computers and Composition* 16 (1999): 25–54.

Takayoshi, P., E. Huot, and M. Huot. "No Boys Allowed: The World Wide Web as a Clubhouse for Girls." *Computers and Composition* 16: 89–106.

Van Gelder, L. "The Strange Case of the Electronic Lover." *Computerization and Controversy: Value Conflicts and Social Choices.* Ed. C. Dunlap and R. Kling. New York: Academic, 1984. 364–75.

Section II:
Learning to Teach
with Technology

Fools Rush In

SCOTT LLOYD DEWITT AND MARCIA DICKSON
The Ohio State University at Marion

There's a narrow line between being foolish and being wise, and the last thing anyone in the academic arena wants to do is to feel or appear foolish. Our acceptance in the academy, not to mention our own self-esteem, depends a great deal upon our ability to present ourselves—both in conversation and in writing—as knowledgeable, rational human beings possessed of intellectual merit. These are matters of identity similar to issues of race, gender, sexual orientation, or ability. Any understanding of identity depends upon an examination of the construction of self—in this case, we are constructing our sense of self as scholars, as teachers. For this identity to be complete, to be authentic, we need to learn to be a bit foolish as well since the learning that comes from taking what others might consider foolish chances is often the basis of innovative thought.

For most of our academic teaching careers, the two of us have engaged in developing courses which have been enhanced by word processing, email, electronic discussion groups, and other computer-based activities—a pursuit that other members of our profession sometimes feel is inherently foolish but that we believe eventually leads to wisdom.

Wise Beyond Our Years

Early research in the field of computers and composition strongly suggested that sound pedagogy should always begin with what we already hold to be true about teaching writing: that the technology should be secondary and used as a means to achieve our primary goal of facilitating student learning. Not only does this sell short the possibilities for inventing pedagogy that grows out of our experiences with various technologies, but it also paints an unrealistic picture of how innovative classroom applications of technology are created. Often, computer-rich assignments and classroom activities grow out of teachers' experiences with the technology itself. In other words, as teachers work with a particular technology, they imagine a classroom application and then shape this application with what they know about teaching writing. Of course, when the assignment or activity is realized in the classroom, the use of technology should be balanced with sound teaching practice—a seamless chicken/egg entity.

Last year, the two of us completely revamped our sections of first-year composition, a reconceptualization of what we were doing with our students. Our early discussions about this course grew out of our desire to try something new with the technology. We both admit to being initially motivated by simple boredom, but as we worked on the course, we began to develop some specific goals.

Technology Goals

For this class, we decided to focus our attention narrowly on the Web, as both a form of technology and a subject of inquiry, integrating it into the writing assignments. We asked students to read, research, and compose using web technologies. All course materials were available online—readings, class documents, and assignments. The final writing assignment required students to create their own web site. To this end, we each used MS FrontPage to create and maintain individual web sites to make available class records and announcements germane to our own students (<http://mrspock.marion.ohio-state/dewitt/> and <http://mrspock.marion.ohio-state.edu/dickson99/>). We also shared responsibility for maintaining a collaborative web site (<http://mrspock.marion.ohio-state.edu/e110assign/>) that contained class assignments, readings that weren't readily available on the Web, schedules, and general feedback for all of our students.

Student Writing Goals

We knew that change in our students' writing would be imminent if we were indeed committed to a new focus on web technology and that such a significant shift would also require an equally significant shift in the type of writing that students would produce. It was important that any new sequence of assignments be equivalent to our previous writing assignments, which asked students to process difficult texts—both as readers and as writers—and to consider carefully the ways in which a writer addresses an audience, establishes purpose, develops an argument, finds and utilizes appropriate forms of evidence, and deliberates on matters of style and form. The final web site assignment—a large-scale web site project—would serve as an opportunity for students to collect and reshape all of the writing and thinking they had done for the course. This assignment would require us to develop a means of valuing and assessing students' graphic designs as well as to consider how this visual rhetoric would blend with the extended written word.

Planning the Course

For our first run through the course, we taught our sections of first-year composition in tandem. Our individual sections were as identical as two sections could possibly be, and our experience was about as close to team teaching as two people can get without actually teaching the same group of students. For example, in addition to collaborating on a great deal of preliminary planning before the term began, we had a standing date on Monday mornings throughout the quarter to converse about our classes, review student writing, and create class schedules, day by day, for the week. We deliberately ran our pilot during the spring quarter so that we could reflect on our invention over the summer, believing that this extended break from the classroom would allow us the time to revise the course as necessary.

Like most of our colleagues, we chose to design our writing course around a particular theme, or content area. "Censorship, Witch-hunts, and Thought Police" asked students to examine critically the complicated issues that shape how we understand (or do not understand) the nature of censorship and free speech. Our thinking was that this topic would force students to think complexly about a subject that they often take for granted or that they treat superficially, at best. Our course consisted of three major writing projects, descriptions of which follow.

Writing Project 1

The first writing project was a collaborative venture that asked students to write in teams of three or four. We created the following rhetorical situation: "In its efforts to prepare for National Anti-Censorship Month in October, the Marion Campus Library is compiling a list of resources for students and teachers about First Amendment issues." Student groups were charged with writing "descriptive evaluations of web sites that feature valuable information and creative viewpoints for those interested in researching various censorship and free speech issues." The intended audience was the library staff. We provided our students with a list of over forty web sites that they were asked to examine outside of class. Then, their writing team needed to choose two sites from this list, one on First Amendment rights *in general*, and the other on a *specific* free speech issue. After spending time writing thick descriptions of these two sites, students were asked to "write a short essay where you make an argument for what makes an effective web site for college students on the issues of censorship and free speech." The assignment was fairly traditional: "First, you must substantiate the claims you make in regards to the criteria that makes a web site effective. Then, you must support your argument with details and examples from the two web sites you [chose to analyze]."

We modeled this assignment for students by having the entire class look at two web sites that mirrored the texts we wanted them to explore: The Center for Democracy and Technology (<www.cdt.org>) and the Xenaverse War Room (<http://www.nutbread.com/warroom.html>). The CDT web site, controlled and tightly organized, takes the form of a newsletter, complete with headlines, side bars, and editorials. The Xenaverse War Room site is an emotional and rambling collection of information devoted to protesting the censorship of a "Xena, Warrior Princess" episode because it featured Xena battling Krishna and Hindu gods. Working in groups, the students drew upon each other's observations and opinions to analyze the censorship sites and tease out what was effective and what was problematic in the presentation of information and opinion. Then, as a class, we created criteria for evaluating the effectiveness of the web sites that they would analyze as part of the first writing project.

The in-class workshop directed students both to describe the sites and to begin making claims about what contributed to effective web writing. Writing teams turned in drafts of this writing project, and we offered extensive written feedback to students that impressed upon them the importance of revision, especially early in the term. We offered both global feedback about their entire drafts as well as specific feedback on distinct areas that needed attention.

Writing Project 2

For their second assignment, students were asked to adopt a more argumentative stance in their writing: "Write an editorial in which you argue for or against the appropriateness of a specific case of censorship." Students were expected to use the Web to locate and study a clearly definable case, situation, or instance of censorship and to "decide whether or not the key players involved were justified in the decisions they made." This assignment moved students toward writing for an audience of a particular forum instead of to an identifiable reader (the campus library staff). Like the first writing project, this assignment also had overtones of traditional academic writing: "Your editorial should forward a strong thesis that clearly states your position on the case, and your position should be supported by logical thinking, carefully constructed arguments, and substantial evidence."

Knowing that our students would need a model for writing, we posted an example of an editorial, "Forget Big Brother; Beware Little Sister: Turning Children Into Spies, or Be Careful of What You Think and Say," by Nat Hentoff, on our common web site. We asked students to read the article, attempting to answer the question "What is the structural makeup—the parts and pieces—of an editorial?" We also presented students with our own annotation of the article after they had completed the assignment.

We hoped that the first assignment would feed into this writing project not only by introducing students to specific cases of censorship and ways of thinking critically about those cases but also by providing them with a foundation in general First Amendment theories and concepts. However, we did not rely upon this hope alone. Knowing how difficult it is for students to develop their own editorial topics, we offered students a number of general suggestions, like the following, to get them started in their research:

Internet—Should schools and libraries be required to place filters on the computers used for public access? Examples: Blocking software for computers used by children; limited computer access for children; filters to eliminate hate sites.

Finally, we forewarned our students: "Make sure you are engaged with this topic. You will be asked to continue working with it in Writing Project 3." As with the first writing project, we provided students with written feedback on their drafts, yet we focused mostly on their overall arguments.

Writing Project 3

The final writing project was clearly the most experimental. Whereas we asked students to pull from their first two assignments extensively, the final product was to be significantly different from the writing they had completed to date:

> Create a web site that a serious undergraduate student could use to conduct research on a narrow topic pertaining to censorship, free speech, and First Amendment rights. Your purpose is to provide these students with a wide variety of resources about your narrow topic that they will, in turn, be able to use in their own research. Your web site should be informative in purpose while also forwarding your perspective, when appropriate, on your chosen topic. Furthermore, your web site should represent the qualities and characteristics of effective web sites that you articulated in Writing Project 1. (In fact, you may find it helpful to imagine that you are creating a web site that could be recommended for the Marion Campus Library's Anti-Censorship Month resources.)

Indeed, we were asking a lot of our students. Not only did they need to consider issues of audience, purpose, and content, but they also had to consider these concepts in regards to composing a web text which included a graphic, visual composition as well as a navigation structure. To provide some guidelines which would help us with assessment, we listed the elements that each site needed to include: a home page of some type, an introduction to the site that would justify its purpose (students were encouraged to think about Writing Project 1 when writing this introduction), a linked annotated bibliography of web sources, and an annotated bibliography of non-web sources. So that students didn't simply "information dump" in their web sites, we also asked them to include "a significant amount of original text and relevant material" that would create an overall argument throughout the site. However, we did allow them to revise and to incorporate Writing Project 2 into their web sites to meet this goal.

To help them complete the project, we taught our students Microsoft FrontPage, and because they needed to use classroom computers to create their web sites, most of our class time was used to work on web sites. Students were instructed to complete certain research and writing tasks outside of class so that their time using the classroom computers was well spent. Most of the web sites were created on diskettes—a few larger sites needed a zip drive—so that the students could work outside class, either at home or in the campus computer labs. We published the completed web sites on the server because we did not wish to give students access to our server password.

We gave our students feedback in two forms. We posted global feedback to all of our students on our class web site, and we held numerous in-class conferences with some students while others worked on their web sites. Midway through the project, we held a "critique workshop," much like an artist's critique, in which small groups of students—three or four in each group—worked with the teacher to provide design feedback to each other. Students loaded their web sites on the computer, and the group spent approximately fifteen minutes looking at each site's design, offering an almost "gut reaction" to issues of layout, alignment, color, typeface, and navigation. As teachers, we asked the participants to refer back to the work they had completed earlier in the quarter to draw upon what they had learned about effective site design. Students whose sites were being critiqued took notes and articulated both the plans that they had for completing their sites and the problems that they were experiencing as they made their original visions concrete.

Reality Strikes

To look at the syllabus, it would appear that we had created a series of great scholarly activities for our students and ourselves. We certainly anticipated a quarter of fast-moving conversations about the complex nature of censorship and looked forward to watching the students respond to difficult but satisfying writing tasks. However, as the quarter progressed, we grew increasingly more puzzled and distressed to discover that we were uncharacteristically isolated from our students and unable to stimulate the level of intellectual endeavor that we usually enjoyed with our classes. Nothing about these classes fit into the patterns we, as seasoned composition instructors, were accustomed to encountering. Although several positive things occurred under our tutelage—students learned quite a bit about analyzing the web texts that have become part of our society's everyday life, about the conventions that govern editorials, and about documenting ideas in their essays—we are not altogether convinced that our students drew upon and increased their potential as writers, thinkers, and learners. Neither class even approached the formation of the sort of intellectual community that would make it possible for all of us to explore a topic thoroughly. The majority of students neither asked nor attempted to answer the complex questions which the topic of censorship should have generated.

It has taken several months of reflection to come to some conclusions about what went wrong. The major problem with the class design was simple: We were continually overwhelmed by the magnitude of the task we had undertaken. We had, in essence, not eased into a new endeavor, trying to add an element or two of technology to our practice. We had instead radically changed most of the pedagogy we found safe and familiar. We were completely reinventing the entire course, forgetting what we already knew and blindly trusting that our new strategies would work.

While one is in the process of invention, it's hard to keep track of what is and isn't working in the classroom. Such information is only gained through reflection. Unfortunately, even after reflection, the reasons why we were so dissatisfied with our experiment can't be neatly categorized into a tidy list of pedagogical dos and don'ts. However, we did come to recognize a series of pedagogical choices which we made which contributed to the problems.

#1: Eliminating the Common Text

One of the pedagogical premises to which the two of us have always adhered is that reading enriches and stimulates the thought behind student writing. The texts we have used in the past have varied: books, sections of readers, special collections of related articles—in short, any material that would prompt thinking, model the conventions of academic texts, and allow students to develop an educated opinion about a topic. This time the reading was different. Seduced, perhaps, by the claims of the Internet and by our own successes with using the Internet as a research tool, we decided to forego using a common text that the students would read together and discuss in class and focused instead on the reading material students could find on the Web. The work we usually do with analysis, we assumed, could be done just as well by concentrating on the rhetoric that is inherent in web construction.

Although the first writing project was successful, in the second and third writing projects—the editorial and the web site—the weakness in our grand scheme began to surface. The first drafts, and eventually the final products, could only be characterized as passionate but shallow. Arguments consisted of appeals to the emotions supported by the simplest possible confirmations of the students' positions. Even those students who attempted to balance their arguments by looking at the other side of the issue gave that opposing viewpoint quick acknowledgment and even quicker dismissal.

The problem, we decided, resulted from the lack of a common reading which would have formed the foundation of recursive study and discussion. Reading a common text together would have allowed us to focus on deepening the students' knowledge base and understanding of discourse. The debate which grows out of such discussions always requires students to consider others' opinions and beliefs. Without the complicated resistance that discussion brings, the students had little compulsion to question their primary beliefs.

#2: Relying on Web Texts

We encountered several problems when relying on web texts:

- *The rich and complex topic of censorship was not well served by the electronic media.* Amazingly, the majority of web sites on censorship proved to agree with each other. What we assumed would emerge as a hearty debate on the evils and virtues of censorship turned out to be a one-sided argument.[1]

- *The abundance of information did not inspire inquiry.* The students uncovered either too much information or not enough. The information and arguments provided by most sites proved to be redundant and undeveloped, denouncing the practice of censorship without examining the reasons why opponents were concerned about it. Other web writing was better suited to print journals than to web sites. Long, scholarly, and extremely dense, both visually and rhetorically, these articles were difficult to read online.

- *The reading style encouraged by the Web caused students to read casually rather than closely.* Students were not presented with an *explicit* argument, and so moved quickly from link to link without fully understanding or considering the merits of the *implied* arguments of the authors of the sites. Although students' surfing endurance was tested, their intellectual powers were seldom engaged or exercised.

#3: *Underestimating the Demands of Technology*

"Writing for the Web," the final project which was supposed to cumulate the students' first-year writing experience, had been planned to allow the expression of the students' newly developed academic selves—an identity that would support them as they continued on their educational journey. Again, we made several foolish assumptions:

- *Technology learning curves won't interfere with rhetorical learning curves.* We now believe—and it is amazing that we did not foresee—that our students' development as writers may have been hampered by the efforts that went into the development of their web sites. Our expectation was that the two types of learning—technological and analytical—would complement each other. As the students learned how to create a web page, we had reasoned, they would be making decisions about the effectiveness of visual representation as well as textual placement. In theory, the process ought to work; in reality, it didn't.

- *Web texts can be responded to in the same manner as print texts.* Although we did schedule small group presentations which required students to explain their design and written rhetorical choices, these critiques tended to be directed toward the visual elements rather than the textual ones. Consequently, we provided far less feedback on the students' written texts than we usually did.

#4: *Losing Interaction*

If the greatest aid to developing intellectual identity is interaction with one's peers and instructors, we failed to create room for that experience. Without meaning to, we had moved the students away from collaborative assignments and toward individual work.

At the start of the quarter, we had used class discussion as we had in the past, and we had gotten the results we had expected. However, when we reached the second writing project, our pedagogy changed—or perhaps slipped. As a result of time constraints, we ended up publishing our own analysis of Hentoff's editorial instead of conducting a whole-group discussion of it. Even at the time, we knew that the published analysis was not a good substitute for classroom interaction, but we were so involved in the momentum of our technological project that we were afraid to interrupt the flow of activities by backtracking to work on Hentoff's piece in class. This first omission of group discussion led to others, and by the end of the quarter, most of the interaction students had experienced was with the technology, which didn't represent the types of intellectual problem-solving that were usually the focus in our first-year writing classrooms. Seldom had our students been so tightly glued to their computers. The casual conversation and laughter that usually become part of our classroom exchanges as students grow comfortable with expressing their ideas weren't exactly absent. However, class bonding instead developed around frustration with misplaced images or delight with some gimmicky aspect of the web site rather than in the discovery of some incongruity of society or self.

Conclusions: Where Angels Fear to Tread

At this stage in our reflections on the first run of our course, we attribute our trials to our extensive use of web technology; however, we attribute nothing to the technology itself or to some imaginary innate or transparent qualities of the Web. We are more concerned with how we *used* the technology and the *assumptions* we made about it. We also realize that we need to examine the ways in which we were seduced by the technology, even after all these years of playing and working with the machines, for seduction involves losing sight of what we already know, not to mention what is right in front of us.

Next year, the course will be different and, we hope, more in line with the goals of our teaching. We plan to make several changes that we feel will address the problems we experienced in our search for adventure and a new way of teaching. We will draw upon what we already know and will modify the course in the following ways:

- Return to using a series of common texts, emphasizing more traditional academic and public discourse rather than depending upon the limited texts employed by most Internet sites
- Once again employ in-class discussion and written responses to these texts in order to push the students intellectually toward a deeper understanding of the topic
- Use collaboration more carefully in order to form a student community which can draw upon the combined knowledge and opinions of peers

- Select a topic which does not allow students to instantly adopt clichéd, even knee-jerk, positions that they cannot bring themselves to question
- Schedule special sessions for teaching web-site design early in the quarter so that students' lack of knowledge about web construction will not interfere with their development of the textual elements of their web sites

Our returning to these course components does not mean that we have abandoned or intend to abandon our search for more effective, more contemporary, and indeed, more useful ways to employ technology in our classes. We have only tested a series of new ideas, some of which worked, others of which need revision.

Call us fools. We have called ourselves that many times. We wear the label proudly. But our response to such a label is quite the opposite of how most would react: Fools rush in—again. In fact, writing this chapter has made both of us extremely eager to start working at it again. We are engaged in the process of inventing pedagogy, which means we need to be committed to and to grow comfortable with asking, "What would happen if . . ." and enthusiastically replying, "Well, let's try it." Learning—for us as well as for our students—requires taking risks and being willing to reflect and re-see. Inventing a new pedagogy requires a willingness to appear a bit foolish. Our intellectual identities depend on it.

Notes

[1] Just in case our readers might attribute the lack of such web information to the students' inability to conduct good web research: once the problem became evident, both of us put our rather extensive experience in web searching to the problem and, much to our surprise, came up with the same results.

Balancing Acts: Tightrope Walking Above an Ever-Changing (Inter)Net

NICHOLAS MAURIELLO
Spelman College

GIAN S. PAGNUCCI
Indiana University of Pennsylvania

Perhaps the greatest of all pedagogical fallacies is the notion that a person learns only the particular thing he is studying at the time.
— John Dewey

If "location, location, location" is the operative phrase in real estate sales, then "timing, timing, timing" have to be the key words in our teacher research into technology and literacy. In 1995, Gian was a first-year Assistant Professor at Indiana University (IUP) of Pennsylvania and Nick was Gian's graduate assistant. As "timing" would have it, the Internet was about to become a mainstay of popular culture, challenging established notions of commerce and culture. Finally, as timing once again dictated, IUP, like most colleges and universities, was beginning to struggle with the hows and whys of introducing the Internet into traditional pedagogy in response to the emerging national agenda to make technology a part of education. Against this background we began to introduce the Internet as a collaborative writing tool into a variety of undergraduate and graduate courses. What we have found is that technology is not easily adapted to the classroom. There are, in fact, a multitude of obstacles to making technology work in the teaching of composition. Applying technology in the classroom means changing from using successful pedagogical practices to using unproven methods (Mauriello, Pagnucci, and Winner), having some students resist and others excel in this new public writing space

79

(Mauriello and Pagnucci), and potentially exposing students to strangers and other unknown dangers of this new networked classroom community (Pagnucci and Mauriello, *Technologies' Impact*).

And yet, despite these problems, there is much potential for technology to help previously silenced students to speak, to engage students in dialogue with a culturally rich and diverse new population, and to help students become real published authors. We are faced, then, with a balancing act between trials and delights, a tightrope walk above an ever-changing (Inter)net.

What we offer in this chapter is a description of our own shaky walk from novice technology teacher to practiced technology teacher. We provide three short narratives of our attempts to make technology work for our composition teaching. As David Schaafsma tells us, stories are "sites of rich descriptive detail, grounded as they are in particular contexts, vehicles to help us think about the real from a constructed exchange of perspectives" (v). We've tried to retell our stories of pedagogical development as honestly as we can, which means that these stories are full of our excitement about curriculum planning, our grand hopes, our many missteps, and our constant search for technological teaching practices that can be successful.

We hope that this combination of stories will serve as a form of encouragement to other teachers taking their first steps toward teaching with technology. Although this is often a messy process, we do believe it is a very rewarding one, and we hope our experiences will provide a form of support to other teachers.

We hope, too, that readers can learn from our mistakes. We were at times overeager, at other times overprotective. These mistakes can be avoided. We also failed to include our students actively in the development of our curriculum. Making students a part of curriculum creation is an approach we now readily endorse. We believe that like writing, the development of pedagogy should be viewed as a process. This means we should learn to embrace, rather than fear, our mistakes, learning from them and using them to reshape our teaching. As we tell our stories, you'll see how we worked through misguided assumptions and the occasional outright blunder. We've learned to see these errors as a natural part of the pedagogy process. The errors have pushed us to reflect constantly on our pedagogy, to seek ways to improve it, and to understand where problems might be hidden. And so we urge readers to become reflective practitioners themselves, to become teachers who see mistakes as nothing more than opportunities to rethink their pedagogy.

Public Discourse versus Private Concerns

We introduced the Internet into our pedagogy in a cautious manner. We decided to experiment first with a graduate seminar in reading theory. This course explores the varied definitions of literacy and asks students to unpack their own beliefs and values about how literacy should be taught. It also places literacy and reading instruction within their social and political contexts.

In 1996, we were becoming increasingly convinced that technology and particularly the Internet were beginning to change conceptions of literacy. We were also noticing increased demands by university administrators and politicians that teachers begin to retool their pedagogical practices through the use of educational technologies. For these reasons, using a reading theory graduate seminar as a starting point for developing an Internet pedagogy seemed appropriate.

We thought we had an advantage in accomplishing these goals since the majority of graduate students in our doctoral program are experienced English teachers. We assumed that these more experienced students would be open to trying new educational technologies and would also appreciate the political ramifications of doing so. We hoped that the students could learn from our pedagogical experimentation and then adapt this technology later for their own teaching practices. Unfortunately, both of our assumptions proved to be quite misguided.

We decided to ask students to write a series of papers which would be circulated in an electronic portfolio. We designed this electronic portfolio as a series of five papers. Two of these papers were to be autobiographical stories, with the other three being syntheses of personal journal entries reflecting upon class readings. The plan was for students to post their work on the Internet and include embedded email links within each individual document for readers to use as a means for responding to the works. Any responses, whether from class members or web surfers, would be added to the students' portfolios to demonstrate the social and public nature of the electronic portfolios. We hoped that use of this portfolio method would encourage the students to view their writing as an ongoing dialogue within a larger community rather than as the standard, isolated teacher-to-student paper exchange. Our vision was that each portfolio would become a repository, remaining in place even after the semester concluded, and would become a reference site for the teacher to use as a model for developing electronic portfolios at his or her home institution.

In many ways the class we planned turned out to be a disaster, but it was a nevertheless informative blunder. The students did write all the papers we assigned, but most only published one or two on the Internet. No one posted an autobiographical story. The students also read and responded to hard copies of the papers, but they did not make email responses. Therefore, our students never established the type of online community we envisioned.

Instead of a vibrant online community, our classroom divided into two ideological camps. On the left stood the less experienced teachers. These teachers embraced the new technology, seeing ways not only to enhance their pedagogy but also to understand the political necessity of doing so. As one younger student, Ally (all student names are pseudonyms), who teaches composition in urban New Jersey, said during one class session, "Distance education is on my doorstep. If I don't use it, I'll be out of a job." Another student, Joey, who teaches tenth-grade English in Western Pennsylvania, commented, "I'm going to try to organize this in my school district. If we can get enough computers."

On the right stood a group of veteran teachers who felt no need to bring technology into their already successful pedagogical practices. These were tenured public-school teachers who could safely resist administrative and political pressures, but who also brought years of experience and thus a critical eye to our new—but unproven—teaching approaches. "Can't we just photocopy our papers instead?" Valerie, a middle school teacher from Pittsburgh, asked one day in class. She felt doing that would be easier than struggling with the computer. A high school English teacher named Mathew wondered, "How do I know that somebody won't steal my paper off the Internet? I've heard about that happening."

These resisting veteran teachers were fearful of the technology and its public nature and distrustful of this new Internet community. The student who wished to photocopy her paper was making a complicated request. She was indicating her frustration and difficulty with the learning curve for using this new pedagogical tool. To her, it seemed like too much work aimed at displacing her already-successful teaching practices (Mauriello, Pagnucci, and Winner). Her resistance highlighted the difficulty in reeducating our existing teaching force about new technology-based methodologies. Haas and Neuwirth describe the problem in this way: "The assertion that 'computers are not our job' distances us from technology by invoking a division of labor: the study of English is our job; the study of computers is the work of others. . . . Adherence to such a limited perspective results in the inadequate training of students" (325). Cynthia Selfe, in her keynote address to the 1998 Conference on College Composition and Communication, claimed this problem was discipline-wide.

Although in early class discussions, Valerie stated that she believed in the potential benefits technology might offer her own students, in a later class meeting she abandoned her exploration when she found that she could not control the technology and the type of classroom it would create. In a class workshop on file transfers, Valerie pushed herself away from her computer in frustration and said, "I give up. How can I ask my students to do this when I can't figure it out? This isn't for English teachers. You have to be a computer scientist." For Valerie, it seemed that being a teacher meant being the expert. Such a view of teaching is based on expert performance, an idea in which knowledge is delivered based on the banking model of education critiqued by Paulo Freire. Tompkins discusses this view, showing the connection between fear and performance in teaching:

> What is behind this model? How did it come to be that our main goal as academicians turned out to be performance? I think the answer to the question is fairly complicated, but here is one way to go. Each person comes into a professional situation dragging behind her a long bag full of desires, fears, expectations, needs, resentments—the list goes on. But the main component is fear. Fear is the driving force behind the performance model. Fear of being shown up for what you are—a fraud, stupid, ignorant, a clod, a dolt, a sap, a weakling, someone who can't cut the mustard. (654)

One of our mistakes in designing this first Internet-based course was not anticipating our graduate students' fears of pedagogical change. To us, the

Internet was a technological tool which could replace the photocopy machine. Our mistake was believing what Haas calls "the straightforward progress model, a new-is-better view in which new technologies are more advanced and therefore more efficient, more powerful, or both" (210). While we discussed the online project with our students, we never thought of discussing the ethical limitations of our endeavor. A more developed Internet-based pedagogy would have included class discussions of how and why students had varied reactions to the technology. In that way, we might have better understood not only Valerie's beliefs, but also our own.

Although dialogue about our new pedagogy might have improved our course, we now see that Internet-based teaching raises ethical concerns about both students' and teachers' rights. Do instructors have the right to ask students to expose personal writing to a global audience? If teachers require doing this, how does it effect the nature of what students write? Many of our students told us that they would have to censor their papers if they were going to post them. Others refused to post them because they said their papers were too personal for a public audience. Still others commented that it was only after reading their papers that they realized how much self-censoring they had done subconsciously once they were informed about the possibility that their autobiographies would be put online. Since our course hoped to foster student empowerment and a sense of community, we were left with this question: To what extent does the self-censorship by these students limit the Freirian principle of empowerment? There can't be genuine dialogue when students are censoring parts of their identity from the conversation.

The concern of Mathew, the student who feared his paper would be stolen from his web page, represents yet another set of issues. While we envisioned the electronic portfolio as a method for fostering student dialogue, we didn't expect Mathew or any other student to be threatened by the notion of sharing his writing outside a protected environment. But although Mathew was willing to give his paper to a teacher, he said he did not want to share his work with an unknown Internet readership.

Mathew's fears are certainly valid. Not only is theft a possibility on the Internet, but so is the threat of receiving untempered criticism, rejection, and alienation. Whereas we wanted our students to value sharing their writing in public and to feel a sense of empowerment by writing to a large audience, the students' concerns about the uncontrolled nature of the World Wide Web made them unwilling to post their papers on the Internet. By not addressing these safety concerns about the Internet, we may have actually created a teaching environment which disempowered students and left them comfortable only when writing for their instructor.

We set out to create a course that would empower students, one that would connect them to new audiences, give freedom to their voices, and create new purposes for their writing. We built this course on the dialogic power we had attributed to Internet technology. But our students cautioned us that because writing has such great personal value, making it public becomes problematic. Our students wanted protection as they entered the global community of the Internet, and we resolved to give it to them as we redesigned our course.

Empowerment versus Identity

As we returned to the drawing board to try to design another Internet-based course, our primary objective remained that of promoting cross-cultural dialogues. The power of the Internet as a tool for pedagogical change, we believe, rests in the medium's ability to facilitate communication with diverse cultural communities, thereby encouraging greater cultural acceptance. Although our first Internet-based pedagogy did not work very well, it was not a total failure. Freire reminds us that "knowledge emerges through invention and reinvention" (Freire 53), and thus creating a successful Internet-based course naturally requires a series of reinventions.

It is a commonly held belief that computer technology is the domain of the young. In fact, this was a repeated refrain that we had heard from our first class of graduate students, whose average age was over thirty-five. Interested in testing this belief, we introduced the Internet to a pair of first-year composition classes. We again planned to post our students' writing on the Web, but we would now add a new element: We would directly seek outside responses to these papers by drawing on students in writing classes at other universities. We called this new course the College Writing Peer Response Project (Mauriello). We were mainly concerned about creating cross-cultural dialogues and wanted to ensure that diverse populations would read our students' papers. Since our graduate students in the first Internet-based course had been experienced writing instructors from six different countries and numerous states, we believed that their participation would help us accomplish this goal, so we asked several of these teachers to allow their students to respond to our students' papers via the Internet. This plan would not only guarantee the cross-cultural dialogues that we were looking for, but it would also adhere to a basic Freirian principle of pedagogy that "education must begin with the solution of the teacher-student contradiction, by reconciling the poles of the contradiction so that both are simultaneously teachers *and* students" (53). With graduate students like Valerie and Mathew now exploring the benefits of educational technology with their own students, we hoped to shorten the poles of contradiction, thus engaging everyone in a bottom-up exploration of knowledge. We hoped that the undergraduates would share their writing as well as their knowledge of technology at the same time that the graduate students/instructors were critiquing this writing and learning to make effective educational use of Internet technology. By reconstructing our pedagogical approach, we were placing students in an environment where power was dispersed and where the students would not be molded by a banking model of education.

We also knew from our first Internet teaching experience that the whole process would break down if our students felt too uncomfortable to post their papers. The students in our first course told us that we needed to address the safety issues connected with placing highly personal writing on the Internet. The obvious answer to our problem seemed to be for students to choose pseudonyms when posting their writing. Faigley finds no detriments to using pseudonyms for online student discussions and Susan Romano reports "several kinds of evidence supporting continued use of pseudonymity: near universality of student participation (formerly fearful students speak out), degree of student enjoyment (students jump in playfully), and increase in students' repertoires of possible discursive positionings (a student tries on different personae to see how the class reacts)" (254).

Yet despite the research in favor of pseudonym use, taking this approach proved to be one of our greatest errors. What we discovered was that when students were given the freedom to choose pseudonyms, they often picked highly troubling identities like Anheuser Busch, Charlie Manson, and Piss. Our first reaction was to say that some pseudonyms were off-limits, but the minute we set parameters on students' identity creation, we also limited their power to name the world. Ideally, of course, we hoped our students would reach a critical consciousness about the implications of their identity choices. However, students told us instead that they were very deliberately picking shocking pseudonyms in order to draw attention to their writing on the Internet. In the currency of the Internet, notoriety, fame, and sex paid dividends in readership. The students who chose these troubling identities received a disproportionately higher number of responses than the students who stuck with their true names, like *Joey* and *Maria*.

Beyond discovering the cross-cultural allure of these distorted identities, we also found that pseudonym use by our students negatively impacted both their writing and their peers' responses to it, a problem Nakamura has studied further in her research. Though a student with a shocking pseudonym could attract a significant readership, the response that student received was often colored by the pseudonym choice and not helpful for revision. In the end, perhaps our students' responses should not have been that surprising. By asking students to work in an environment of masked identities and gendered stereotypes, we inadvertently helped to sanitize their responses. Surface-level critiques are safe and easy. They involve little risk and become just another course assignment (Pagnucci and Mauriello, "Masquerade" 149).

The introduction of pseudonyms into the design of the Internet-based course did make students feel safe enough to post their writing, but in the end, it proved to be our greatest mistake. Freirian philosophy encourages "teachers and students to become Subjects of the educational process by overcoming authoritarianism and an alienating intellectualism; it also enables people to overcome their false perception of reality" (67). By asking students to write behind pseudonyms, we reified this false perception of reality. Instead of sheltering the students with pseudonyms, we should have encouraged them to look directly at their own, unfiltered existences, confronting, analyzing, and learning to value their own genders, ethnicities, and unique personal identities. Freire tells us that we need to create an environment in which "the world—no longer something to be described with deceptive words—becomes the object of that transforming action by men and women which results in their humanization" (67). If you cannot say, "This is who I am, I exist," then you are never truly empowered. If you cannot sign your real name to your own words, then no one else will ever know what you think and believe. Your existence will always be marginal, lacking the ownership so important to Freirian self-reflection.

Revelation versus Censorship

Our experiment with allowing students to use pseudonyms clearly had impacted the ways in which our students wrote and responded online. We had learned that creating a safe online writing environment was essential, but now we could see that if students were to produce meaningful writing, preserving student identity was just as essential. Taking both concerns into account, we once again redesigned our course. We would still offer students the option of using pseudonyms when publishing online; however, we would now deliberately limit the types of identities students could choose. We wanted students to move away from using cartoonish characters and cultural icons that distorted readers' responses and writers' self-images. Offering an alternative to adopting culturally loaded pseudonyms, we encouraged students foremost to use their real identity or, as a secondary option, to pick a name which preserved their gender and ethnicity for Internet readers. In this way, all the student authors at our web site would possess ordinary names, but no reader other than a student's writing classmates would be able to tell which names were authentic and which were pseudonyms. We hoped that this new policy would make all our students feel safe, would keep responders accountable, and would lead to genuine writer-reader dialogue.

In this improved environment, we found that students seemed more willing to share personal writing with each other. It is only when both writer and reader are perceived as real people that a human dialogue begins. In Henry Giroux's work, human community building is a cornerstone of critical pedagogy:

> A pedagogy of critical literacy and voice needs to be developed around a politics of difference and community that is not simply grounded in a celebration of plurality. Such a pedagogy must be derived from a particular form of human community in which plurality becomes dignified through the construction of classroom social relations in which all voices in their differences become unified both in their efforts to identify and recall moments of human suffering and in their attempts to overcome the conditions that perpetuate such suffering. (21)

As one student told us in an email:

> The best part of exchanging papers on the Internet was the fact that people actually responded to our work. I liked this because I normally hate letting people read my work, but this way I didn't have to see them, and they didn't know who I was. It was also good reading others' essays. *I feel like there are certain people that I really got to know through their work*, even though I have never met them. (emphasis added)

Having used this course design during the last three years, we've seen students like the writer of this email benefiting from this Internet-based writing course. However, despite many students' gaining from the exchange of writing, there have also been a number of problems, two of which especially cause us concern: students who use the public medium for self-revelation and students who see the public medium as a need for self-censorship.

With our current course design, we believe many students are empowered to write for a global audience. Yet in facilitating this dialogue, we've also encountered some new, disturbing situations. Consider this student's motivations for making her writing public:

> Letting others whom you don't know read your papers can be very beneficial. Plus, it helps shy people come out of their shells and discuss very private things that they normally wouldn't talk about. This project really helped me mature in both my writing and in my mind. It allowed me to talk about being a crime victim and finally tell someone my story. I could have never done this if just our class would have been reading it.

When asked to publish an online narrative about a life experience that helped shape her identity, this student wrote a graphic account of having been raped as a child. Even more troubling is her detailed account of the rapist's death from AIDS and her ongoing medical testing for the disease. In her own words, being able to share this story for the first time went beyond empowerment. As other people responded to her story, not only sympathizing but sharing their own stories of abuse, this student found that a community of human dialogue helped to remove some of the isolation of the past and the stigma of being a victim.

Although we welcomed these benefits for our student, the revelatory nature of this piece of writing pushed us into the role of therapists, a role for which writing teachers are not professionally trained. Morgan, in fact, has discussed the problem of the expanding demands being placed upon teachers:

> To me, the inescapable conclusion is that the very nature of teaching itself has changed, especially in a field such as composition, where "content" is most often the students' own writing. With all the safeguards possible—legal, ethical, professional—our interaction with students, our responses to their work, have become more personal.
>
>   A teacher's responsibilities always did entail more than content expertise and classroom management, always did include listening, encouraging, mentoring, and even, occasionally, some degree of informal counseling. But we now live in a time when many more college students have "special needs," when we see a much higher proportion of students who have led nontraditional lives, a larger number of what I call "broken wing" students. And so, our roles have

of necessity become even more time-consuming and challenging. (321)

In Morgan's view, when students tell revelatory tales, they are moving through highly sensitive emotional ground, and we must proceed with great caution.

In addition, there is a danger that once one revelatory story has been told, other writers may feel obliged to meet that standard, perhaps even fictionalizing some experiences for dramatic effect. As Shalynne told us in an email reflecting upon this type of assignment, "Sharing these personal stories allows us students to express ourselves to others while in return reading about other people's lives and experiences. It's absolutely brilliant. It is a great experience that allows people to open their hearts and minds. It's like watching Oprah . . . Sometimes the topics can leave the viewer in tears."

Because many of the students were writing such highly revealing personal stories, we held several class discussions about the ambiguous boundaries of public writing. At what point has an author compromised her story by revealing too much personal detail? Do we need to read such revelations in an academic classroom? Do we want to shoulder the emotional burden of such writing? Students differed in their opinions on what limits breached acceptability. Faye, for example, was moved to tears as she told the class how important it was for her to write about the death of a friend, but other students, in private emails to us, said they felt silenced. As Jason, for instance, wrote:

> I enjoyed the conversation we had in class today because we got the opportunity to express our ideas on a personal level. I didn't say anything, though, because I wasn't quite sure how to approach the subjects discussed on a level appropriate for a whole classroom of students to hear. I also don't like to tell my personal business to a room full of strangers. I don't have a problem with sharing things on a personal level as long as it doesn't get too deep. I, too, withheld my emotion from my assignment in order for me to feel comfortable sharing this with complete strangers.

We found that not only were some students silenced, but other students created writing which was so self-censored that it was essentially silent. In a response to one personal essay, a reader said:

> The thing I most noticed about your essay was that you went on and on about how influential your father is to you and how you've learned so much from him. You made it very clear that your father was important to you, but you didn't show ANY examples of how he would do that. Maybe think of an example of when your dad did something specific for you to show that he cared. I could copy your essay exactly, put my name up at the top, and it would fit me exactly. You need to personalize. I'm sure you and your father have had times together that are unique to you two. How about using

some examples? I would have been much more interested in your paper had you used some of these examples. It sounds like you're just rambling on with no real mass to the essay. You could easily fix this by just doing some personal typing.

When we asked the student author his reaction to this reader's response, the student told us that he didn't realize how much he had censored his own voice. He said that he assumed he had done this because he had been worried about posting the writing on the Internet. In fact, although this student revised his essay three times to include more intimate details, he declined to post any of these later drafts online.

This is the blunder that keeps recurring for us. Too often, when we get a student to write, the student cannot or will not share that writing. In many ways, we're back where we started with our initial class. In the face of the unknown audiences of the Internet, too many students are silenced. bell hooks puts the dilemma this way:

> Encouraging students to speak, I tell them to imagine what it must mean to live in a culture where to speak one risks brutal punishment—imprisonment, torture, death. I ask them to think about what it means that they lack the courage to speak in a culture where there are few if any consequences. Can their fear be understood solely as shyness or is it an expression of deeply embedded, socially constructed restrictions against speech in a culture of domination, a fear of owning one's words, or taking a stand? (57–58)

If we ever hope to empower students, indeed if we really can, they must embrace the power of free speech. Yet throughout our Internet-based teaching, we've come to see that achieving this simple goal is a monumental task.

Maintaining Our Balance

As we reflect back upon our experiences of learning to use technology for teaching composition, we can clearly see the tightrope we have been walking. In retrospect, our course may have suffered from what Ellen Barton (1994) calls "the dominant discourse of technology" (57). According to Barton, we often assume that "first, technology, particularly computer technology, is here to stay; second, that technology ultimately benefits most individuals and all of society" (58). While others have also cautioned against this type of unguarded optimism (Heim, 1993; Stoll, 1995), perhaps we were misled by this overly positive belief in technology. What the dominant discourse obscures are the critical pedagogical and ethical questions that our students have helped us to see. We worried initially that our students were the ones being constrained by their fear, their distrust of the Internet, and their resistance to bringing technology into the writing classroom. We now understand that these are issues that teachers must address in cooperation with their students in order to make Internet technologies an effective part of the curriculum.

What we have learned from our teaching experiences is that one question is paramount—How do we ethically implement an Internet-based writing class?

To answer this question, we need to formulate an ethics of technology. When the subject of technology is addressed in the classroom, it must be broached in a way that considers the philosophical, sociopolitical, and cultural underpinnings of the media from the student-user perspective. Before teachers put students in front of computers, they have an ethical obligation to consider what that balancing act means. Failure to do so will subjugate the students' identities and impose the dominant technological discourse upon them. If technology is truly a conduit for student empowerment, teachers must learn to walk the tightrope between curriculum failure and a pedagogy of possibility.

Works Cited

Barton, Ellen L. "Interpreting the Discourses of Technology." *Literacy and Computers: The Complications of Teaching and Learning with Technology*. Ed. Cynthia L. Selfe and Susan Hilligoss. New York: MLA, 1994. 56–75.

Dewey, John. *Experience and Education*. New York: Macmillan, 1938.

Faigley, Lester. *Fragments of Rationality: Postmodernity and the Subject of Composition*. Pittsburgh: University of Pittsburgh P, 1995.

Freire, Paulo. *Pedagogy of the Oppressed*. Trans. Myra Berman Ramos. Rev. 20th ed. New York: Continuum, 1995.

Giroux, Henry A. "Literacy and the Pedagogy of Political Empowerment." *Literacy: Reading the Word and the World*. Ed. Paulo Freire and Donaldo Macedo. Westport, CT: Bergin and Garvey, 1987.

Haas, Christina. "On the Relationship Between Old and New Technologies." *Computers and Composition* 16 (1999): 209–28.

Haas, Christina, and Christine M. Neuwirth. "Writing the Technology That Writes Us: Research on Literacy and the Shape of Technology." *Literacy and Computers. The Complications of Teaching and Learning with Technology*. Ed. Cynthia L. Selfe and Susan Hilligoss. New York: MLA, 1994. 319–35.

Heim, Michael. *The Metaphysics of Virtual Reality*. New York: Oxford UP, 1993.

hooks, bell. "'When I Was a Young Soldier for the Revolution': Coming to Voice." *Landmark Essays on Voice and Writing*. Ed. Peter Elbow. Davis, CA: Hermagoras, 1994. 51–58.

Mauriello, Nicholas. *The College Writing Peer Response Project*. 6 April 1999 <http://www.iup.edu/~nickm/peer.htm>.

Mauriello, Nicholas, and Gian S. Pagnucci. *Public Works*. Portsmouth, NH: Heinemann, 2001. 44–52.

Mauriello, Nicholas, Gian S. Pagnucci, and Tammy S. Winner. "Reading Between the Code: The Teaching of HTML and the Displacement of Writing Instruction." *Computers and Composition* 16 (1999): 409–19.

Morgan, Dan. "Ethical Issues Raised by Students' Personal Writing." *College English* 60 (1998): 318–25.

Nakamura, Lisa "Race in/for Cyberspace: Identity Tourism and Racial Passing on the Internet." *Works and Days* 25/26.13 (1995): 181–93.

Pagnucci, Gian S., and Nicholas Mauriello. "The Masquerade: Gender, Identity, and Writing for the Web." *Computers and Composition* 16 (1999): 141–51.

Pagnucci, Gian S., and Nicholas Mauriello. *The Future of Narrative Discourse: Technologies' Impact on the Way We Write*. Cresskill, NJ: Hampton, 2002.

Romano, Susan. "On Becoming a Woman: Pedagogies of the Self." *Passions, Pedagogies, and Twenty-first Century Technologies*. Ed. Gail E. Hawisher and Cynthia L. Selfe. Logan: Utah State UP, 1999. 249–67.

Schaafsma, David. "Telling Stories, Drawing Maps." *The Future of Narrative Discourse: Technologies' Impact on the Way We Write*. Ed. Gian S. Pagnucci and Nicholas Mauriello. Cresskill, NJ: Hampton, 2002.

Selfe, Cynthia L. "Technology and Literacy: A Story about the Perils of Not Paying Attention." *College Composition and Communication* 50 (1999): 411–36.

Stoll, Clifford. *Silicon Snake Oil*. New York: Doubleday, 1995.

Tompkins, Jane. "Pedagogy of the Distressed." *College English* 52.6 (1990): 653–60.

"But I'm *Just* White" or How "Other" Pedagogies Can Benefit All Students

SAMANTHA BLACKMON
Purdue University

I walked into my computer-mediated freshman composition class like I had many of my previous classes. I started with introductions and my descriptive spiel. This year it went a little like this: "In this course we are going to interrogate discourse communities. We are going to look at racial, ethnic, socioeconomic, regional, and religious discourse communities, just to name a few. We are going to spend some time looking at each of these communities individually and then looking at how they function to form the whole (that would be you) and how they influence and are influenced by the other discourse communities that you belong to." I looked around the room and saw a few looks of pure horror on faces of differing hues. One male student in the back row raised his hand and voiced the horror that was present on those faces. He said, "But I'm just white!" I looked at the student who was wearing the same baseball cap, t-shirt, and jeans as all of the other "just white" male students in the room and nodded because I could see why he would believe this, and then I said, "Not quite *just* white."

Why We Need "Other" Pedagogies

Many readers may wonder why I am beginning a paper about pedagogies of inclusion for minority students with an anecdote about a white male student (just about as nonminority as you can get), but I do so to illustrate that what I have learned about using a more inclusive and reflexive pedagogy is that African-American students and *just white* students alike can benefit from it. At the end of a first-year composition course that I had taught, I distributed a survey to students about their level of satisfaction with the course. The responses from the questionnaire showed that the three African-American

92

students in that course felt that neither African Americans as a whole nor they as young African Americans were correctly portrayed on the World Wide Web. One of the male students, Marcus,[1] wrote:

> It seems young black men are only associated with rap . . . Young black males, such as myself, need to start making web sites that aren't music based. We need to start making web sites that educate people of other things that young black males are involved in (ex. Big Brothers, Big Sisters).

A nineteen-year-old African-American woman, Kim, wrote:

> Most of the web sites that I have seen that are about African Americans like me[2] seem to concentrate on sports. They talk about how great sports are and how we are great at them . . . But that isn't me. I don't play sports. I don't even like sports.

For Marcus, there is no connection between how he defines himself as a young black man and the way that he sees himself defined on the WWW. He seems to feel that young black men are culturally reduced to *being* rap music and all of the negative stereotypes that typically go along with it rather than being a positive role model for African-American children. The same seems to hold true for Kim, who feels that she, as an African-American woman is being misrepresented and subjected to a cultural bias which is not accurate. I believe that if two of my African-American students felt this way, there must be other African-American students and minority students who share these feelings. For this reason, I designed a class that gives students the opportunity to focus on, think critically about, and represent their individual identities on the WWW as they see fit.

Thomas Fox writes:

> [S]chools have failed to make good on the promise that literacy instruction in the schools will reward African American students socially and economically. Equally serious is the fact that schools have failed to change the perception (and reality in most cases) that for African American students literacy instruction entails 'deculturation without true assimilation.' (<http://nosferatu.cas.usf.edu/JAC/122/fox.html>)

If, as Fox claims, "literacy instruction entails the deculturation without true assimilation," the same rules are at play in web-based literacy instruction of African-American students. They are being asked to see themselves as either rappers and sports stars or as a part of the raceless, white majority represented on the Web without ever actually having the ability to become one of the majority because of the thing(s) that make them "Other" (i.e., race, ethnicity, and sexual orientation). Let me make it plain here that this representation of the raceless majority is not tied to an actual declaration of whiteness but rather to the fact that in the absence of a specific race, white is considered the "default."

What stuck out for me most when reading these questionnaire responses was Marcus's proclamation that African Americans need to create their own web sites in order to be accurately represented. A third African-American student, Justin, although recognizing the need for representation, was more cautious about the power African Americans might assume vis-à-vis the Web:

> I'm sure things could be changed for the worse. At least black peo-
> ple are allowed to even have web sites. I'm sure the Internet world
> is run mostly by whites, and they have the power to allow and not
> allow people to make web sites.

These student responses are simultaneously tentative about the hidden power structure behind the Internet and hopeful about the possibility of making the World Wide Web a place where African Americans can see themselves represented in a positive and accurate manner.

In response to these findings from my survey, I developed a class curriculum and a series of assignments which build upon one another in such a way that they ask students to think and write about different facets of their identities before they complete a final paper that focuses on their identities holistically. The underlying hope in my students' survey responses that things could improve led me to create this course based upon student identity; the course was cumulative in that students thought about themselves in compartmentalized ways (i.e., in terms of class or gender) and then used those understandings to think about themselves as a whole. Over the course of the semester, I asked that students do the following:

- Think specifically about their home discourse communities in terms of their race or ethnicity
- Analyze a number of the discourse communities of which they considered themselves members
- Analyze how they saw race (or a lack thereof) portrayed on the World Wide Web
- Interrogate how computers in the classroom helped or hindered the education process for students from different socioeconomic strata
- Discuss their experiences with online community-building in comparison to real-world community building
- Create a final webbed project that put together all of the various discourse communities in a way that reflected how they made up the student as an individual

These assignments were facilitated by readings focusing on building real-world communities in two composition readers: Richard Marback and others' *Cities, Cultures, Conversations: Readings for Writers* and Gail Hawisher and Cynthia Selfe's *Literacy, Technology, and Society: Confronting the Issues.* The pieces I chose from these collections focus on various discourse communities in large urban areas like Detroit, Michigan, where the class took place, and community building in cyberspace. In discussions of these readings, students shared stories about online comfort zones as places where they could discuss those things that they were too afraid or ashamed to discuss in the real world.

The weekly assignments that stem from these readings are progressive in that they build up to a final project in which students connect their individual identities to a variety of discourse communities. The first of the weekly assignments asks students to read a series of online articles dealing with web site evaluation (see the resources housed on the University of North Carolina server) and then evaluate a series of web sites for content and credibility while considering the aspects of the sites that make them "credible." After completing the evaluation of the sites, students are asked to think about the content of the sites that they did not find credible and whether or not a universal "web advisory board" of sorts should be established to monitor and control web content. I designed this assignment to introduce students to the range of quality and content of the web sites available and to prepare them for more in-depth analysis of web content, which begins with the second assignment.

The second assignment follows an in-class synchronous chat session in which students are asked to think of one tradition that they feel defines their culture for them. Using the transcript from this chat, students are asked to think about the diversity present in their own classroom and to think about how their classmates' traditions and values are similar to or different from those in their own home discourse communities. Students are asked to think and write about how these traditions add to the richness of the conversation and whether or not they feel these different and differing traditions should be retained by a group of people that all label themselves "American." The purpose of this assignment is to get students to think about the differences that exist among "Americans" and how these differences enrich rather than detract from the idea of a national community.

Feeling Erased in Cyberspace

This assignment asks students to look at a series of random personal web sites created in free web communities such as Yahoo/Geocities, Tripod, or Angelfire. After looking at these sites, students are asked to think about what the Web does to humans, not as racial or ethnic groups (Americans, Asians, or Africans) but as human beings. After receiving general definitions in a classroom lecture, they are asked to consider the terms *cyberspace*[3] and *cyberhuman*[4] and what each of those terms means regarding the portrayal or erasure of difference in order for a person to fit into these categories. They are also to write about issues of access. The prompt for this assignment asks, "Is technology equally accessible to all people? What happens to those who don't have access to technology?" Students also are to consider, in their writing, the repercussions of the formation and maintenance of a universal cyberrace in terms of a sense of community. Could these homeplaces and fortified ghettos be recreated in cyberspace, and would the real world (and its lack of connection to cyberspace) become the newest ghetto? This virtual loss of cultural affiliation in favor of none (or many, if you hold to the cyberspace melting-pot theory) mimics the cultural schizophrenia that theorists like Victor Villanueva discuss:

> "Sink or swim" suggests a resignation to let some sink. Too many already do. And when they do, they don't tend to blame a system that fails them; they tend to blame themselves. Those who swim all too often find they have lost sight of their original homelands . . . alienated from the first culture, not quite a part of the new culture, "Tonto in both languages." (48)

It is this alienation of self as cultural being that gets replicated all too often in cyberspace. I use this exercise to challenge and establish working definitions of *community* and to have students think about how real-life communities, difference, and prejudices are replicated rather than erased in cyberspace.

Access Denied

In the next assignment I ask students to write about how they are aided or hindered by the use of technology in the classroom and how this situation might be different for a student who is at the opposite end of the socioeconomic spectrum. After spending several weeks discussing cyberspace and real-world communities and how they break down, students are asked to define, in writing, their own specific community affiliations.

This assignment stems from Elspeth Stuckey's argument that rather than being libratory as promised:

> Literacy, like communication, is a matter of access, a matter of opportunity, a matter of economic security—a total matter. The violence of literacy is the violence of the milieu it comes from, promises, recapitulates. It is attached inextricably to the world of food, shelter, and human equality. When literacy harbors violence, society harbors violence. To elucidate the violence of literacy is to understand the distance it forces between people and the possibilities for their lives. (94)

If this holds true for traditional literacy, the violence of literacy is amplified when literacy is computer mediated. Computer-mediated literacy holds not only the promise of socioeconomic equality that Fox suggests but also the promise of inclusion (or assimilation) in the realm of cyberspace. Unfortunately for the nonmajority student, these promises do not get fulfilled because of the maintenance of a connection to the real world and the violence that it "harbors." Although many students are not naturally critical of the world around them, working in the classroom with "texts" (their own identities) with which they are familiar offers them the opportunity to develop critical-thinking skills without requiring them to work with new and unfamiliar texts. Students need to be educated to be aware and critical of this fact so that the addition of computer technology to education does not serve as fuel added to an already raging fire of inequity in literacy education.

Community Connections

After the students read a series of essays on sexual orientation and gender issues in cyberspace,[5] the fifth assignment asks them to pick the one discourse community to which they feel most connected (race, class, gender, sexual orientation, or what we called "x-factor"[6] communities like religion or profession). I then have students write descriptions explaining why they feel most connected to this community and what things about this community are most important to them. This is done to facilitate a face-to-face discussion of how difference is necessary for the formation of the individual. This discussion leads to the next assignment, which asks students to find a visual component to their real-life community.

Images on the Web

This next assignment invites students to use the Web in order to find three images that reflect their connection to the community which they chose in the previous assignment. The selection of the types of images is left to the discretion of the student. After studying the "Images of Gender" section in Hawisher and Selfe and discussing how images speak and what these specific images say about gender and technology, students are asked to write a short (100–250 words) description of how each image they have collected reflects their connection to their community. Students use these images and descriptions to create their final web projects. One student chose clip-art spotlights to reflect the connection that she felt to the Roman Catholic Church. She had spent much of the semester interrogating feelings she had never previously expressed about Church-defined "sins": homosexuality, abortion, and premarital sex. Her reflections on religion and the fact that her parents still require that she go to Mass every week like a "good little girl" offer us some insight into her feelings for the first time:

> One of the things that really bothers me is their [church representatives'] tendency to want the one thing that they tell me will destroy the world, my soul, and send me straight to hell. Money. They ask for more donations every time I show up there . . . Other than the money, they're into the brainwashing thing too. Sure, God created us with free will, but it doesn't matter, because they tell you what to do. If you don't do what they say, then you are a bad person, and must go tell your sins to the priest, who forgives you, since they say you can't just talk to God, and get forgiveness that

way. Too bad they also tell you that you should have a close relationship with God, and should be able to talk to him about
anything. Oops, but that's another contradiction . . . I don't want to
get off my topic. Anyhow, they want to control your life, tell you
how to live it, with who, where, and when. No, thank you, I can
think for myself. Hmmm, now, as to modern day issues such as abortion and all that . . . would you like to know where I stand? That's
good, so would I. I don't care what my supposed religion tells me, I
can make up my own mind . . . I just haven't managed to do that yet.
HA! so there . . .

For this student, the image of spotlights seems to illustrate the fact that for
the first time she is publicly scrutinizing her "supposed" religion and putting
her own beliefs on the World Wide Web for all to see.

Oh, What a Tangled Web

The final web project is simultaneously analytical and informative in nature.
The three images from the last assignment are pulled together to serve as a
gateway to more detailed discussions of the students' chosen discourse communities. Students are to research their discourse communities and then discuss
how the various communities affect them as individuals, how their relationship with one community affects their relationships with other communities,
and how they affect the community. It is this interaction with cyberspace and
the act of thinking critically about who they are as people and how they
affect and are affected by their surroundings that can lead students to become
more critically aware and socially conscious individuals. After reading about
gender in the course, one Lebanese student began to question the gender-biased
practices in her own family:

> Gender is a large part of my world. My parents' gender-biased
> upbringing has influenced the way they treat their children. Sons
> are treated differently than daughters. The unfair practices of
> gender bias are so numerous [that] my whole paper could be dedi-
> cated to this community . . . My two older brothers have a life I can
> only dream of. According to my parents, young women should not be
> seen out after dark . . . My older brothers, on the other hand, have
> a two to three o'clock curfew. This curfew is never met, meaning
> they're home a lot later if they choose to come home. I am one of
> the elite whose enthusiasm for Spring Break is diminished by the
> fact that I must take on my brothers' shifts at the family business so
> they can enjoy themselves in sunny Cancun. The only vacations my
> sibling sisters and I take are family vacations to see our grandpar-
> ents in the next town[;] as exciting as that may seem[,] please re-
> frain from becoming green with envy.

This individual is no longer "just" white, "just" black, or "just" Lebanese but is
also a student, a Muslim, a woman, and an aspiring nurse who is aware of the

gender inequities in her own life, and, we might hypothesize and hope, unlikely to duplicate them because of this awareness.

Thoughts

This series of readings and assignments led to discussions (face-to-face and those held in synchronous chat environments) that I believe would never have taken place if I had not asked students to place themselves within the discussion of community building and social identity. The three Indian/Asian students in this class were able to share information about their cultures (marriage, dating, and holiday customs) and were able to analyze and critique them without fear of familial and cultural objections. GLBT (gay, lesbian, bisexual, and transgendered) students were able to explore their sexual orientation as a discourse community in a space where they were safe from ridicule and gay bashing. African-American students were able to share their feelings freely about the history of oppression of African Americans in North America, and the "just white" students were able to explore German and Scottish traditions that were previously regarded as so "normal" by them that they just assumed that these were "American" traditions. Theories of cultural critique gave the students the language that they needed to express themselves in ways that they may not have previously been able to do.[7] For these students, seeing their own ideas and issues in print and openly discussed in class seemed to validate them and leave them open to personal connection. Reading Barbara Kantrowitz's discussion of the problems posed by a lack of material access to computers in "The Information Gap" led one African-American student to share with the class that as a single mother who worked the afternoon shift, she often found herself taking public transportation to campus after midnight in order to complete her assignments. It was this sort of disclosure that made the issue of unequal access and the problems that it causes in higher education more real (and more personal) for the class as a whole.

The final projects that came out of the class led students to discover more about themselves as people. The projects led them to trace their roots, to do research on what it means to be African American, Asian, Christian, healthcare professionals, and yes, white. While students in this diverse classroom learned about Hindu customs and Kwanzaa ceremonies from their classmates, they also learned new things about themselves, their communities, and their own beliefs. For this reason, I argue that this course could be equally valuable for an apparently "homogenous" student population. The "just white" student whose story begins this essay learned that there was a castle in Scotland that bore his surname and that his family has a rich Scottish history:

> The research that I have done on my family background really interested me quite a bit. In the past, I only thought of myself as strictly American. I have realized that my family has a deep history in Scotland. Before I did research I had no idea that there is actually a city in Scotland with my last name in it. Not only is my last name in the title, but that is the family [from] which I am

descended ... originally. I plan on visiting Scotland one day and
hopefully find out a little more about the history of my family.

Although he may not be royalty, the revelation made this student more interested in his Scottish heritage and more aware of the fact that this heritage
was not "just American" and by default "just white" (at least for the moment).

Afterthoughts and Critical Possibilities

Although it is usually better to be proactive than reactive, reaction is often
very important and necessary. In order to be more proactive, we must look for
sensitive issues in our classrooms before they become obvious problems and use
them as subject matter in courses in order to get our students to think critically
about them. The course that I have described here originated from my reaction
to a student survey which revealed to me that African-American students in
one of my classes felt alienated by technology and cyberspace. Even more
important than their fear of technology, some of them seemed to feel that
there is some kind of conspiracy that keeps them in their marginalized positions in cyberspace in much the same way that minorities have traditionally
and historically been oppressed by the hegemonic power structure. For them,
the use of technology in the classroom (the same technology to which historically few racial and socioeconomic minorities have had access because of its
prohibitive cost) adds another layer to the oppression that they experience.
In the computer classroom "other" students are not only disadvantaged because
of race and socioeconomic status but also because historically they have had
little or no interaction with technology. This lack of familiarity with technology means that they are further behind their majority classmates before
the course even begins. It is as if we educators are "raising the bar" of education before all of the students are able to clear the original height.

As a whole, this pedagogy seeks to diminish the feeling of disconnected-
ness that some students can feel toward computers in an attempt to make
technology a more effective teaching tool and in order to provide all students
with a more equal educational playing field. More important than learning
technological skills is adopting the practice of thinking critically about
technology, its uses (and limits) in higher education, and what all of this
means for and to students of different and differing discourse communities.

Rather than simply giving a few minority students the opportunity to
build web sites and successfully navigate the World Wide Web so that they
can make their presence known to students like Marcus, Justin, and Kim, I ask
students to interrogate why minorities fear some sort of "cyber conspiracy" in
the first place. It is only with this new knowledge that students and educators, regardless of their race, gender, or ethnicity, can realize the need for and
work toward both social and educational reform.

Notes

[1] The names of the students have been changed in order to protect their privacy.

[2] Here we can assume not just a similar race but a similar age as well.

[3] Cyberspace is a term coined by William Gibson in his 1984 text *Neuromancer* and is most commonly defined as the medium of computer networks in which online communication and community building take place.

[4] Here I am defining *cyberhuman* as a raceless, sexless, genderless, and classless entity that, because of its lack of descriptive features, is the same as every other person in the virtual world.

[5] Steve Silberman, "We're Teen, We're Queer, and We've Got Email"; Julie Peterson, "Sex and the Cybergirl"; and Elizabeth Gerver, "Computers and Gender" in Hawisher and Selfe.

[6] The term *x-factor* is one that the class coined collectively to describe variable discourse communities that we had not focused on in class. The X comes from the mathematical symbol used to signify a missing variable.

[7] I believe that this is evidenced by the fact that students felt free to share their feelings and thoughts on some very personal issues such as sex, gender bias, religion, and sexual orientation in their webbed assignments, chat sessions, and classroom discussions.

Works Cited

Center for Instructional Technology. "Evaluating Websites for Educational Uses: Bibliography and Checklist." 2001 <http://www.unc.edu/cit/guides/irg-49.html>.

Fox, Tom. "Repositioning the Profession: Teaching Writing to African American Students." *Journal of Advanced Composition* 12.2 (1992) <http://nosferatu.cas.usf.edu/JAC/122/fox.html>.

Gerver, Elizabeth. "Computers and Gender." *Literacy, Technology and Society: Confronting the Issues*. Ed. Gail Hawisher and Cynthia L. Selfe. Upper Saddle River, NJ: Prentice-Hall, 1996. 361–83.

Hawisher, Gail, and Cynthia L. Selfe, eds. *Literacy, Technology and Society: Confronting the Issues*. Upper Saddle River, NJ: Prentice-Hall, 1996.

hooks, bell. "Homeplace: A Site of Resistance." *Cities, Cultures, and Conversations: Readings for Writers*. Ed. Richard Marback, Patrick Bruch, and Jill Eicher. Boston: Allyn and Bacon, 1998. 68–76.

Kantrowitz, Barbara. "The Information Gap." *Literacy, Technology and Society: Confronting the Issues*. Ed. Gail Hawisher and Cynthia L. Selfe. Upper Saddle River, NJ: Prentice-Hall, 1996. 212–14.

Marback, Richard, Patrick Bruch, and Jill Eicher, eds. *Cities, Cultures, and Conversations: Readings for Writers*. Boston: Allyn and Bacon, 1998.

Peterson, Julie. "Sex and the Cybergirl." *Literacy, Technology and Society: Confronting the Issues*. Ed. Gail Hawisher and Cynthia L. Selfe. Upper Saddle River, NJ: Prentice-Hall, 1996. 359–60.

Silberman, Steve. "We're Teen, We're Queer, and We've Got Email." *Literacy, Technology and Society: Confronting the Issues*. Ed. Gail Hawisher and Cynthia L. Selfe. Upper Saddle River, NJ: Prentice-Hall, 1996. 58–63.

Stuckey, J. Elspeth. *The Violence of Literacy*. Portsmouth, NH: Boynton/Cook, 1991.

Vergara, Camille J. "Our Fortified Ghettos." *Cities, Cultures, and Conversations: Readings for Writers*. Ed. Richard Marback, Patrick Bruch, and Jill Eicher. Boston: Allyn and Bacon, 1998. 82–88.

Villanueva, Victor. *Bootstraps: From an American Academic of Color*. Urbana, IL: NCTE, 1993.

Section III:
Teaching Beyond
Physical Boundaries

The Pleasures of Digital Discussions: Lessons, Challenges, Recommendations, and Reflections

KATHLEEN BLAKE YANCEY
Clemson University

It's not a question of whether you'll use technology to help students learn. It's a question of what kind of technology you will include— and when.

In a first-year seminar, students prepare to email their drafts to each other for electronic peer review. Down the hall, first-year composition students are ehosting a visiting guest expert from across the country on their closed class listserv. Across campus, writers in a computer lab log onto a national listserv to hear the concerns of practicing teachers as they wrestle with the challenges evoked by the events of September 11 and whether or how they should include in their writing classrooms issues like the ones raised by this tragedy.

Although these situations differ, in each the students are engaging in an increasingly common practice: participating in electronic discussions. As Stuart Blythe explains, such discussions—in MOOs and MUDs, via bulletin boards and email listservers—can take various forms and serve diverse purposes. And, as Blythe also explains, choosing which of these to use for which purpose poses a myriad of challenges.

To think more specifically about the kinds of pedagogical issues these forums can evoke—from determining which structures we need to design to make listservers "work" to deciding what kinds of response to them would be most valuable—I'll consider here, as a kind of follow-up to Blythe's general discussion, some particular applications of two kinds of electronic discussion: email and listservers. Electronic mail—otherwise known as *email*—connects one individual with another much as a letter does, although as we'll see, email also differs from a letter in significant ways. The second type of electronic discussion, the listserver, is what we might consider "email plus" since it acts as a large distribution system, sending one individual's email to a list of recipients typically called *subscribers.* Although listservers come in several flavors, I'll here detail two that are particularly appropriate for the first-year writing classroom: (1) the closed class listserv, a classroom distribution list open only to members of the class, and (2) the open and unmoderated public listserv to which a class makes some kind of connection. There are other applications for electronic discussions, of course, but I'll focus on email and listservers in order to illustrate some specific purposes, some assignments, and some axioms that guide the best use of these media for first-year composition classes.

My premise is that taken together, these digital forums offer teachers new ways to connect students, new ways for students to communicate with each other and the world at large, and, not least, new genres in which to learn.

Email Simple: Email as an Extension of Ordinary Practice

Ordinarily, we tend, I think, to prefer that new technologies and new genres do new kinds of work. At the same time, however, it's often easier *to begin trying out the new*—or the unfamiliar—*by using it to extend what we already do*—that is, to use it in a familiar context or for a familiar purpose. Accordingly, one "natural" way to begin using email is simply to use it as another medium through which to perform an activity that we already do, i. e., offering typical pedagogical practices in another venue. Beginning this way is fairly easy: It allows us to try out the new without adding a novel dimension to a course or revamping it. It also permits us to see in a small way the kinds of challenges a new technology can bring with it so that before we implement it on a broader scale, we can see how it works in a microcosm.

Perhaps the simplest kind of email extension is the "e-office hour," which, of course, isn't really an "hour" in the conventional sense. In addition to holding RL—"real-life"—office hours, a faculty member also commits to being available for consultation through email. In this sense, then, the use of email is merely an extension of what we already do. As for specifics, both the form and the substance of e-office hours will vary. You can offer to be online for a set period of time, as we do with office hours, or you can leave it more open. As with RL office hours, the material addressed during ehours can also range from the serious to the silly. Some students will want to notify you when a genuine emergency (a sick child, an auto accident) prevents their attending class, others may tell you that they need to skip class because they can't miss tonight's fraternity rush, and still others will want clarification of an assignment. The virtue of these e-office hours is that they provide another, more flexible venue for students to use, one that some students may find more convenient and more comfortable than your RL office time.

Another advantage of setting up email office hours is that they provide a class channel that you may find convenient as well. In other words, email is a two-way channel—and part of its charm is exactly that: Built into the medium is an expectation of response. Sometimes you'll want to contact a student about a late assignment; at other times you'll want to remind a student to come by your office during regular hours. Such a medium can be very useful precisely because *you* can initiate a message, and you can send it when it suits you. In terms of purpose, then, you can use e-office hours both ways: (1) to create a channel outside of RL office hours that replaces an RL office hour and (2) to augment RL hours.

Occasionally, such email can also help when an emergency arises—as a quick anecdote can illustrate. Once my son became quite ill right before class, and since it was too late to arrange for a colleague to step in, I knew I'd have to cancel the class. Still, I had to find a colleague to notify the students that class was cancelled. Everyone I could think of was either in class or off campus. Taking a chance, I sent an email to a number of students who were online often, asking them, if they got the message, both to announce the cancellation to the class and to outline what we would do during the next class period. As I pondered what to do next, I received two replies from students. Not only did they cancel the class, but they also shared the next assignment with their colleagues. So email isn't merely convenient for students; making it a routine part of our classroom practice, even minimally, can assist us as well.

Another now fairly routine use of email is to facilitate regular conferencing on drafts, particularly to review student drafts. Even if you teach on a residential campus where students can come by for an RL meeting, many of them—about half, in my experience—will be just as happy (indeed happier) with a draft review conducted by email. I arrange this by circulating a sign-up sheet in class with two options—one for a conference in my office during office hours and a second for an email review. (A third option, of course, is no review since I don't require one.) For the email option, I stipulate certain conditions, such as requiring that the draft arrive in my emailbox by a certain time. Also, I explain that the response I provide will be global, addressing items like purpose, development, and so on. Although draft conferencing is available in my office, some students prefer the email venue at least for three reasons:

- They would rather receive what they expect to be bad news more anonymously than my physical office permits.
- They can access email at their convenience.
- They can have a written record of my response that is composed in my words, and they can feel more secure revising from that record than from their transcription of my oral suggestions.

"Email simple," then, allows us to extend what we already do, enabling us to provide more venues in which to connect and teach and learn, and therefore to make our pedagogy more accessible to a wider variety of students.

The Listserv Discussion Group: Enrichment, Integral Class Activity, New Forum

Listservers, otherwise known as distributed email systems, offer other kinds of pedagogical opportunities. Here I'll focus on three, and again, I've located them according to purpose: (1) the listserv as *enrichment* to the class, (2) the listserv as *integral* to the class, and (3) the listserv as a *new forum* for the class.

Listserver as a Source of Enrichment

Listserv conversations can *enrich* a class in ways that differ from the ways in which conversations held in real time and in face-to-face mode can, as a simple comparison can illustrate. Let's say, for instance, that you are teaching a class in document design for your first-year writers, and you would like them to hear about current practices from someone in the field, someone working as a communications consultant. To accomplish this kind of goal, to create an offering that enriches the course, I've often invited outside speakers, frequently a panel of speakers. Whereas such a session is valuable—I think so, and the students concur in their evaluations—it does present problems. For one thing, the session only lasts about sixty to seventy-five minutes, so there isn't sustained contact between students and teachers; there's not a lot of opportunity even for follow-up questions. Worse, my class is typically scheduled during the (working) day, which is the same time when the consultants are at work. Accordingly, because I've had to offer this session after school and thus outside of class time, I can only offer it as an option. The logistics, in other words, frustrate my intentions.

To meet this same goal, I could try another venue, the Internet—which also has its own pluses and minuses. But one plus is that I can invite the consultant (or consultants) to log on for a longer period of time—typically for a week—so that sustained discussion can occur. Doing this tends to result in a much more meaningful exchange, in part because there *is* time for exchange. Also, because there is time and the written record that a listserver permits, I can be sure that each student has a chance to communicate with the consultant. Also as important, I can ask students as an entire class, when the session is over, to talk about it—about how what they have heard from "real" communicators corresponds with what we have produced and with their other experiences on campus. Since the entire class has participated, the entire class benefits. Interestingly, I've also had consultants thank me for inviting them to participate and then offer to log on with another class. Class evaluations as well as anecdotal evidence, then, tell us that this pedagogical application of a listserver is enriching students' learning experiences.

The key to making the enrichment version of listserver pedagogy work is twofold: provide structure and outline appropriate expectations. Both students and guests will want to know how this enrichment "works," including knowing

- how long the guest appearance will last
- who the students are
- what the students are studying in class
- what kinds of questions will be discussed
- what kind of credit will be awarded for this activity (will it "count" for a grade, and if so, for how much?)

One way to address all of these concerns, except the credit issue (which is discussed later in the chapter), is to make an opening listserver introduction, in which you can set an appropriate context, indicating who the guest is and why you've asked this person to participate, how long the session will last, and what topics and assignments the class has already discussed. You'll also need to close the session—or you might ask a student or team of students to do so—and that would be a good time for an in-class summary discussion.

It's important to note, though, that these kinds of activities—for example, the RL consultant panel and the consultant-expert listserv guest visit—are neither incompatible nor mutually exclusive. In some situations, one may be better than another, but often it's best to offer both. In fact, one of the crucial observations that even proponents of corporate e-learning make is that it's not an either/or situation in terms of medium used but rather a *blend* of media—f2f *and* digital—that is best for most students, regardless of their age or occupation.[1]

Using a Listserv as an Integral Class Activity

A listserv also offers opportunities for several kinds of student interactions that are *central* to a course. I'll highlight two, primarily to illustrate the kinds of activities that are possible.

STUDENT EDISCUSSIONS

Students can use a closed listserver for discussion outside class. Again, the values of using it include the fact that everyone can take a turn and that you will have a record of the discussion. Such a record is especially helpful if students want to use the material generated there for a formal assignment, as in a writing class for which the listserv can function as a site for invention. For instance, one assignment I use in first-year composition classes asks students to select an image and trace its development across time or culture: How does it morph? Why or why doesn't it? To prepare for this formal assignment, we engage in several informal activities, including a listserver discussion of (1) the image associated with their high schools (what was it, why was it selected, and what does it suggest about the school?) and (2) images they are drawn to and why. This kind of activity helps students think on the screen and together with others about the topic they will address in a formal assignment. Students like it because email feels "normal" and is fun for many of them. As important, since the students are talking to others, they are more inclined to explain and elaborate. From our perspective, as they work together, students create a kind of collective knowledge, one that is written and thus accessible and from which they can all draw as they work on a formal assignment.

Another kind of integral class activity conducted by listserv calls on students to participate in a type of behavior we are hoping to foster. Thus, in a first-year writing class that addresses research issues, you can ask students to select the best piece of research that you as a class have read so far—when you have read five or seven and have a sense of the range and possibility— and to explain why they think it's the best. This is a useful exercise for several reasons. First, just to answer the question, students have to read well, they have to understand how each article embodies an important research question, and they often have to synthesize the readings in their responses. Second, this assignment requires students, again, to talk to each other at least as often as they talk to the teacher—and this is especially so if students are directed to "build on previous posts to the listserv," that is, to include in their thinking and comments the observations that have already been posted. Third, and not least, this kind of activity can be fun for students; they like the sense of play and contest that develops as they consider which article really is best—and they often find that no one is best overall but that each has something to recommend it. At the conclusion of the activity, the teacher can again bring it back to the RL class, summarizing the claims that students made and indicating which seems strongest. In this way, a teacher can create a vital connection between class activities and eclass activities. In the terms I stipulated earlier, such a curricular design is thereby *blended*.

PROFESSIONAL LISTSERVS

Another activity, one that connects students with others outside the academy, is to ask students to sign on to a listserver that hosts members of a professional community. For example, one assignment asks students to log on to a listserv on which writing is discussed by writers—copy editors, for instance, or web designers or tech communicators (the possibilities here are nearly infinite). A second iteration of this assignment asks students to log on to a listserv that relates to their major. After a limited time—a week to two—students report back to the class on their observations via oral presentation, PowerPoint presentation, and/or print report or review. Such an assignment accomplishes several aims. First, it allows students to see members of a community communicating with each other about issues important to them, thus providing a window into both acceptable email demeanor (or not) and current questions engaging the community. Second, as they observe, students learn about something that is important to them, about a topic on which they have expertise, and about material that they then need to share with their colleagues. This assignment, then, is real in both purpose and audience, and it widens students' resources as they complete it.

Listserver as a New Forum

A final way to use listservers is modeled by Victor Vitanza's Pretext Re/Interviews (see <http://www.pre-text.com/ptlist/reinvw.html>). As the title suggests, a "re-interview" is a process through which an author discusses a book or article with what Vitanza defines as a *study group.* Borrowing from Vitanza, we can set up our own re/interviews (for a published version of such an exercise, see Nedra Reynolds's account in *CCC*). Last spring, for instance, my coteacher Barbara Heifferon and I invited James Zebroski to meet via email with a graduate student class to discuss his article "The Expressivist Menace." The article had both appealed to and mystified the students: They liked the claims, but they didn't understand why Zebroski had chosen to use the form of research reported in the piece, nor did they understand why it was "reported out" as it is—in intervals that didn't seem to make sense to them. Raising these kinds of questions with Zebroski gave the author a chance to contextualize his research much more fully. For their part, the students— because they could talk to the author—began to understand the research quite differently—as one piece in a continuing line of research—and they also began to read the assumptions that Zebroski had made about his readers more accurately. For our part, as teachers, Barbara and I saw how students processed new pieces of research and why they raised the kinds of questions that they did. We were all seeing things we hadn't before—through an email forum. What's interesting about such an exercise, then, is multifold: (1) It offers students more contexts for interpretation while (2) affording an author a chance to revisit a composition and (3) offering teachers—through the written record of the listserv—a chance to (quite literally) *see* how students learn.

    This exercise, of course, was tailored for a graduate class. But it's a quick leap to see how it would work for other classes. For instance, as I write this, I am a guest expert for undergraduates in Jenna Rossi's class, at SUNY Buffalo, who are enrolled in a class on feminist pedagogy. The students are interested in applications of my work in reflection to feminist pedagogy, and they are raising terrific questions—some showing me what I haven't made clear in my writing, others showing me where else I might take my writing. Likewise, when I teach first year comp again, I'll be inviting Victor Villanueva to visit with my students as they read his *Bootstraps*. So the opportunities for this kind of new practice are several.

A Heuristic for Planning Ediscourse

We have only begun to understand the various uses to which email might be put, but what is exemplified here begins to outline some options. So how shall we choose among them? One way is to think about what's needed and is most useful by means of a heuristic, a set of questions that can be quite useful for planning purposes. To that end, I've provided these brief heuristics, with annotations following:

- What's the exigence?
- How will you manage what could be a large volume of email?
- What are your expectations for this exercise?
- How will you convey those expectations?
- How will you connect the e-activity to the RL class?
- How will you reward student e-activity?
- How will you know if it "works"?

What's the Exigence?

In all rhetorical situations, Lloyd Bitzer argues, there is an exigence, an urgency or occasion that calls for action and discourse. Teaching is, of course, a kind of rhetorical situation, and when we use email or listservs, we need to know why we're doing so. Knowing why involves both the teacher (What effect is intended and what purpose is served?) and the student (Why do this at all?). Like any pedagogical approach, ediscourse is not the answer to all curricular questions. It's a good answer (1) if the question is about connecting students to each other in new ways, (2) if the question is about connecting students to relevant practitioners or professionals outside the classroom, or (3) if the question is about making new kinds of knowledge together.

How will you manage what could be a large volume of email?

The good news is that students do like ediscourse; the bad is that if it works, you could be up to your eyeballs in it. Therefore, you need to consider in advance how many classes you teach and how many students you have in each, how you'll use email and/or listservs with each of the classes, how you'll stagger this use so that the emails don't hit your inbox at the same time, how much you can actually read, and how much response your use will require. In general, it's best to start small, figure out what works best for you, and then build on that success. Also, you might want to check with your sysop to determine if your institution has an email appliance that will allow you to sort your email.

What are your expectations for this exercise?

Again, the good news is that students do like ediscourse, but another piece of bad news is that liking something doesn't guarantee that it will work in the ways that we intend. Making it work requires two moves: (1) stipulating the parameters and (2) outlining expectations. On parameters, for instance, do you want a weekly post? What constitutes a post? Is it one screen? Three? How much depth do you expect in postings? In other words, is summary enough? Do you want analysis and interpretation? And in the case of listservs, each is a forum composed of others. What are the role and the value that we assign to participation—that is, to the response to others as well as to a prompt of some kind?

What I'm calling expectations here generally fall under two rubrics: edecorum and intellectual work. As we know, the world of email, even on a closed class listserv, isn't innocent; it's not protected from flames, from sexual harassment, or from homophobic discourse. Accordingly, it's best, then, to *describe* what you expect in terms of edecorum. Moreover, since what we expect isn't always clear in any medium, and since the world of ediscourse is still under construction, we need both (1) to articulate what we expect (and permit) and (2) to model what is appropriate. Sometimes, this isn't even obvious to us. For instance, you probably don't want responses that look just like print— what I've called elsewhere *print uploaded*—but exactly how un-print-like and informal should posts be? Likewise, a lot of learning can emerge from play. How much and what kinds of "playfulness" are you comfortable with? These are the kinds of clarifications that students need. Outlining expectations in advance will help students as will replying to those who are participating as we'd like. When we respond to what we like, we shape in a powerful and favorable way what we want students to emulate.

For help in establishing these expectations, you might want to consult the University of Hawaii web site at <http://www.hawaii.edu/infotech/policies/itpolicy.html>. It explains well what appropriate expectations for email decorum are. And once you decide what your expectations are, it's also a good idea to include them on your syllabus where you have included other important expectations.

One last note about expectations, especially those related to intellectual work. To date, members of the profession have not yet established anything we might consider norms for student email expectations. As a recent discussion on the WPA listserver demonstrates (see <http://lists.asu.edu/cgi-bin/wa?A1=ind0111&L=wpa->), neither do we regard them the same way for ourselves. On one side is a view of email as casual conversation, and on the other, a view of email as epistemological activity. In this latter view, email is conceptualized as a medium through which new knowledge is created collectively before our eyes. Bill Condon has summarized this view:

> Lists operate cumulatively. What I say, I develop over several shorter messages, and it's interleaved with what others say. As a community, we have quite an extended, varied, detailed, deep, and rich conversation. That whole conversation is what contains "things that matter"—not one single, mono-voiced long turn, such as one sees in a journal article. So we do have long and probing conversations . . . and those conversations often morph into other long and probing conversations. . . .

> It's easy to mistake what happens on a listserv as chatting, as light and inconsequential. Much of what passes on this listserv is just that, because this listserv also functions as a community of people who like each other, who tease each other, who congratulate

each other, who criticize each other, etc. . . . SOMEone needs to teach people how to interact in these environments. We are talking about literacy, certainly, and it does matter.

<Tue, 6 Nov 2001 16:45:18 +0800>

If indeed this is the kind of "email literacy" that we expect, we need, as Condon suggests, to think of it in terms of a new kind of literacy, and then, very quickly, we need to define, explain, and model it for students.

How will you convey those expectations?

It's best to convey expectations in a variety of forms and modes. Including the email/listserver assignments on the syllabus attests to their importance— likewise for attaching a grade to them. Outlining the e-activity in a one-page assignment sheet, as we often do for a formal assignment, provides another opportunity to suggest goals, procedures, and outcomes. And, of course, outlining expectations digitally—at the outset and at the closing of activities— underscores your expectations.

How will you connect the e-activity to the RL class?

Although it's not clear from research that connecting the e-activity to the class will ensure its success, it is clear, as Yagelski and Grabill have shown, that when we *don't* make this connection, students quite rightly won't necessarily see one. In other words, if we outline an email or listserver activity but fail to connect it to the class writ large, students are likely to see it as superfluous and thus ignore it. Ways of connecting the two modes of activity, as the earlier illustrations show, are numerous—from an instructor's making that connection to asking students to complete an invention activity together or to reporting out observations to the class.

How will you reward student e-activity?

Expectations, of course, are themselves integral to what we value, and we should reward what we value. Explaining what we reward is tricky; we don't want to be so precise that we determine response or "script" postings. On the other hand, failing to provide guidance isn't very helpful, and in the final analysis, most of us do prefer some kinds of responses to others. A good starting point is to think about what we ourselves respond to favorably in other posts. Items we might consider include the number and size of posts, and the ability to communicate well online by

- connecting with earlier posts by providing sufficient context and by synthesizing

- responding specifically to issues already raised
- taking issues already raised and extending or complicating them
- raising new questions for the group to consider
- reflecting—working metacognitively—to think about what has been learned through ediscussion and through this new medium

I suspect that for some, there will be the temptation to "count" the number of posts, although that's not a very strong measure of what we are looking for. It's better, then—as in the case of evaluating journals—to avoid mere quantity as a measure and instead to articulate the criteria that more accurately speak to what we value.

Another way to think about the "reward" issue includes determining how to grade such participation. Several options are available:

- Using the previously listed criteria—which include both new contributions and responses to earlier postings—to count email participation the way we do class participation, for 10 percent of the grade, for instance. The advantage of doing this rather than evaluating class participation, by the way, is that unless we keep very careful records of in-class participation, this method provides much better evidence of contributions and responses.
- Using the previous criteria, "count" the email activity as we might a journal grade or even an essay assignment.

In either case, you won't want to keep track of student contributions; in any class, students outnumber us! But there are several ways to keep track, both of which ask students to assume an appropriate responsibility and to made a reflective judgment:

- Ask students to keep a tally of the number of times they have posted. Ask them likewise to present to you a limited number—three to five, perhaps—of their best postings (either electronically or in print) with a one-page reflection on what they contributed to the email discussion and what they learned from it. This "portfolio" can provide the basis for your grade.
- You might also ask students to write to you about which students seemed to make the best contributions to the list and why they valued those the most. With this set of criteria in hand, ask students to present their best case in these terms.

How will you know if it "works"?

Since we are using email and listservs for new purposes, it's important to know if and how these new discourses help us succeed. For instance, if you begin to use e-office hours, how will you know if they work? How many students will need to contact you via email for the method to be a success for your teaching—a single student? 20 percent? What kinds of concerns should they bring? And, regarding a listserver discussion, how will you determine if it's contributing to student learning? Here are some quick ideas: Include items from a listserv discussion on a test (in fact, you can use a listserv discussion to have students generate test questions!), or review students' portfolios to see if they have included printouts of listserver discussions as evidence of their own learning. Similarly, we can do a "thematic analysis" of listserver-generated insights in their formal assignments or of comments *they* make in their final portfolio reflections. Unprompted, do students connect this activity to their claims about what they have learned? Course evaluations offer yet another venue. We can, simply enough, ask them what they have learned. Deciding what "counts" for us as evidence of the success of new practices provides a foundation that we can use once an initial implementation of email and/or a listserv is complete. It supplies the criteria that can help us understand whether or not our new application has succeeded in the ways that we had hoped.

Conclusion

I began this chapter by remarking, "It's not a question of whether you'll use technology to help students learn. It's a question of what kind of technology you will include—and when." A hundred years ago the principal technology for the teacher was the blackboard, for the student, the pencil. Forty years ago, television was the technology that would finally make the difference in education. Like earlier technologies, however, TV was more transmission of knowledge than its construction, and it understood such knowledge as less rather than more social. As a technology, email relies on a different set of assumptions. Even its design suggests that communication is collaborative and that knowledge is constructive; it is a social medium. In these ways, then, email as a medium is congruent with the theories informing many of our writing classrooms.

Put another way, and as is no doubt evident, I'm an advocate of using email and listservers for learning. But I'm also an advocate of using common sense, I think, because I think the choice of which medium to use for which purpose and for which audience is a rhetorical one. It requires some understanding of the differences among media, and it requires planning. Like other good teaching, it requires some experience; we learn through trial and, alas, error. And after we've given it a try, it needs review, analysis, reflection—and a new design and a new iteration.

Using email and listservers for learning is a new practice that is itself still very much under construction. Working together, among ourselves and with our students, it will be interesting, challenging, and rewarding, too, to see what we construct.

Notes

[1] For an excellent discussion of the role of online learning in higher education, see Amy Harmon, "Cyberclasses in Session," *New York Times Education Life* 11 Nov. 2001, Sec. 4A: 31–32.

Works Cited

Bitzer, Lloyd. "The Rhetorical Situation." *Philosophy and Rhetoric* 1 (1967): 1–14.

Harmon, Amy. "Cyberclasses in Session." *New York Times Education Life* 11 Nov. 2001, Sec. 4A: 30–32.

Reynolds, Nedra. "Fragments in Response: An Electronic Discussion of Lester Faigley's *Fragments of Rationality*." CCC 45.2 (1994): 264–73.

Yagelski, Robert P., and Jeffrey Grabill. "Computer-mediated Communication in the Undergraduate Writing Classroom: A Study of the Relationship of Online Discourse and Classroom Discourse in Two Writing Classes." *Computers and Composition* 15.1 (1998): 11–40.

Web Sites Consulted

<http://lists.asu.edu/cgi-bin/wa?A2=ind0111&L=wpa-l&D=1&P=16736>

<http://www.pre-text.com/ptlist/reinvw.html>

<http://www.hawaii.edu/infotech/policies/itpolicy.html>

Meeting the Paradox of Computer-Mediated Communication in Writing Instruction

Stuart Blythe
Indiana University—Purdue University Fort Wayne

As is often true with something unfamiliar, computer-mediated communication (CMC) can seem intimidating and difficult at first—enough so that the drawbacks of the inevitable learning curve may seem to outweigh any benefits. However, CMC can affect you and your students in ways that make the learning curve worthwhile. In fact, some instructors (including me) wonder how we ever lived without it—which is the same kind of wonder many feel about, say, the microwave or air conditioning. The purpose of this chapter is to describe some of those benefits and to offer advice on ways to integrate CMC into your courses.

What is Computer-Mediated Communication?

CMC is one of those slippery terms used to refer to a wide range of phenomena. In some cases, *CMC* refers to any kind of information sent via networked computers. Almost anything is considered a form of CMC, according to this definition—from a dialogue in a chat room, to a digital audio recording, to an email message or a copy of an *Atlantic Monthly* article made available online. In other cases, the term is used to refer only to instances that approximate unpublished or face-to-face communication—that which approximates talk or informal correspondence between two or more individuals. If you adopt the latter definition in the classroom, communication that approximates in-class discussion is characterized as CMC, while communication that approximates more formal written documents (e.g., handouts, essays, and books) is not. Although each definition has its uses, I use the latter conception of CMC in

Figure 1
MUD/MOO Interface: Stu's Room

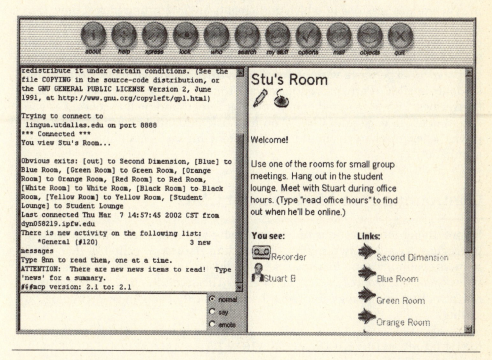

this chapter because other parts of this book deal with web pages and other forms of computer-mediated writing.

Whatever the definition, CMC can be characterized both technologically and linguistically. Technologically, CMC can be characterized in terms of the functions of a given application, such as email, a listserv, a chat room, or a MUD/MOO. (See Figure 1 for a sample of a MUD/MOO interface.) Each application allows users to complete specific tasks—such as creating and sending a message, storing files, or creating mailing lists—and requires specific types of hardware and software—such as network connections and computer-processing speed. Although technological issues are inevitable, you should not dwell on them. Let technically trained people handle technological questions. Make friends with computer support staff personnel. What is more important for you to consider is how CMC may be characterized as a language practice and how that may fit in your classroom.

Linguistically, CMC can be characterized as a hybrid that sits somewhere between talk and writing. Even though most CMC is written—whether it be a message posted via email or shared in a chat room—it shares several characteristics with oral communication. Chat-room exchanges, for example, often seem as fleeting as the spoken word, and they occur synchronously (with partners communicating at much the same time). Another sign of the hybrid nature of CMC is many writers' attitudes toward conventional rules of grammar when sending email or engaging in online chat. Many writers are more lax about applying such rules than they would be, say, when publishing a formal essay. Or, seen another way, many readers exhibit a greater tolerance for grammatical deviation in CMC than in printed media. This is especially true in synchronous sessions in which participants are interacting in real time. (See Figure 1 for an example of an application that makes this happen.) In these cases, people may be typing too quickly to check their work; they would fall behind in the "conversation" if they did. All of which means you should be prepared to experience various forms of written language when you engage students in CMC. Perhaps you may want to use CMC for exercises for which "correctness" is not required or else consider foregrounding that concept as you ask students to engage in CMC. You may ask students to consider for themselves when mechanics should be important in, say, email and when they should not.

Confronting Two Myths About CMC

Before diving into questions of how and why you might use CMC in writing instruction, consider two myths surrounding its use. The first is that CMC reduces communication to a small set of exclusively verbal cues. (This is sometimes called the *reduced context hypothesis*.) The second is that using computers introduces technology into what had previously been an un-technological setting.

MYTH 1: CMC REDUCES COMMUNICATION TO A SMALL SET OF EXCLUSIVELY VERBAL CUES. Some have asserted that issues of gender, race, and class get masked online because of the lack of visual, nonverbal cues available there. Consider how many cues available in a face-to-face session (e.g., sex, skin color, spoken accent, and so on) do indeed get masked when you can't see the person with whom you're communicating. Some believe that online exchanges are more egalitarian as a consequence, that people are more likely to attend to another's words rather than to what they look like or to the way they talk. This would be a good thing—if it were true. As Janet Eldred and Gail Hawisher point out, though, CMC does not reduce such cues as much as one might expect. In order for such cues to be lost completely, (1) participants would have to have no prior concept of each other, and (2) verbal and visual cues could not get reinscribed online. Neither contingency is usually true. It is possible, for instance, that students may have met previously; it is inevitable in a class that combines face-to-face sessions with CMC. Although such students may not see each other when they are interacting via computer, they still retain visual images of their classmates.

Even when students have never seen or heard their partners, they can still take certain cues from online exchanges. Names with gendered or ethnic markers, for instance, might predispose online participants toward certain assumptions and consequent behaviors. Students' writing styles can also carry "accents," as anyone who has read papers by second-language writers can attest. Even the information one attaches to the end of one's email message can carry with it a certain amount of authority. Consider the difference between a signature line like this in email:

Stuart
Office: Classroom-Medical Building, 555
Phone: 555.555.5555

and a signature line like this:

Dr. Stuart Blythe
Assistant Professor, Department of English and Linguistics
Indiana University—Purdue University Fort Wayne
Office: Classroom-Medical Building, 555
Phone: 555.555.5555

Don't count on CMC to create a more equal exchange between students. It has other values, as is made apparent in this book, but don't expect an exchange free of all bias to be one of them.

MYTH 2: INCORPORATING CMC INTRODUCES TECHNOLOGY INTO WHAT WAS AN UNTECHNOLOGICAL SETTING. Some teachers claim that working in computer-mediated settings is "artificial," as if technology were intruding on a once-natural activity. This assumption ignores the technologies that already exist in a traditional classroom. Though networked computers complicate writing and writing instruction, it is important to see that we are adding new technologies to *already technological practices* and that we are not "technologizing" something that was once "natural." Writing classrooms are already technological because both writing (even with pen and paper) and instruction rely on material artifacts. "Technology and writing are not distinct phenomena," Christina Haas writes. "That is, writing has never been and cannot be separate from technology" (p. x). Writing can occur only if one has artifacts that enable the inscription and display of information (e.g., paper and pencil, blackboard and chalk, computer with keyboard and monitor). Moreover, even an in-class discussion can occur only in environments that enable such an encounter. Good discussions occur in settings conducive to talk and may be inhibited otherwise (as anyone knows who has tried to work with another person while standing in a busy stairwell or who has tried to hold a class discussion outdoors). Good discussion relies, in other words, on technologies that work so well that we need not attend to them.

Just as you should reject the notion that communication becomes more egalitarian online, so should you also reject the notion that good conversation cannot take place there. Good conversation can take place online if the technologies are working well. What you should expect with CMC are similarities and differences when it is compared to the traditional classroom. That's the paradox of teaching using CMC. On the one hand, it is in many ways similar to face-to-face communication or informal writing. Many aspects transfer to the new medium. On the other hand, it does indeed differ from face-to-face and print media, which means that it offers options that other forms of communication could not. CMC simultaneously is the same as and differs from those forms.

How Might CMC Be Used in Writing Instruction?

Up to this point, I have argued that CMC is often treated as an informal type of writing akin to conversation or unpublished correspondence. I have also suggested that CMC is simultaneously similar to, and different from, more traditional forms of speaking and writing. You may well ask, "How might I use CMC in the classroom?" Let me answer that in two ways. First, let me suggest ways it can be used; then, let me suggest ways to get started.

Because there are various forms of CMC, it may help to think of several analogies to familiar forms of communication. As Table 1 illustrates, CMC can be thought of as a form of letter writing, or as a form of mass mailing, or as a method of posting messages for others to see, as is the case with hallway bulletin boards or kiosks on campus malls. Finally, CMC can be thought of as a hybrid of face-to-face communication. What application you choose ought to depend on the kinds of communication you want to foster among students.

Why Use CMC in Writing Instruction?

There are several reasons to consider integrating CMC into instruction. What follows is an incomplete list. The ideas mentioned cover some of the more basic benefits. For a summary, see Table 2.

CMC OFTEN MAKES IT EASIER TO GET MORE STUDENTS INVOLVED IN CON-VERSATION. This can happen in two ways. First, some students get more involved online than in face-to-face encounters and vice versa. It is inevitable that some student who rarely contributes to face-to-face discussions becomes the most prolific writer in online discussions. Perhaps that student feels more secure communicating online. Perhaps she wants the time to compose a message to the class rather than having to think on her toes in the press of a face-to-face discussion. Likewise, the student who contributes little to online discussions may be inhibited by a distrust of the technology or by poor typing skills. If you can combine face-to-face and CMC sessions, you give different students a chance to take part in a way that's more comfortable for each. Second, you can require all students to post to a computer-mediated session, thereby requiring everyone to participate. No one can sit silently in the back of the room when everyone is required to post, say, responses to a reading or a response to each other's texts. In CMC, those who take longer to compose a message, or to think of a reply, don't lose out to those who speak more loudly or who think more quickly.

CMC CAN BE USED FOR ONLINE JOURNALS. You can ask students to post journals a few times per week. You may assign journal topics or encourage students to post messages on a topic of their own choosing. You can even encourage students to post a journal responding to a fellow student's journal. (You must, of course, set some parameters about what may be posted and which ways students may respond properly to one another.) Such online journals can be used not only to promote reflection on class material but also to help stu-

Table 1: A Comparison of Analogies Regarding Computer-mediated Communication, and the Applications Most Pertinent to Each.

Analogy	*Characteristics*	*Applications*
CMC can be like writing a letter or memo.	*One-to-one*, with the writer delivering a message directly to a reader	*Email.* Most email applications follow a memo format and function like letters and memos.
CMC can be like creating a mass mailing.	*One-to-many*, with the writer delivering a message directly to many readers	*Listservs and Email.* Listservs allow members to send an email message to one address, which in turn forwards that message to the email addresses of all other members.
CMC can be like posting a message on a bulletin board or kiosk.	*One-to-many*, with the writer leaving a text so that others may wander by and read it	*Online bulletin board systems* (BBS). These often appear as web pages where a reader can browse through a collection of messages left by others.
CMC can be like engaging in a face-to-face conversation.	*One-to-one or many-to-many.* Two or more people can meet and converse at the same time. All must be "present" simultaneously.	*Chats rooms and MUDs/MOOs.* Such applications allow participants to send messages which others see immediately. See Figure 1.

dents see that they are in certain respects not alone. Students are often pleasantly surprised to see, for instance, that their classmates also are struggling with certain writing assignments or have similar reactions to an assigned reading.

CMC CAN BE USED TO ENCOURAGE BRAINSTORMING. CMC often feels informal, as has been mentioned. Moreover, many people experience a sense of playfulness when engaging in certain kinds of activities such as online chats. The sense of "role playing" online can encourage a certain volubility in many students. Because of their informal, playful feel, many CMC applications are good for brainstorming. You might present a small group with a series of questions or a particular task designed to get students started. For example, you could ask students to describe their first memories about reading, asking something like, "What's the first book you remember reading?" or "What's the first book you remember liking as a child?" or "Why did you (dis)like reading as a child?" You might ask each student to respond, read partners' responses, and then ask at least two additional questions of each partner. Such exchanges are especially helpful when students can save transcripts of them. In addition, the brainstorming is a richer, collaborative product rather than the work of an isolated writer.

Table 2: A Brief List of Classroom Activities and the CMC Applications That Best Support Them.

If you want students to . . .	Then use . . .
Be able to exchange private messages with each other and with the instructor	Email
Share copies of their papers only with a few small-group partners for the purposes of peer review	Email or bulletin board systems
Share copies of their papers with every student in a class	Listservs or bulletin board systems
Correspond publicly with a "guest speaker" or others outside the class or with the entire class as part of a discussion	Listservs or bulletin board systems (*Note:* MUDs/MOOs can overwhelm students if too many people are logged on at once. Consider using those applications for small-group work only.)
Take part in real-time brainstorming sessions with small-group partners	MUDs/MOOs, chat

CMC CAN BE USED TO FACILITATE PEER REVIEW. If a student uses email, she can send a copy of her paper to a few members of her small group. Or the student can use a listserv to send a paper to the entire class. Or the student can use a bulletin board system to post a paper that other students can stop by to review. Reviewers, in turn, could send a private reply directly to the writer (using email) or could leave a reply for others to see on the bulletin board page. That reply would appear as a link directly below the link to the student's page, which helps others see the relationships among various messages. Also, you could critique students' reviews, thus coaching students during the review process. What combination you use should depend, of course, on the amount of privacy you want to ensure each student. Certain papers may be handled privately while others may be handled more publicly. (See "How Can CMC Be Integrated Smoothly?") In cases in which all small-group partners see everyone else's comments, reviewers can add to comments made by classmates. As with the use of CMC and brainstorming, online peer review can seem more collaborative and less isolating. Review can also be handled beyond the constraints of a classroom.

CMC CAN BE USED TO EXTEND TEMPORAL BOUNDARIES. Many times, you or your students may have an idea that could contribute to a classroom conversation, but that idea may have arrived after class was dismissed. CMC could be used to enable students to follow up on the conversation, regardless of whether or not the class was meeting. Moreover, CMC allows students to complete some course work at times that meet their schedules. If a student wants to work at midnight, she can (unless she is engaging in an online chat with an unwilling partner). With classes of working adults, for instance, it often helps to require a series of bulletin board or listserv postings in lieu of a face-to-face class meeting.

CMC CAN BE USED TO EXTEND SPATIAL BOUNDARIES. Just as students need not always adhere to one schedule in order to exchange ideas or review work, so should they not be limited to communicating only among themselves. Students may communicate with students from different parts of the country, from different countries altogether, or from different parts of the same city. All sorts of combinations are possible. One teacher may want her rural students, for example, to communicate with urban students; another may want high school seniors to communicate with students about to enter high school. "Guest speakers" may be invited to join in a series of exchanges—speakers who would otherwise have to travel to reach the students. For instance, a speaker may agree to post an initial statement via an online bulletin board and then agree to field questions sent by students for two additional days.

How Can CMC Be Integrated Smoothly?

In the previous section, I shared some ways that CMC might benefit you and your students. In this section, I offer advice on integrating CMC for the first time. The most important piece of advice I can offer is to *think first about what you want students to be able to do.* "English composition teachers need to start with what they know about writing and teaching," writes Cynthia Selfe (1989), "rather than [with] what they know about technology" (p. xxi). In other words, "forget about computers and concentrate on writing" (Selfe, 1989, p. 7). Think first about the types of communication you would like to foster among students. Do you want to enable peer review, correspondence among students and others outside their classroom, brainstorming in small groups, or collaborative writing? How much privacy do you want to allow during review processes? Decide first what you want students to do; then think about what types of arrangements will enable doing that.

Consider some examples of thinking about teaching first. (See Table 2 for a summary.) If you want students to be able to exchange messages with each other, and with you, when it's convenient for them, if you want them to be able to extend conversations beyond class time, then you ought to consider using asynchronous technologies such as email or bulletin board systems. Further, if you want students to be able to communicate *directly* with other individual students, or with you, then you ought to use email. If you want students to post papers or general announcements to small groups or to an entire class, but you don't think it's necessary for them to be communicating directly with each other individually, then you may want to use a bulletin board application. (You may want to use email for some types of communication and a bulletin board for others.) If you want the synchronicity that often seems to come from the heat of a face-to-face, real-time exchange, then you ought to use some sort of synchronous application in which participants can log on to a network at the same time and share messages. The speed of such exchanges will be limited primarily by typing skill and reading ability.

Whatever type of application you use, *integrate CMC by having students begin with simple tasks that are relevant to assignments.* In other words, don't regard the learning of CMC as "lost time." Kill two birds with one stone. For instance, you can introduce students to a bulletin board application at the beginning of the semester by having each student post an introduction to herself and then read other students' introductions. Such an exercise combines the learning of a computer application with an icebreaker that helps students get to know one another. If you're feeling ambitious, you could even offer some sort of quiz with questions that can only be answered if students have read their classmates' messages. You might ask questions like "Who in this class graduated from X high school?" or "Who in this class worked for Y last summer?" (One caveat: Do not ask students to use an application for a complicated task, one crucial to a course grade, without offering them practice with that application first.)

Finally, *rely on some of your students for computer advice.* Remember that your expertise is writing, not technology. You need not claim to be all knowledgeable with computers. Most students have grown up with computers and are comfortable with them in ways that many teachers are not. Use that strength. In fact, realize that many students are flattered to be identified as computer experts. You may even begin a semester by asking students about their computer strengths. Consider asking who knows how to use specific applications that will be used in class. It helps to know, for instance, who has used a bulletin board system before or who knows how to fix crashed disks. Make sure classmates understand who the experts are, and don't be afraid to ask those experts for advice from time to time during class. (For students who consider themselves to be poor writers, this is a way for them to build self-esteem in a writing class.) Again, *your* expertise should be in writing.

Other Questions to Consider

There are always a host of questions to consider when integrating CMC. I hope that the preceding sections have addressed the main ones you're likely to encounter. In closing, I present a grab bag of other questions you should be prepared to address when integrating CMC for the first time.

- How quickly do you want to start? In other words, do you want to integrate CMC into an entire semester's curriculum, or do you want to try a few CMC exercises with a class before using it more extensively in subsequent semesters? I personally recommend that you integrate CMC slowly. Don't try to master it all in one semester. Try a few exercises one semester; then add more in later courses.
- Do you want to monitor discussions? A teacher's presence influences student discussions. By monitoring discussions, you may ensure that students avoid inappropriate topics and act civilly toward one another;

at the same time, your presence may inhibit certain fruitful discussions as well.

- Do you want to record discussions? Many applications allow students to create records of synchronous exchanges. This has the advantage of allowing students to review an exchange. On the other hand, you must be sure to set parameters for the fair use of such exchanges.
- How do you handle the line between CMC transcripts and students' papers? This is a question that addresses traditional notions of plagiarism. To what extent can students cite discussions held online? How should such discussions be handled? Be prepared to set some parameters on this issue.
- Should students post anonymously or sign their names? In some applications, students can log on under a pseudonym. Although this option may allow a certain playfulness, it may also prompt inappropriate behaviors. As with the decision to monitor discussions, you may want to base your decision regarding anonymity on your level of trust regarding any given group of students.
- How do you measure involvement? In some cases, such as journal postings, you may simply count the number of posts as a way of measuring involvement. In other cases, you may need to focus on content. If you feel compelled to measure involvement through quantity of posts, be prepared to talk in terms of "screens" rather than pages. In other words, you might require students to post at least two journal entries per week, and each entry may have to be fill at least one screen. Word count is still appropriate as well, depending on your goals.

Works Cited

Eldred, Janet C., and Gail Hawisher. "Researching Electronic Networks." *Written Communication* 12 (1995): 330–59.

Haas, Christina. *Writing Technology: Studies on the Materiality of Literacy.* Hillsdale, NJ: Erlbaum, 1996.

Selfe, Cynthia L. *Creating a Computer-Supported Writing Facility: A Blueprint for Action.* Houghton, MI: Computers and Composition, 1989.

Teaching Writing at a Distance: What's Gender Got to Do With It?

GAIL E. HAWISHER
University of Illinois at Urbana-Champaign

CYNTHIA L. SELFE
Michigan Technological University

> *Recently, I got involved in my class's Blackboard discussion in a very heated debate about sexism in advertising. I was accused in several posts of not thinking clearly, or of oversimplifying, and of misreading the ads. Finally, at my wit's end, I tried to agree to disagree—thinking that the class could all have different opinions on the matter if they wanted. And then a guy emailed me privately to say that was okay—he was glad I was beginning to see things more clearly, as if he were an expert on this issue of gender and advertising. I was so mad, but finally gave up. I was surprised my instructor didn't jump in when they were all attacking me. At least that's how I felt. By the time she did say something, the damage had been done. I have very little to say these days in online class discussions.*
>
> —Sandra Morton[1]

Over the past fifteen years or so, there have been several studies that have looked at women and their experiences in the online teaching and learning environments associated with writing classrooms. Each, in its own way, has tried to ascertain what happens to classroom dynamics of gender when the online world comes into play. Are women students (or women instructors) treated differently in online contexts than otherwise? Do the uneven relations among the genders carry over into class discussions more markedly online than outside of electronic writing classes? Do email discussion lists, listservs, chat

128

rooms, IRCs, MOOs and other forms of asynchronous and synchronous online discussions make a difference in how some women learn and how some women teach? What happens when the World Wide Web with its preponderance of images is added to this mix of new technologies?

All these questions take on added importance when classes—especially composition classes—are taught online *and* at a distance. In this chapter, we focus our discussion on the gendered experiences of women in composition classes taught at a distance.

Several key assumptions provide a foundation for our work. First, we acknowledge that online spaces, in general, have not proven to be the egalitarian spaces that teachers had hoped for in the early 1990s (cf., Hawisher and Selfe; Faigley; Cooper and Selfe). They do not, generally, afford people equal opportunities to speak up and out, and they often serve to instantiate—and sometimes exacerbate—many of the same problems that women and others have always encountered in their day-to-day relations in the home, community, workplace, and, not surprisingly, school (Selfe and Meyer; Selfe and Selfe). As Hawisher and Sullivan point out, our most optimistic assessment suggests that these new espaces are "neither egalitarian utopias nor sites devoid of power and influence for women" (173).

Second, we work from a belief that individual differences between women and men preclude essentializing their experiences simplistically along the lines of gender alone (cf., hooks; Anzaldua; Flax; Gruber, forthcoming; Jarrett). Although women share many common experiences associated with their gender and are influenced by many common cultural and social forces that bear on, and are affected by, gender relations (e.g., class, race, religion), they are far from a homogenous group. As much as they share in the experiences of a gendered world, individual women—and groups of women—also differ from one another in terms of personal experience, background, education, technological preparation, geographical location, socioeconomic status, race, and so on.

Finally, we work from the recognition that distance education, increasingly, involves a complex set of global practices and values (Thompson) and that any examination of women's experiences must be situated clearly in a cultural and geographical context. In the case of this chapter, we review research on students' online experiences from both the United States and Canada (where some recent studies bearing on gender have been conducted and published, for instance, Care and Udod; Burge and Lenksyj). Our surveys of women teachers focus exclusively on teachers within the United States.

When we started exploring the new educational spaces of distance-education classes, we were curious to see what sort of research was being conducted to assess the effects of moving writing classes, and classes in general, entirely—or primarily—*online*. We were curious about the challenges that both women students and teachers have encountered in these online environments and about the steps they have taken to address these challenges. As we began to look into the research literature, however, we realized that if we were to adequately represent gender issues in distance-learning environments, we needed to do more than look at computer-based distance-education classes. We needed, as well, to look at distance-education classes supported by multiple technologies. As a recent government report on distance education (*Distance Education*) notes:

> While postsecondary education institutions employed a wide variety of distance education technologies, in 1997–98, courses were likely to use several types of video technologies and the Internet-based technologies more than any other modes of delivery. (v)

In line with the data of this report, we found that classes using interactive, instructional television were often, but not always, accompanied by online interactions over email, the Internet, or a computer-supported conferencing system, and that the online interactions in such settings affected students' and teachers' experiences in these classes in some of the same ways that they did in courses without televised components.

In the first of the three major sections that follow, we provide some statistics that should help readers gain some sense of distance education as an educational effort and offer a working definition of *distance education* or "teaching at a distance." In the second section, we offer a review of some of the recent research on distance-education environments. Without exception, readers will find that these studies report on either the pedagogical strategies used in such environments or on the experiences of women *students* and provide very little information about the experiences or attitudes of women *teachers* in distance-education classes. Hence, in the third section of this paper, to address this gap, we offer the observations of five women faculty members who teach composition classes at a distance. The responses of these women were gathered in a pilot email survey that we conducted in the summer of 2001. We end this chapter with a third major section that identifies some basic concerns for teachers, students, and programs interested in establishing a feminist-informed pedagogy for composition courses taught online and at a distance.

Distance Learning/Distance Education: What Is It?

First and foremost, the growth of distance learning, like the electronic world in general, is not merely a trend—a phenomenon that may be here today and gone tomorrow. A recent American Council on Education (ACE) document predicts "that distance education demand will increase from 5 percent of all higher education students in 1998 to 15 percent by 2002" (*Distributed Education* 11). Predictions also suggest that the number of colleges and universities offering distance-learning courses will increase to over 3,300 in 2004, when the market for these courses in higher education will be worth about 750 million dollars, and that during the next four years the number of students enrolling in these courses will jump 33 percent each year (Burger, Boggs, and Webber). It is also worth noting that, of those institutions offering courses at a distance, 70 percent have chosen to do so within the fields of English, humanities, and social sciences (*Distance Education* iv).

Distance-learning courses have also helped to create a shift in the population of students working in institutions of higher education. No longer restricted primarily to eighteen- to twenty-four-year-old college residential students who largely populate four-year, traditional university campuses, distance-learning courses usually attract older, working students. Eighty-five percent of the five hundred students enrolled in Western Governors University, for example, are employed full-time, and average forty years of age (Spangler and Thalman).

Perhaps equally important for this chapter, however, is the fact that studies of distance-learning environments in North American colleges and universities indicate that women outnumber men as students in such classes, with female students accounting for 60 percent to 77.9 percent of the population. (Thompson). Even on a global scale, the proportion of women enrolled in distance-education courses is significant. In Canada, for example, 60 to 70 percent of distance learners are women; in the British Open University, 50 percent are women undergraduates; 54.7 percent are women enrolled in such classes in Spain; 38 percent in the Netherlands; and 31 percent in Germany (Burge). That these women—here and in other countries—tend to enroll more frequently in humanities courses increases their representation in the classes that we teach. Thus, it is imperative that we pay attention to these distance-learning environments and scrutinize them as carefully as we have the more conventional classroom-based electronic writing classes.

The American Association of University Professors (AAUP) defines *distance education* and *distance learning*—which we use interchangeably in this chapter—in these terms: "In distance education (or distance learning) the teacher and the student are separated geographically so that face-to-face communication is absent; communication is accomplished instead by one or more technological media, most often electronic (interactive television, satellite television, computers, and the like)." The statement goes on to say that "[t]he geographic separation between teacher and student may be considerable (for example, in a course offered over the World Wide Web), or the distance may be slight (for example, from the teacher's computer to the student's in a nearby campus building). Hence distance education may apply to both on- and off-campus courses and programs." For our purposes, however, we define *distance education* and *distance learning* a bit more narrowly: as that instruction which is accompanied by online interactions—that is, accomplished over the Internet—and at a distance—that is, not including only those students on our campuses. It is in these contexts that few studies have looked at gender issues.

Pedagogically, we believe that what distinguishes these new electronic classes from the more conventional classroom-based, online learning environments is that the instructor-to-student relationship, as well as the student-to-student relationship, is almost always conducted online or over video, and, in the cases in which we're most interested, the classes provide no or little opportunity for participants to meet face to face. Up to now, much of our collaborative and individual research has looked at online classes that, for the most part, meet in face-to-face environments. Here, for the first time, we step back and look at those classes taught from afar or, in other words, at classes in which the face-to-face component is mostly absent. Hence, an appropriate working definition for distance learning as presented in this chapter includes only those classes accompanied by Internet and web instruction, even when conducted through interactive and satellite television, and only those online classes with little or no face-to-face component with the instructor.

Even with these restrictions on our definition, however, distance-learning classes vary tremendously across the spectrum. Some rely primarily on interactive television, which broadcasts the class to various electronically connected sites. Others are taught primarily online by using a course management package such as Blackboard or WebCT with which students consult their syllabus, access readings and assignments, participate in online discussions, and submit their essays. Still others augment such classes with MOOs (object-oriented, synchronous communication spaces), email, and sometimes streaming audio, streaming video, or web-authoring programs. Here's one description of the technology requirements for a distance-learning course:

> To take an online course, you will need specific hardware or software. . . . Typical requirements include: Windows 95/98 software, at least 32 Mb of RAM, a sound card and speakers, a Pentium 90 or higher processor, a color monitor, a keyboard and mouse, access to the Internet, and a graphic web browser that is Java capable. Internet Explorer and Netscape Navigator are two major browsers that may be downloaded for free at www.microsoft.com or www. netscape.com. (Boyer 40)

Although many would argue that these requirements are relatively basic, each instance in which additional software is required makes access for students more difficult. Not only must they have the wherewithal to purchase the software, but they must also have the time to learn how to install it and to use it. It is perhaps significant, then, that the few studies looking at women participating in online discussions report consistently that women view time as a scarce commodity (Hawisher and Sullivan; Blum; Burge), something we write more about in the next section. Finally, we need to note that the costs of distance-education courses are often considerable, especially those that lead to a degree or certificate. Students pay 40 to 100 percent more for classes leading to a two-year degree at Western Governors University, for instance, than they would at a local community college (Spangler and Thalman).

Distance Learning and Women: Where's the Research?

When we turned to the research to learn what findings we might use to inform a feminist approach to composition classes taught at a distance, we were surprised at the dearth of studies related to gender issues. It should not have surprised us, however, for in the journal we edit, *Computers and Composition*, Susan Kay Miller tells us that there have been twelve articles since 1994 discussing the impact of distance learning on writing instruction, and we note that none of these articles deals explicitly with gender issues.

Nor do the articles in *Computers and Composition*'s recent special issue on distance learning address gender specifically. Although we would argue that all the articles offer the field a wealth of well considered, theoretical, and practical approaches to teaching online at a distance, they nevertheless seem to pay less attention to important issues related to our differences than they might. And this observation seems true of the field of distance education in general. Although articles like "Seven Principles of Effective Teaching: A Practical Lens for Evaluating Online Courses" (Graham et al.) are full of excellent suggestions for online teaching—some of which might address problems related to women—the research neglects specific or particular concerns associated with gender. Other documents we located showed similar lapses. The September 2000 draft Statement of the Regional Accrediting Commissions on the Evaluation of Electronically Offered Degree and Certificate Programs and the Guidelines that they present include no recommendations regarding possible special needs of women or of others. (See Western Interstate Commission for full document.) Although there are specific recommendations designed to address "faculty support" and "student support," no recommendation takes women into its field of vision. Similarly, on a global level, the "Policy and Programs" section of the World Bank's Global Distance EducatioNet <http://wbweb4.worldbank.org/disted/Policy/policy.html> offers no specific references to the needs of women students in distance-education contexts.

The uniform absence of references in such sources simply corroborates what Care and Udod term a "general lack of attention to the needs of women distance learners," and give credence to these authors' claim that "one of the biggest barriers to effective distance education for women is that courses are often designed without due consideration of women's needs, interests or learning styles." (Pym 387)

Most distance-learning studies, even the few that include gender issues in one way or another, attempt to evaluate the distance-learning context, in part, by asking students about their experiences in the course. John Ory, Cheryl Bullock, and Kristine Burnaska, for example, surveyed 895 students at the University of Illinois to determine whether the uses of asynchronous learning networks (ALN) in classes were the same for men and women and whether the two sexes' attitudes toward using ALN in courses differed. Student surveys, course monitoring, and group interviews comprised the researchers' method, which focused on students enrolled in forty courses. Although the abstract of the study indicates that no statistically significant gender differences were found in analyzing primarily student self-reports, there were some important differences reported in the study itself. In contrast to the men's responses, women students reported the following:

- They used computers more often for conferencing with the instructor and other students but less often for exploring resources on the Web.
- They found that using computers became slightly more difficult throughout the semester.
- They were more likely to use personal computers in computer labs.
- They learned more about using computers as a result of the course.

As the researchers themselves acknowledge, these findings have implications for instructors as far as pedagogy is concerned. At the very least, it would seem that women students often have less experience with technology and would benefit from more explicit teaching or discussion of technology matters at various times during the semester.

The only study of which we are aware that looks specifically at online interactions within the discourse of a distance-learning course took place at an unnamed "U.S.-based higher education distance organization" (Blum). An online doctoral student herself, Kimberly Blum analyzed 149 messages of non-traditional graduate and undergraduate students. Collected over one month, the messages were culled from an electronic student forum promoted as the school's student union, that is, as a place for students to gather online and discuss school-related issues that might not be discussed in their classes. Here are some of the discourse patterns that characterized the research. Women contributed

- 81% of all messages containing the words *thanks* or *thank you*
- 83.3% of personal remarks added to absolute statements
- 80.8% of all questions asked
- 87.5% of all messages containing _ or <G>
- 21% of responses to questions

Blum also noted that women

- asked more technical questions and evinced more concern about technical matters that had a bearing on the course
- commented more frequently on worries having to do with success in school, course pacing, time, and the cost of education

Importantly for this chapter, Blum documented a conversational pattern similar to that which was described anecdotally by writing studies' women faculty and graduate students in Hawisher and Sullivan's study. She notes that

> male students tended to dominate the online discussion for a time period (many times over days). When a female interjected a message, the resulting trend was an abundance of more female messages. Time after time this female pattern of communication was stopped by a male message of an extraordinary length (usually pages and pages), a message containing a female "put-down," or a message of an arrogant nature. After this occurred, it was often days before female students would post any messages.

Men, Blum noted, used a variety of techniques to dominate the online class conversation: for example, more males than females posted and answered messages (males posted 9 percent more messages than females did and posted 79 percent of the responses to questions). Males also sent 95.5 percent of the messages containing jokes of a "sexual nature," used all capital letters to "shout" in their email messages, and accused females of "whining" about technical difficulties. Thus, as Blum concludes, despite the polite, sometimes personal messages and questions women submitted, men got more air time in online discussions. Less air time, we believe, in most instances also means less learning. It also suggests that women contribute less frequently to class discussions, thus depriving all the members of the class of their needed perspectives.

Blum's findings are remarkably similar to those which Cynthia Selfe and Paul Meyer report in their now more than ten-year-old study of writing instructors' messages on a listserv within the field of computers and composition. During the twenty-day periods in which Selfe and Meyer collected and analyzed 296 messages, men also tended to dominate the discourse. According to the researchers, men consistently contributed more messages, introduced more new topics, and disagreed more frequently with others. They conclude, like Blum, that patterns in online educational forums tend to reflect the gendered styles of language documented in the larger society.

Also looking at gendered conversation patterns in online contexts, Susan Herring attributes the findings we have noted to different styles of posting and different values associated with what the two sexes regard as appropriate online interactions. According to Herring, the "female-gendered style" exhibits a degree of both "supportiveness" and "attenuation." She argues that supportiveness has to do with "expressions of appreciation, thanking, and community-building activities that make other participants feel accepted and welcome," whereas "attenuation" is marked by "hedging and expressing doubt, apologizing, asking questions, and contributing ideas in the form of suggestions." That this type of conversational style characterizes the women's contributions in both Blum's and Selfe and Meyer's studies suggests that our face-to-face gendered world makes a strong showing in online contexts. It behooves us, then, to craft a feminist pedagogy that acknowledges and endorses women's virtual contributions while, at the same time, valuing men's participation in these contexts as well, admittedly not an easy task.

We should add that these studies consistently note that women express more concern about having enough time to participate in the distance discourse, even as they appreciate the fact that the distance classroom has made course work more flexible and learning opportunities more accessible within their lives (Blum, Burge, Care and Udod). The adult, professional women in Hawisher and Sullivan's study found discussion groups time-consuming and often remarked that in this stage of their lives they simply lacked the time to play; Blum's participants noted that in addition to holding down full-time jobs, these women also were the persons mainly responsible for the children and household, both obligations that reduced the number of hours that they could spend online. Blum adds that although time may also be a scarce commodity for the adult men in her study, they voiced this concern far less frequently than women. And, as one woman graduate student we queried related, "I wasn't expecting the amount of time the course would take. . . . I found that I had to make a lot of time for this course, and I sacrificed other things to do so" (Ann Kane, personal email). The student was also taken aback by having to spend hours as she "scrambled to get a working FTP program onto [her] computer and . . . untangl[ed] problems with [her] password that prevented . . . uploading materials to the shared team and course spaces" (Ann Kane, personal email). Thus, whatever the configuration of distance-learning courses, it is a sure bet that some students will have less time than others, along with a greater number of technology problems in the course, and that often those with the greatest number of problems will be women (Blum). In a new report from the Association of American University Women, entitled "The Third Shift," Cheris Kramarae also tells us that distance-learning classes tend to add another layer to women's already full days—that women do their online class work before and after their real-world jobs, along with attending to their homemaking and childcare responsibilities.[2]

Stories About Teaching at a Distance: What Do Women Faculty Say?

To identify the experiences women faculty have had with composition courses offered at a distance, we asked twelve women instructors who had some background with using computer technology (most of these subjects had recently attended a summer institute for integrating technology into composition classes) if they had had experience with online classes and if they would be willing to respond to a standard set of questions. Five women from different kinds of institutions, programs, and backgrounds reported having experience in teaching such courses, and all five completed our survey. Although we found prior research in distance education to be useful, much of what we read lacked detailed descriptions of individual women's experiences; these studies were, moreover, especially silent about the experiences of female faculty.

We recognize that the comments of the women in this chapter represent only a partial, sketchy, and preliminary picture of the challenges that women faculty face in distance-education classes—an incomplete picture characterized both by the complexity and contradictory attitudes that one might expect. However, although these stories are far from representative of women's experiences in distance-education classes, they do add some information and range to the data we currently have about students' experiences, and they provide a fruitful direction in which to focus further studies that will add more information about distance learning and women.

The women we asked to respond to our survey questions have taught writing-intensive courses in distance-education environments sponsored by a range of different institutions. In the following accounts, we provide short snapshots of the individuals who responded so generously to our survey queries:

Sarah Carpenter, Assistant Professor: In her first tenure-track job at a mid-sized university in the Southwest, Sarah agreed to teach a distance-education class because her field was computers and composition studies, and because state education officials were pressuring her home institution to offer more courses to students in remote locations. Her school offered a training program that she took advantage of, but it was disappointing in its approach. In her words: "Most of the information we got was on support services (library, statewide office, sending materials, etc.). We were told also—which I consider rather sexist—to avoid wearing bright colors, dangling beads and necklaces, or anything that would hurt the eyes of the viewers." Little time was actually devoted to developing a pedagogy.

Beverly Moller, Full Professor: A former high school English teacher and an experienced university faculty member, Beverly taught her first distance-education course at a large Southern university. This university provided faculty associates in each college with training to help colleagues design and teach distance-education courses, as well as technical support for these efforts, both within her college and in a central campus office. In addition, Beverly taught her first distance-education course as part of a team of three. In her words: "In my early years I was occasionally involved in a school production or jazzercise class or other event where I was in a chorus line with other nonprofessional dancers. There were always those who were shown a series of steps once and [who] then deftly repeated them with seeming ease. I often stumbled through the first one or two steps and then stood there mutely waiting for assistance. That is how I felt in distance education teaching experiences. . . . I was fortunate to be a member of a team of three for my first teaching, and my two colleagues had more experience than I with distance ed. They helped me limp through the initial attempts, and finally I achieved some small successes."

Diana Deneuve, Adjunct: An experienced online teacher, Diana has taught multiple sections of both technical writing and creative writing courses (as well as a literature course) at a distance, often through her university's Extension Services Division. She describes her early efforts in online teaching like this: "In the beginning of setting up these classes, I prepared the entire semester based upon regular class teaching experiences of the same courses, and thought: How can I give a distance student learning exercises that will cover material that I usually direct in the classroom?" Diana eventually designed all three courses that she teaches at a distance, and, on short notice, she has also used the materials of other teachers who have experience in distance education. Diana uses a popular course-management program as a platform for her distance-education teaching, which the university supports.

Celeste Baron, Associate Professor: As a writing program administrator at a large urban university, Celeste courageously experimented several years ago with teaching a portfolio development course online. In her words, the course was "a disaster." At the time, her university, inexperienced in offering distance-education courses, hindered her teaching efforts as much as it helped them. As she describes the experience: "[To prepare,] I attended several workshops, conducted by different people who gave us some handouts and a book with no page numbers (???) and no index—very useful!

Computer technicians had to be contacted separately and appoint-
ments made to schedule assistance. Very 'removed' and difficult
process that contributed to my sense of floundering, clueless. . . . In
my institution, the initial enrollments in DL were handled out of
one office which did not collect email addresses or check for computer competence. I was simply given a list of names, with social
security and PHONE numbers whom I had to CALL to give a code
number to access the course on line. WHAT A MESS! Leaving messages with kids, etc."

Devina Dunham, Assistant Professor: Having just completed teaching her first fully online course at a large urban university in the
Southeast, Devina notes that her school's administration "tends to
get excited over anything that involves technology" and provides
reasonable support for such efforts. In her words: "In order to prepare to teach the course I took a seven-week workshop in the fall of
2000. This involved working with an instructional designer and
learning about the system our school uses for Web courses, etc. I was
compensated with use (for as long as I'm employed at this university) of a . . . laptop computer and a web camera. In addition I was
allowed to choose between a $2000 stipend and (my choice) a course
release. I did not receive any additional compensation during the
semester in which I taught the course, but I do have ongoing technical support from our Course Development office. They are a bit slow
to get things done but ultimately professional. . . ."

What did we learn from these women? We can identify three major clus-
ters of observations that we gleaned from a study of their completed surveys.

Observation #1:
**Some women faculty believe that distance-education courses can
provide an environment different from face-to-face teaching environments—one that is more flexible and more effective in terms of
feminist pedagogical goals like increasing equity, paying attention
to the needs of individuals, and working toward nonauthoritarian
teaching models.**

Corroborating research findings cited earlier in this paper (e.g., Care
and Udod; Blum), four of the five women teachers we contacted noted that
distance-education courses allowed them to provide a more flexible learning
environment for students. They also liked the fact that such flexibility
provided an increasingly diverse population of students more equitable access
to educational opportunities. Beverly, for instance, said, "I especially like
the opportunity to involve students who otherwise would be unable to participate in course work." And Davina concurred, "I'm just really excited about . . .
the flexibility of these kinds of programs for all kinds of people."
A second strength of distance-education courses identified by these
women faculty had to do with the fact that such courses allowed them to pay

more attention to the needs of individual students and helped them teach students to be increasingly responsible for their own learning. As Diana noted,

> I realize with distance education I think much more about the students' learning process than I did in previous classroom teaching. But here's the rub: I now will think more about these learning processes (formerly intuitive or inherent) in classrooms than I have done previously. . . . I celebrate distance education for flex time, self-pacing, individuated assignments, personal feedback (my courses, anyway), and support for individual development in a non-threatening atmosphere (this is particularly important to hesitant creative writers).

She also told us of how she had changed her thinking about pedagogy. For Diana, distance teaching moves away from the teacher as mere dispenser of knowledge. Instead, she sees it as "a process of exposing students to information for their own use, with a creative emphasis on how each student will use the information to 1) complete a task, 2) develop an area of learning, or 3) create unique work congruent with their own desire for self-expression." We find this last comment especially interesting in that today's distance-learning system really grew out of old correspondence courses, which were marked, of course, by a strong emphasis on teaching as a delivery system. Diana, however, has tapped into the interactive capabilities computers afford and has radically moved away from the dispenser-of-knowledge model.

A third strength of distance-education classes identified by these women faculty focused on the nontraditional, nonauthoritarian teaching and learning styles that such environments could support when used with care. Celeste also mentioned that online environments seemed particularly effective, in her experience, in supporting student-to-student collaborations:

> I . . . experimented with emailed collaborative exercises, in which students were to share/edit/peer review a collaboratively designed letter. It worked really well, and was BETTER than classroom-based collaboration for students who work and have lives and needed to meet outside of class time to work on an assignment. As an aside, in a technical writing class that started this summer, students who collaborated this way on an assignment in which they were given an option of collaborating did noticeably better than those who choose to work alone. Their work was more sophisticated, more audience-appropriate, and more technically accurate. While these four students are all fairly capable, their grade on the collaborative assignment was higher than grades each had received previously when working alone.

Such collaborations, Devina speculated, were successful because students who knew each other only through their interactions in online environments were forced to pay increasing amounts of attention to the texts their classmates produced. For Devina, the absence of face-to-face encounters with their inherent physical distractions encouraged students to know their classmates only through their texts. Hence, for her and her students, writing took on a value and seriousness of purpose that was less apparent in her traditional classes.

These comments bode well for women students. If women do indeed work best in distance-education environments that allow for personal interaction and cooperative exchanges—as suggested by Blum and by Care and Udod—then they would find such environments readily available in the classes designed by the female faculty members we contacted.

> **Observation #2:**
> **Like women students in distance-education classes, women faculty may struggle with the format of distance education for a range of reasons—including primitive and ineffective technology, lack of technical support, and increased time commitments. Distance learning also tends to keep students and women faculty if not housebound certainly isolated from human interaction. But many women also see distance education as an important challenge for women faculty to take up.**

Sarah Carpenter noted that she continued to have a "love-hate relationship with distance ed courses"—with the edge going to "hate." As she explained,

> I find them [distance-education environments] essential in situations where students can't come to campus because of their jobs, family issues, or economic issues. But they only work when the teachers are really dedicated to making them work. And that takes a lot of effort and time. . . .

In addition, planning an interactive television or web course takes up a lot of time. Not only do you have to get comfortable with the various technologies, but you also have to rethink your teaching strategies. And then, since most of the communication outside of class takes place through email, the time commitment during the semester is also much higher. It would help teachers if they got reimbursed for this extra time commitment through a course release or through a stipend.

Sarah's comment—especially in its focus on the increased time commitment demanded by distance-education efforts—was echoed by every one of the teachers with whom we worked. Davina noted, for example, that "the biggest downside of this whole business is the workload—distance teaching is a major time suck." She explained:

> I guess the biggest downside of this whole business is the workload.
> . . . I have a tendency to overrespond to questions. I do this with student work, too. . . . I always do this, but with the technology hassles and the need for me to keep learning new tricks for posting course materials, etc., it compounded into a major time suck. I'm sure

I could have trimmed some of this, but by and large I'd say this is seriously hard work.

Similarly, technology problems—and the lack of expertise and confidence to deal with these problems productively—was mentioned by all five women as a major downside of distance-education courses. As Celeste told us,

> Though I had attended several university-offered workshops, I was still unfamiliar with what had to be done to set up assignment boards, chat rooms, etc. My own caution with the computer impeded more aggressive attack of the equipment; my more "passive" approach and my seeming need for "experts" to help me created an atmosphere of frustration and intimidation. Whether this can be attributed to gender or personality issues I do not know. Many of the other workshop participants were male and they did seem more able, more comfortable, more adventuresome than I was. Naively, I had told myself that if others could do this, I should be able to succeed, too. Most of the time [that] I taught the course I thought I was part of a massive ruse, on a slim edge from "being discovered" to be incapable of teaching the course.

Devina, though she was more confident about her technology skills than Celeste, also identified technology as a serious trouble spot in her distance-education class. She mentions the "unavoidable technology problems" especially prevalent when she wanted students to engage in peer review exercises. Thus, distance teaching tends to push teachers into subject positions they would rather avoid. None of the instructors liked the role of technology troubleshooter. They continuously needed to stress to the students that they were professors and writing instructors.

These comments resonate, for us, with the findings of the research studies cited earlier in this chapter (Blum; Care and Udod): Women students in distance-education classes also experienced frustration with technology use, a concern that technology issues would affect their performance in class, and a lack of confidence in relation to their technology skills. However, as Beverly pointed out, such concerns do not prevent women students from experimenting with—and succeeding in—distance-education classes. This observation may help explain the research results cited by Thompson, who noted that women students in distance-education courses often have a higher success rate than male students, despite their concerns about technology issues and their difficulties with technology. Among the additional explanations for this phenomenon that Thompson noted was a "higher level of motivation among women, who often work in occupational sectors in which career advancement is closely tied to academic upgrading," as well as the "appeal" of flexible distance-education courses for women whose "lives are characterized by multiple roles." Not surprisingly, a direct relationship also seems to exist between the troubles women faculty identified with technology and their concern about the increased time commitment demanded by distance-education courses.

A final problem that at least one woman faculty member noted in connection with distance-education courses was that such virtual courses could seem impersonal—an insightful observation that tempered and complicated claims about the advantages these spaces could have for collaborative work and personal interaction. As Sarah Carpenter explained:

> Taking a distance ed course through the Web can be very impersonal. Women, and men too, can feel very disconnected when they work on their assignments and readings without having contact with their peers and their teacher. Also, taking a web course at home doesn't solve the issue of "getting out of the house" for women who feel restricted to their four walls because of children or other responsibilities.

Thus what at first feels like flexibility—participating in a course anytime, anyplace—may soon feel all too confining and may deprive women of needed face-to-face interactions. As Susan Miller has noted, "Distance classes do not socialize students into an academic personae of any sort. . . ." In other words, both women and men remain outsiders in academe if distant online courses are their only higher education experience.

Observation #3:
The women faculty to whom we spoke corroborated several key findings about women students in distance-education courses, but they also complicated our understanding of these findings.

At first glance, we were struck by what seemed to be close matches between the observations offered by women faculty in this project and key research findings published about female students who had participated in distance-education classes. However, although this correspondence offered a consistent and coherent picture of gender and distance learning, other comments and stories from the women faculty we interviewed complicated this picture and made us wonder, like Susan Miller, how much the cultural narratives we have constructed about students and gender—as a profession and a society—had shaped our understanding of the dynamics in distance-education courses.

Diana's comment, for example, that "women students are more likely to need help where computers are involved" corroborated the findings of Blum and of Care and Udod which suggest that women students in distance-education classes may have more concerns about technology and may need more help with technological problems than do men in such courses.

This coherent narrative about technologically underprepared women, however, was complicated by Celeste's and Beverly's observations that the female students in their distance-education courses were becoming increasingly savvy about technology. The narrative gained additional dimensionality, moreover, with the following story that Devina told:

I regret to admit that I probably interacted differently with male and female students in the area of problems with technology. I know that while I think I provided all students the same level of assistance with technology problems, I usually was more sympathetic to the female students who had them than to the males. I tended to have a kind of "deal with it" attitude toward the two men in our class, even as I did the extra work to deal with their glitches. I think I went further out of my way to offer kind words to female students who hit these barriers than to my male students. I recall one example in particular. One of my students was a female public school teacher who had repeated difficulties with sending documents and opening them, etc. I went far out of my way to help her; I even loaned her some of my personal software to help her get up to speed. For whatever reason she wasn't able to use it, and I ended up resending several emails from her, which implied that I simply wasn't trying to help her get things figured out. She would always write back a day or two later to apologize, but my frustration remained. I wonder now if the "deal with it" approach with which I handled the male students' complaints might not have been healthier with her, too.

Thus, a feminist pedagogy that prizes nurturing might not be effective or even warranted in working with women—a more directive but nevertheless feminist stance by the instructor might have produced better results. We should note, however, that like distance-learning approaches, feminist pedagogies can take multiple forms, depending upon the instructor and the contexts in which she teaches.

We found a similar situation in the contention, offered by several of the women faculty, that female students were more likely to seek and depend on interpersonal exchanges and support than were male students, an observation corroborating the findings of Blum and Herring. Beverly, for instance, noted, "Women often have greater inclination/ability to share, talk in groups etc." Diana, too, noted that the women students in her classes "tend to be highly motivated achievers, with many anxieties (particularly if they are older students), and they like a lot of personal contact, personal commenting." Celeste, however, complicated this picture, noting that the women students she had encountered in distance-education classes "seemed more able to work with limited input[,] but this may have been because they had more college experience behind them when taking DL." And Davina agreed that her female students were probably more independent than the male students, but she attributed their independence to their having had more experience with distance-learning courses in general. As these stories suggest, though, this was not always the case.

In sum, this project reminded us how important it is to collect and analyze a range of stories about individuals' experiences in both teaching and learning situations. These recountings—because they are multiplied and enhanced by differences of situation, gender, race, class, ideology, and background—provide a rich set of perspectives that can contribute to a robust and dimensionally complicated representation of distance-education experiences. They also caution us about drawing conclusions too quickly, thereby contributing to stereotypical representations of women in technological settings. If, for example, we endorse visions of women as less competent with technology, more hesitant with online discourse, and more dependent on fellow classmates and instructors, we do them a tremendous disservice. It is incumbent upon us as feminist teachers to remain open to the strengths women bring to these new online classes. To present women primarily as victims serves only to undermine the many contributions they make as students and instructors in distance settings.

Feminist Interventions: How Do We Teach and Learn at a Distance?

In this chapter, we have begun to assemble a picture of teachers' and learners' experiences in writing courses taught at a distance. What does this picture—as yet quite partial and incomplete—tell us about teaching and learning in such venues? Does it suggest anything about how we can, for instance, overcome "one of the biggest barriers to effective distance education for women" by identifying a pedagogical framework informed by feminist principles for teaching (Care and Udod) that would help us "pay due consideration" to "women's needs and interests and learning styles" (Pym 387)? And does it suggest anything about designing and implementing such writing courses while maintaining "an equitable learning environment" (Blum) for male students as well?

For us, the outlines of such a framework emerge from the collection of information we have assembled. At this stage, we consider this framework to be both tentative and incomplete. It will change as we learn more about distance education and continue to collect the stories of women faculty and students who participate in distance-education environments. And it will change as the educational environments themselves change and as the technologies on which these environments depend change as well. We also invite readers to suggest changes, additions, and deletions to this framework as they gain additional experience with distance education. The following are some of the suggestions we have drawn from our reading and preliminary research.

Faculty—both women and men—teaching writing in distance-education environments should:

- "Take the specifics of women's experiences into account" (Burge and Lenksyj), as well as those of male students. Among these are factors of class, race, needs, interests, experiences, technological expertise, learning style, and conversation styles.
- Be sensitive to specific technology concerns of women and include information in the course syllabus about how and where students—both female and male—can seek answers to their technology questions, a list of

minimal technology skills and equipment required of students before they enroll in the course, and a list of frequently asked questions about common concerns raised by the distance-education venue for the course.

- Diagnose students' technological literacy backgrounds, values, and skills by asking both female and male students to complete a technological literacy autobiography and use this information to assist students who have difficulties with technology or to pose advanced assignments for students who need additional technological challenges.
- Foster in students not only technological literacy skills (e.g., reading, composing, and exchanging information in online environments; conducting research online, navigating online environments) but also a *critical understanding of technological literacy* (i.e., an understanding of the cultural consequences and implications of technological literacy practices and values as well as of the ways in which technology functions in specific social, political, economic, and cultural contexts) (Selfe).
- Articulate the differences between teachers' and students' responsibilities in the classroom, clearly identify instructional goals for the class and strategies of students' active learning, provide timely feedback on students' writing, allow for both collaborative and individual participation in online assignments (recognizing the preference that some women students may have for social interaction), take full advantage of institutional systems of support for technology-based learning, provide students adequate time for responding at a distance, and make sure that students practice responsible forms of communicating with a diverse range of people in online environments (recognizing the tendency of some males to silence some females in some online environments).

Students—both women and men—who enroll in writing courses offered in distance-education environments should:

- Talk to their teachers early in the term about their needs, interests, preferred learning styles, and technological expertise/problems/questions (acknowledging that women may have specific needs in online learning situations that faculty should know about).
- Make sure to meet the minimal requirements for technological skills and equipment *before* enrolling in a distance-education class, and, *after* enrolling in a distance-education course, make sure that they understand and follow procedures for seeking assistance with technology problems (recognizing that female faculty, while often sensitive to students' needs, are not necessarily the technical support staff of the institution).
- Provide instructors—both women and men—with information about their technological literacy experiences, expertise, and backgrounds as they apply to the requirements and activities of the class.
- Take an active responsibility for their own learning and maintain active communication with the teacher of the course about their learning; meet their responsibilities as stated in the course syllabus, understand the instructional goals for the class or ask the instructor about these goals, seek and use the feedback that the teacher and other students provide on

their writing, participate responsibly and with attention to the responses of others in online exchanges (recognizing that males' conversational patterns may serve to silence females in such environments), take full advantage of institutional systems of support for technology-based learning, and turn in assignments on time and in a form accessible to the teacher and other students.

Departments and institutions that offer writing courses in distance-education environments should:

- Offer instructors—both women and men—not only the opportunity to teach distance-learning classes but also ongoing professional development focused on technological literacy practices as well as on online teaching and learning (recognizing that women faculty may have special needs when learning to teach with technology).
- Provide instructors—both women and men—adequate time to prepare for distance-education courses, the technical support they need to teach distance-education courses, appropriate compensation for preparing and teaching distance-education courses, policies designed to protect the intellectual property that teachers contribute to distance-education courses, and equitable compensation for their distance-education efforts (recognizing that women have a history of inequitable treatment both within and outside the academy).
- Involve instructors and other stakeholders—both men and women—in decision making about distance-education policies and procedures, including the development and revision of such policies (recognizing that women may have different needs than do men in distance-education venues).
- Adequately reward faculty—both women and men—who are asked to pioneer and teach distance-education courses, using tenure, promotion, reappointment, merit, salary, and equipment policies/procedures that specifically address contributions to distance-education efforts (recognizing that women have a history of inequitable treatment both within and outside the academy).

In Sum

Cross and Bailey, among other scholars, indicate that an *equitable learning environment* is one in which women and men are given the opportunity to participate on an equal basis. The scenario with which this chapter begins focuses on one woman's experience in an online writing environment. How we handle such a scenario—or, better yet, how we conduct classes to head off such a scenario—requires study, reflection, and discussion, with the goal of establishing equitable learning and teaching environments in composition programs taught at a distance. As we further our understanding of such contexts, it behooves us to act upon them pedagogically. Our overarching goal is to present possible designs for productive action that ensure all our students—both women and men—a better chance of learning and thriving from afar in these new, totally electronic-based writing classes.

Notes

[1] All names used in this chapter are pseudonyms. Minor details have been omitted or changed in quotations to ensure anonymity and privacy of participants.

[2] Although the full report was not available as this volume goes to press, a short summary of its findings can be found in Scott Carlson's *Chronicle of Higher Education* article at <http://chronicle.com/free/2001/09/2001090501 u.htm>.

Works Cited

American Association of University Professors. "Statement on Distance Education." 25 July 2001 <http://www.aaup.org/spcdistn.htm>.

Bailey, Susan M. "Shortcomings of Girls and Boys." *Educational Leadership* 53.8 (1996): 75–79.

Blum, Kimberly D. "Gender Differences in Asynchronous Learning in Higher Education: Learning Styles, Participation Barriers and Communication Patterns." *Journal of Asynchronous Learning Networks* 3.1 (May 1999). 28 July 2001 <http://www.aln.org/alnweb/journal/jaln-vol3issue1.htm>.

Boyer, Dawn. "The Digital Campus Goes Online." *Springfield Magazine*. March 2001: 39–43.

Burge, Elizabeth. "Gender in Distance Education." *Distance in Higher Education: Institutional Responses for Quality Outcomes*. Ed. Chère Campbell Gibson. Madison, WI: Atwood, 1998. 25–45.

Burge, Elizabeth, and Helen Lenksyj. "Women Studying in Distance Education: Issues and Principles." *CADE: Journal of Distance Education* 14.2 (2000) 3 August <http://www.nova.edu/~aed/horizons/vol14n2.html>.

Burger, Jill, Ray Boggs, and Stephen Webber. "Distance Learning in Higher Education: Forecast and Analysis, 1999–2004." Framingham, MA: International Data Corporation, 2000. 26 July 2001 <http://www.itresearch.com/alfatst4.nsf/unitabsx/W23539>.

Care, Dean L., and Sonia A. Udod. "Women in Distance Education: Overcoming Barriers to Learning." *New Horizons in Adult Education* 14(2) (2000) 3 August <http://www.nova.edu/~aed/horizons/vol14n2.html>.

Carlson, Scott. "Distance Education Is Harder on Women Than on Men, Study Finds." 6 September 2001 <http://chronicle.com/free/2001/09/20010905 01u.htm>.

Cooper, Marilyn M., and Selfe, Cynthia L. "Computer Conferencing and Learning: Authority, Resistance, and Internally Persuasive Discourse." *College English* 52(8): 847–69.

Cross, J. P. *Adults as Learners*. London: Jossey-Bass, 1981.

Distance Education at Postsecondary Education Institutions: 1997–1998. U.S. Department of Education, Office of Educational Research and Improvement, NCES 2000-013. Washington, DC: Government Printing Office, 1999.

Faigley, Lester. "Subverting the Electronic Workbook: Teaching Writing Using Computers." *The Writing Teacher as Researcher: Essays in the Theory and Practice of Class-based Research*. Ed. D. A. Daiker and M. Morenberg. Portsmouth, NH: Boynton/Cook, 1990. 290–311.

Flax, Jane. "Postmodernism and Gender Relations in Feminist Theory." *Feminism/Postmodernism*. Ed. L. J. Nicholson. New York: Routledge, 1990. 39–62.

Graham, Charles, and Kursat Cagiltay, Byung-Ro Lim, Joni Craner, and Thomas M. Duffy. "Seven Principles of Effective Teaching: A Practical Lens for Evaluating Online Courses." *The Technology Source*. March/April 2001. 28 July 2001 <http://horizon.unc.edu/TS/default.asp?show=article&id=839>.

Gruber, Sibylle. "Challenges to Cyberfeminism: Voices, Contradictions, and Identity Constructions." *Fractured Feminism*. Ed. Gil Harootunian and Laura Gray-Rosendale. Albany: SUNY P, forthcoming.

Hawisher, Gail E., and Cynthia L. Selfe. "Letter from the Editors." *Computers and Composition* 7(2) (1990): 5–13.

Hawisher, Gail E., and Patricia Sullivan. "Women on the Network: Searching for E-Spaces of Their Own." *Feminism and Composition: In Other Words*. Ed. Susan C. Jarratt and Lynn Worsham. New York: MLA, 1998.

Herring, Susan. "Gender Differences in Computer-Mediated Communication: Bringing Familiar Baggage to the New Frontier." Keynote speech presented at the American Library Association Annual Convention, Miami, FL 27 June 1994. 28 July 2001 <http://www.cpsr.org/cpsr/gender/herring.txt>.

hooks, bell. *Talking Back: Thinking Feminist, Thinking Black*. Boston: South End, 1989.

Jarret, Susan C. "Feminism and Composition: The Case for Conflict." *Contending with Words: Composition and Rhetoric in a Postmodern Age*. Ed. P. Harkin and J. Shilb. New York: MLA. 105–23.

Kane, Ann. Email to the authors. 1 August 2001.

Miller, Susan K. "A Review of Research on Distance Education in *Computers and Composition*." *Computers and Composition* 18.4 (2001).

Oblinger, Diana G., Carole A. Barone, and Brian L. Hawkins. *Distributed Education and Its Challenges: An Overview*. Washington, DC: American

Council on Education, 2001. (A free electronic version of this report is available through <http://www.acenet.edu/bookstore>.)

Ory, John, Cheryl Bullock, and Kristine Burnaska. "Gender Similarity in the Use and Attitudes About ALN in a University Setting." *Journal of Asynchronous Learning Networks* 1.1 (March 1997). <http://www.aln.org/alnweb/journal/issue1/ory.htm>.

"Policy and Programs." World Bank Global Distance EducatioNet. 8 August 2001 <http://wbweb4.worldbank.org/disted/Policy/policy.html>.

Pym, Frances R. "Women in Distance Education: A Nursing Perspective." *Journal of Advanced Nursing* 17 (1992): 383–89.

Selfe, Cynthia L., and Paul Meyer. "Testing Claims for Online Conferences." *Written Communication* 8.2 (April 1991): 163–92.

Selfe, Cynthia L., and Richard J. Selfe. "The Politics of the Interface: Power and Its Exercise in Electronic Contact Zones." *College Composition and Communication* 4.45 (1994): 480–504.

Spangler, Jerry D., and James Thalman. "Going the Distance: Grand Vision Is Scaled Back, but WGU Chugs On." *Deseret News.* 25 July 2001 <http://deseretnews.com/dn/view/0,1249,295010792,00.html>.

Thompson, Melody M. "Distance Learners in Higher Education." *Distance Learners in Higher Education: Institutional Responses for Quality Outcomes.* Ed. Chère Campbell Gibson. Madison, WI: Atwood, 1998. 10–18. 3 August 2001 at World Bank, Global Distance Education Net <http://wbweb4.worldbank.org/disted/Teaching/Design/kn-02.html>.

Trends in Educational Equity of Girls and Women. U.S. Department of Education, Office of Educational Research and Improvement, 2000. NCES 2000-030. 6 August 2001 <http://nces.ed.gov/pubsearch/pubsinfo.asp?pubid=2000030>.

Western Interstate Commission for Higher Education. "Statement of the Regional Accrediting Commissions on the Evaluation of Electronically Offered Degree and Certificate Programs and the Guidelines for the Evaluation of Electronically Offered Degree and Certificate Programs." 25 July 2001 <http://www.wiche.edu/telecom/Guidelines.htm>.

Section IV:
Teaching and Learning
New Media

The Language of Web Texts: Teaching Rhetorical Analysis of Web Material Through Scaffolding

SIBYLLE GRUBER
Northern Arizona University

The computer, Dennis Baron writes, "has indeed changed the ways some of us do things with words, and the rapid changes in technological development suggest that it will continue to do so in ways we cannot yet foresee" (31). Instead of worrying about a possible loss of textual literacy, Baron encourages his readers through his explorations of the histories of pens and pixels to see "computer communications" such as the World Wide Web as increasing "text exposure even more. . . . The simplest one-word Web search returns pages of documents which themselves link to the expanding universe of text in cyberspace" (32).

Baron's comment is a valuable reminder for writing teachers that new communications technologies are not necessarily undermining or replacing "traditional" or text-based literacy skills. Instead, new technologies can be approached as an extension and transformation of literacies already valued by teachers and students. In this paper, then, I show how teachers can incorporate web analysis as an innovative—but not alien—tool into the composition curriculum. After a brief exploration of the potential uses of the World Wide Web in the composition classroom, I demonstrate a scaffolding exercise that teachers can adapt for their own purposes. I show how I used NARTH (National Association for Research and Therapy of Homosexuality) to teach purpose and audience analysis, the importance of exploring authorship, the need for looking critically at emotional appeals, and the potential problems with faulty logical reasoning. This exercise is intended to coach students on how to transfer their analytical skills to the Web. The processes of web analysis that I show here are illustrative, not conclusive, and by no means prescriptive.

Step 1: Addressing Enthusiasm, Resistance, and Online Literacy

Despite inequities in computer access and computer expertise—often based on economic, political, gender, and racial biases—and despite justified uncertainties about the effects of new technologies on well-established values and ideologies, "computer communications are not going to go away" (Baron 32). This situation can lead to technological enthusiasm and unconditional acceptance of technology in some teachers and students, or, at the other extreme, to an antitechnology perspective and a technological value determinism. Albert Borgmann and Andrew Feenberg consider both extremes especially detrimental to the critical analysis of new technologies (Borgmann 10; Feenberg 8). Instead, they encourage users to take on the challenge of looking critically at the complexity of new information technologies and to look at technology not just technology," as Bertram Bruce puts it (225). For Bruce, technology "is an expression of the ideologies, the cultural norms, and the value systems of a society" (225). Once we change and modify social practices, we also "reshape both ourselves and the new technologies" (Bruce 225). The advent of cell phones, PlayStations, TV, radio, and cars is an obvious illustration of the constant shifting of social practices over the last century. Despite some reluctant individuals, the phone is now a feature in most U.S. homes, and cars are an undeniably ubiquitous commodity in America. Similarly, computers are increasingly becoming an integral part of "social practices."

Many scholars interested in new information technologies have looked closely at *why* computers are being used to an ever-increasing extent in the workplace, in educational settings, and in the home. Although this discussion is by no means exhausted, and although there is no conclusive answer to the *why* of computer use, another question is taking on an important role in current discussions—*how* technology is being used by hardware and software specialists, web publishers, or readers/browsers. The focus on the *how* makes obvious the need for teaching a critical approach to technology. This need is also apparent when one looks at the constantly increasing amount of Internet use by U.S. children and teens. According to a UNESCO report, the number of U.S. children age 3 through 17 who regularly access the Net will rise from 10 million in 1998 to 38 million by the year 2002. Furthermore, about 50 percent (9 million) of U.S. teens age 12 through 17 were online in 1998 (Tawfik), and 2002 will see an even larger percentage of teens online.

According to these statistics, a large number of children in the United States are already versed in the use of new technologies and are communicating via email or other online means. However, they often do not take a critical approach to the sites they visit, the information they download, or the manipulation inherent in the use of text, graphics, and sound. Thus, even though some students may be fluent web users, they often have not learned how to be critical users of the new technology. There are many possible causes for students' lack of awareness of web literacy skills: Teachers might assume that students can transfer already known strategies to the Web without further coaching, or they may not have found time to teach these skills, or they themselves may not have the training to teach web analysis.

An additional reason for relegating the Web to the periphery of many educational efforts is that students' interest in and fascination with the Web is often thought to be connected with a degeneration of their reading and writing skills, a catering to a shortened attention span, and a general loss of traditional educational values. David Chapman, for example, sees the Web as a "siren," a distraction to students' educational efforts and a waste of time in a teacher's and student's life (252). Katherine Kellen articulates a related anxiety: "I had been afraid hypertext would be small bites of reading, partially digested, that did not ask for reader stamina" (unpublished ms). However, Kellen also points out that teachers need to move beyond seeing technology as a menacing and pernicious force in their own and their students' lives in order to help students acquire critical technological literacy skills. Taking a critical and proactive stance can help establish new approaches to teaching writing which can, in the end, create "opportunities to propose new social arrangements" (Romano 252) by teaching students to question knowledge, authority, social systems, and political and economic assumptions. Such teaching can additionally lead to a more immediate but similar goal, as Jean Boreen has pointed out in a recent article: "Using the Internet as a research tool can be one of the most effective ways not only to heighten student enthusiasm for computer use itself but also as a way to influence how students explore and conceptualize what they want to accomplish with their writing" (79).

In addition to helping with research questions, the Web can fulfill numerous other purposes. It can be used for work or for play; it can bring together expert opinions; it can be used for collaboration and for communication; it can be a tool for publishing old and new ideas. Although not "everybody" can publish online for numerous reasons, many have taken on the challenge of being a web publisher. In 2000, for example, the World Wide Web consisted of about twenty-one terabytes of static HTML pages (Quéau). This vast array of information can certainly be confusing to most experts and is definitely a challenge for the novice. A search for "literacy" in a web search engine can result in more than a million hits that could all be useful. But how can this information be sorted out? How can a reader avoid getting lost in the morass of information? Certainly, narrowing the search terms is a first vital step (see Boreen for more details). However, we can help students in other ways as well: We can teach them to figure out 1) what information is trustworthy, 2) when they are being taken in by the graphics instead of the content of a page, and 3) how to be critical about a web author's point of view.[1]

Step 2: Analyzing Web Sources—A Sample Project

Similar to imparting any new knowledge, teachers need to establish guidelines to help in the evaluation of web sources. Once students are comfortable with critically analyzing online information, they will also be more likely to become critical writers of web pages. To offer some general guidelines for teachers, this section provides some specific ideas on how to analyze the strengths and weaknesses of a specific web source. An integral part of this exercise is a close rhetorical reading of the site which is examined throughout the chapter. Teachers should use sites that fit their curricular requirements and that are contextualized within the larger framework of the course. The site for this sample analysis represents at one extreme of a controversial issue; examining a site of this type can be quite useful for showing students how language can be employed very convincingly to establish a very specific position.

To scaffold the critical analysis of web sites, I have used NARTH (National Association for Research and Therapy of Homosexuality) for a variety of reasons. Homosexuality is a highly controversial and often hotly debated and emotional issue. It is an issue that is discussed in many households and is also addressed at religious gatherings, at social get-togethers, and in political campaign speeches. Students hear many perspectives and are prompted or sometimes even required (because of social, political, cultural, or religious reasons) to take a specific position on the issue. Rarely, however, are they asked to look critically at the arguments made by those supporting or challenging homosexual lifestyles. Taking a step back from *what* is being said to *how* it is being said can lead to a more critical approach to a highly charged issue. This shift in focus (from *what* to *how*) requires that students learn to rely on their own analytical skills. Furthermore, they can learn to move beyond their own opinions and instead to look closely at the presentation of material, the impact it has on the reader, and the techniques used to convince the reader of a particular perspective.

Before asking students to log on to a specific site, teachers need to consider the goals and objectives of the lesson. In my case, I wanted to provide students with the tools for critically analyzing web sites. To achieve this, I included the following:

- Teach students to analyze critically the use of text, graphics, links, and sound.
- Teach students to rhetorically analyze a web site by looking closely at the audience addressed, the purpose explored, and the language used to create a believable *ethos*, *logos*, and *pathos*.
- Help students to gain a greater awareness of the diverse and often contradictory information present on the Web.
- Help students to become familiar and comfortable with analyzing web sources by using a scaffolding exercise.
- Encourage students to become critical readers of web sites inside and outside the classroom.

Certainly, teachers can incorporate additional or different goals, depending on the curriculum and on the specific class objectives that need to be met over the course of the semester. What remains important, however, is that students be exposed to a critical analysis of web sites, a skill which will help them in their research on various topics, in their own development of web pages, and in their general ability to look critically at information presented on the Web or in print text.

In addition to settling on some goals and objectives, teachers also need to decide on a focus for the lesson. For this exercise, I asked students to focus on the following questions:

- What is the purpose of this site? Is it intended to inform you about something, convince you of something, interest you in something, or change your mind about something?
- Who is the intended audience for this site? What strategies do the authors use to appeal to their audience? What strategies make the authors' comments/arguments convincing/unconvincing?
- What are some of the rhetorical strategies that are used on this site? What kinds of arguments are used? How are the arguments developed? How do the page layout and the graphic design influence the argument? What appeals are used? What types of support can you find? How does the word choice affect your reading? How does the visual presentation influence your reading?
- How objective/subjective are the authors? What are some specific instances of biases? Are there any flaws in the argument?

Again, teachers can shift the focus of their questions or ask different questions. Teachers can adapt questions that they already use for a close analysis of print text, making sure that students understand the inevitable connections between a well-argued, well-written paper text and a well-constructed web site. Furthermore, some issues might get explored in more depth than others, as the analysis in the next section shows. What is important, though, is that teachers and students realize that analyzing a web site requires using skills similar to those used when analyzing a print text while also challenging students to engage in new ways of browsing, reading, or responding to a text.

Scaffolding Exercise: Exploring Purpose and Audience

Although a web site can attract potentially unlimited numbers of readers, most web authors hope to address a specific audience—an audience that largely agrees with the author or is willing to be convinced by specific arguments. In my class, I ask students to pay specific attention to the purpose of the site (what do the authors try to achieve, and how are they going about it?) and at the audience that the authors try to influence (who do the authors try to influence, and why?). When we analyzed NARTH, we looked very carefully at the rhetorical strategies that were used to try to convince the audience of the value of the site.

A first glance at the home page of the National Association for Research and Therapy of Homosexuality (NARTH) shows a professional layout that includes the association's logo, a picture showing protesters in front of the American Psychiatric Association convention, links to more information and resources, and a short description of the association's mission. It is easy for a reader to link to additional pages and to select various topics based on his or her interests. The web site looks informative and seems to be geared toward a large audience of people who might be unsure about their perspective on homosexuality but who are generally interested in finding out about how to "help" gay men and lesbians become "normal," which is explained as "that which functions according to its design" (NARTH's purpose).

NARTH's purpose is described on the introductory page—it is a "non-profit, educational organization dedicated to affirming a complementary, male-female model of gender and sexuality." Later on, the association enlarges on its initial statement in a linked page titled "NARTH's Purpose." Its function, the page explains, is "to provide psychological understanding of the cause, treatment and behavior patterns associated with homosexuality, within the boundaries of a civil public dialogue" (NARTH's Purpose). Furthermore, the page maintains that the association does not support coercive therapy and that it is the client who chooses her/his lifestyle; however, association members do reserve the right to voice their own opinions. As they point out:

> The fact that we respect and welcome intellectual diversity does not mean that we have no opinions—or that we consider all conflicting viewpoints to be equally valid. Toleration of difference does not require intellectual apathy. A respect for *pluralism* does not mandate *relativism*. (NARTH's Purpose).

The next paragraph, however, moves in a slightly different direction. Although the association advocates a respect for pluralism, representatives also argue that they will make their case "for what we believe to be the truth" without being intimidated by the "angry tenor of the debate" (NARTH's Purpose). Furthermore, they allude to the erosion of scientific study of homosexuality because of the strong—and angry—backing of supporters of homosexual lifestyles. But despite these implicitly voiced threats to their organization, NARTH promises to trade "the truth for silence" (NARTH's Purpose).

Based on what they have read up to this point, students can assess that NARTH uses a scientific and respectful tone in its explanations. NARTH acknowledges different positions, and it would hardly see itself as being associated with or supporting the fringe elements of the anti-homosexual movement which are not averse to using hate-crime methods. Instead, the association wants to convince its audience with well-articulated arguments, facts, and authority figures. From an initial reading, it appears that NARTH intends to inform its readers about a specific issue. And since it calls itself an "educational organization," it can also be assumed that NARTH intends to educate its readers about the association and the issue at hand.

However, students should also become aware of some problematic rhetorical strategies. Despite NARTH's insistence that it welcomes diversity of opinions, it also insists that the "truth" is on its side. Furthermore, the association points to the "angry tenor" of the debate which has led to intimidation on the side of those who support the treatment of homosexuality.

NARTH's insistence that its proponents are the only ones being victimized omits mention of the victimization of those who are persecuted for living or supporting homosexual lifestyles, and it ensures that the purpose of the site will be restricted to promoting one specific kind of truth—the truth promoted by NARTH.

Scaffolding Exercise: Exploring Authorship

To teach the importance of responsible authorship, instructors can bring in excerpts from books, magazines, advertisements, religious manifestos, political speeches, or newspaper commentary and explore the need for *ethos* in any text that is intended to convince readers of its integrity. Teachers can then move from the more familiar print texts to the web site and ask students to analyze the reliability, reputation, or trustworthiness of NARTH's authors.

The vast array of experts mentioned—"psychiatrists, psychoanalytically informed psychologists, certified social workers, and other behavioral scientists, as well as laymen in fields such as law, religion, and education"—is intended to further ensure the reader of the legitimacy of the association. However, despite the numerous experts referred to in the initial web page and despite the initial *ethos* built up by mentioning the experts' supporting the association, it is important to note that no specific authors are mentioned in these documents. Although the writers refer to themselves as "we," the authorship of the pages remains unclear. Readers are left to assume that the document's content was created by the head of the organization, the twenty-six-member Scientific Advisory Board, or the clinicians who are mentioned later on. The continuous use of "we" suggests multiple authors. However, readers are not provided with any specific information. Students have to evaluate for themselves whether the absence of the "author(s)" changes their interpretation of the site's value.[2]

Scaffolding Exercise: Exploring Emotions

It is easy to appeal to emotions. But it is difficult to justify emotional exploitation. Although *pathos* is an integral part of most arguments, I have emphasized to my students that emotional appeals can easily be overdone. *Pathos* alone, they have learned, usually does not make for a convincing argument, especially when the authors also do not follow the principles of sound reasoning. When we look at NARTH, students focus not only on the language but also on the graphics used by the web authors.

An interesting example of the authors' attempt at graphic emotional argument is the eye-catching and very *pathos*-laden introductory picture of protesters. What readers see is men and women marching to protest the convention of the American Psychiatric Association, holding signs that propose that "Thousands have changed. . . . It's Possible," "It's my right to change," "Reparative Therapy is ethical," and "I love my ex-gay husband." Students should find the use of this emotional appeal an interesting strategy to catch readers' attention. They can analyze the purpose of the juxtaposition of the scientific approach mentioned various times throughout the document with the picture's call for an emotional reaction. Furthermore, the reference to "ex-gay men and women" should alert students to the implicit association of homosexuality with acts such as divorce (ex-husband/ex-wife) or leaving a position (ex-marine, ex-president). From this rhetorical standpoint, then, being homosexual is not biologically or genetically encoded, but it is a social phenomenon that can easily be reversed and changed, similar to getting a divorce or changing a job.

Through a further rhetorical analysis of this section, students can find out that NARTH's initial move toward toleration is further called into question when the web site discusses the "intense suffering caused by homosexuality." Accordingly, "homosexuality distorts the natural bond of friendship that would naturally unite persons of the same sex. It threatens the continuity of traditional male-female marriage—a bond which is naturally anchored by the complementarity of the sexes, and has long been considered essential for the protection of children" (NARTH's Purpose).

Students will note that suffering is not attributed to any specific person, but instead the more abstract notion of homosexuality is identified as the cause of suffering, most likely in those who are homosexual and those who know or live with homosexuals. Furthermore, the argument put forth by NARTH repeatedly uses the word *natural* as opposed to *homosexual*, thereby emphasizing homosexuality as the "failure to function according to design" (NARTH's Purpose). Although much of this argument is conveyed in a detached tone, students will be able to point out the emotional undertone evident in using the "protection of children" and the "threatening" of continuity as part of the argument.

Scaffolding Exercise: Exploring Logic

In my class, at this point students have already been exposed to an intense exploration of the logical fallacies that can be found in many texts we read in class. Students have brought advertisements to class and have explained the problems with the logical development of each ad's argument. When we analyze the previous web site section, students approach the task from a similar angle: They bring in their page-long handout on logical fallacies and look carefully—argument by argument—to determine whether NARTH engages in logical reasoning or whether the reasoning employed only seems to be reasonable and logical.

Students, looking closely at the final section of "NARTH's Purpose," will see a continuation of value-laden and highly charged comments. However, we now focus on the logic of the argument instead of the emotional appeals used throughout the site. Again, NARTH uses children as the starting point for continuing its argument promoting sexual reorientation. The association points out the misguided advice of educators who teach that "homosexuality is a normal, healthy lifestyle option with no disadvantages other than society's disapproval." Furthermore, NARTH argues that teenagers are too young to make decisions about their lifestyles, including their sexuality. In addition, gay advocates are blamed for having moved the discussion from "what one does" to "who one is." This shift, NARTH argues, presented dissenters (NARTH supporters) as being "personally bigoted and hateful" (NARTH's Purpose).

At this juncture, teachers can help students to focus on how NARTH uses language to discredit gay advocates while at the same time putting NARTH supporters into the position of blameless victims. Students can follow the problems with the logic of this argument by first evaluating the underlying conclusion that NARTH advocates: Homosexuality is not normal. Similarly, students can use their knowledge of rhetorical strategies to explore the role of victim in this text. Does the supposed change of focus away from "what one does" warrant the assumption that this shift led to the belief that reorientation supporters are "bigoted and hateful"? And they can look carefully at the implications of focusing on "what one does" and "who one is." How does a focus on the act—as opposed to a focus on individuals—change the discussion about homosexuality?

NARTH maintains its professionalism by relating more details about its mission, interviews, stories, and scholarly material from members of the association, former homosexuals, and authority figures. It also provides a list of books and reviews, and it lists numerous resources for interested individuals and friends of NARTH.

One of the supporting arguments is included in "The Three Myths About Homosexuality." Here, NARTH reinforces its mission by refuting three commonly-held beliefs about homosexuality:

Myth #1
Homosexuality is normal and biologically determined.

Myth #2
Homosexuals cannot change, and if they try, they will suffer great emotional distress and become suicidal. Therefore, treatment to change homosexuality must be stopped.

Myth #3
We must teach our children that homosexuality is as normal and healthy as heterosexuality. Teenagers should be encouraged to celebrate their same-sex attractions.

To replace these myths with what NARTH calls "the truth," the association first points out that "there is no scientific research indicating a biological or genetic *cause* for homosexuality." Instead, "research suggests that *social and psychological factors* are strongly influential." Second, NARTH argues that "psychotherapists around the world" have reported significant healing in former homosexuals through psychological therapy, spirituality, and ex-gay support groups. Finally, it points out that homosexuality "is *not* a healthy, natural alternative to heterosexuality" (The Three Myths).

When analyzing the rhetorical strategies used in refuting the myths about homosexuality, students can explore how each argument is presented and how it is supported. NARTH, for example, juxtaposes "myth" and "truth," arguing that its perspective represents the truth. Noticing this could lead students to comment on NARTH's previous willingness to engage in open discussions about the subject. They can question how, if one side already knows "the truth," it can engage in a substantive conversation. Furthermore, students can be asked to look closely at a possible either/or flaw in the argument presented by NARTH. In addition, teachers can ask students to find supporting evidence for the assumptions made about the truth and the myth of homosexuality in a manner similar to the exploration discussed in the following paragraphs.

NARTH allows that "biological factors may play a role in the *predisposition* to homosexuality." However, it discredits such predisposition by arguing that many other psychological conditions could also be considered biologically predisposed. To displace the second myth, NARTH argues that change is possible through "*desire, persistence,* and a willingness to investigate the *conscious and unconscious conflicts* from which the condition originated." This—for NARTH—positive solution allows homosexuals "who yearn for freedom" to change their sexual preferences. Here again, students can analyze the lack of alternatives presented in the argument, and they can question the generalized assumptions that are made about the possibilities for change.

To refute Myth #3, NARTH argues that "age-old cultural norms show that homosexuality is not a natural alternative to heterosexuality." Without further specificity, this comment leaves readers to question the specific "age-old" norms—what time period, what continent, what cultural group?—to which the authors of the document are referring. Students can again question the conclusion—that heterosexuality is the normal lifestyle—by questioning the premise of the argument.

An additional argument against Myth #3 mentions that teens need counseling instead of "a push in the direction of a potentially deadly lifestyle" (The Three Myths). NARTH leaves it up to the readers to find out who "pushes" teens and why this lifestyle could be deadly. One can think of AIDS, hate crimes, suicide, and partner abuse, among other severe consequences. Students can argue for or against the value of leaving the particulars to be interpreted by the reader. They can also point out in their analysis the merits or problems of reinforcing stereotypical perceptions about homosexual lifestyles.

An interesting rhetorical strategy used in the rebuttals of the three myths, and a strategy that students often use themselves, is making reference to authorities and research in the field without providing specific information and data about this research. Statements such as "scientific research supports," "psychotherapists around the world report," and "research suggests" generate initial support but also create doubts about the reliability or existence of such unspecified research. They leave doubts about the ethical nature of the argument since there is no specific support for the opinions brought forth. Students can also point out that the appeal to authority can weaken the strength of the argument, especially when there is not sufficient reason to trust those authorities.

NARTH and Schools: Student Explorations

NARTH includes numerous other links which can be explored to examine a number of rhetorical strategies used by the association. To move students away from the initial scaffolding exercise used to introduce them to a rhetorical analysis of a web site, teachers can ask students to provide their own analysis of other web pages. For example, students could look at one of NARTH's subsequent pages, "Activism in the Schools," which can be accessed from the association's home page. This page contains numerous links to stories and articles that relate closely to students' own worlds. Students can find articles that discuss the impact of gay activism in high schools; they can read about the changes in the prefrontal neural cortex that occur during the teenage years and their relation to sex, can find out how to speak against gay-affirmative programs, and can read about the hazards of a gay lifestyle and the possibilities of reorientation.

Although students should be able to analyze these sites without additional help, teachers can provide the same guidelines that were used in the scaffolding exercise. In addition, they can ask students to explore the following issues:

- Do the authors exhibit adequate knowledge of the subject, make logical arguments, include a proper perspective, and show integrity?
- Do the authors follow the principles of sound reasoning without suppressing evidence or using ad hominem attacks, bandwagon arguments, either-or fallacies, overgeneralizations, hasty conclusions, or questionable statistics?
- Do the authors address the issues with an appropriate but not misleading appeal to emotions?

Exploring "traditional" elements of a good argument can provide students with a familiar starting point for analysis. Although hypertext has often been described as nonlinear, nonhierarchical, and nontextual, on the surface appearing to defy the elements included in the classical approach to discourse, many hypertext documents exhibit a tendency to be linear and hierarchical within their hypertextual variations. Students will find it interesting to determine whether a "traditional" essay structure can be applied to web documents and whether such an approach is even useful. They can also, based on their findings, create a revised structure which takes into account the hypertextuality of the online documents that they are reading but which is still grounded in the principles of sound argument.

Teachers can use a variety of approaches to these individualized exercises. What can be especially helpful is to ask two or three students to analyze the same site individually and then to discuss their findings as a small group in class. Doing this can sharpen students' analytical skills since a comparison of findings will inevitably reveal different approaches to the task.

Concluding Critically

Although teachers might expect students to already have good analytical skills since they have previously worked closely with print texts, it is essential that they provide students with similar models and guidelines for online materials. We might think that students can easily transfer their skills onto a different medium. However, my experience in the classroom has shown that additional scaffolding is needed early on in the exploration of web materials. We just need to remember our own excitement when first exploring the Web, and our trust in the validity of the information presented online. We only became more careful when we later found out—often through trial and error—that the quality of online material differs widely and that web authors can publish without the restrictions imposed on print material. We can prepare our students to become critical readers of hypertext more quickly if we work with them to hone their skills. Hopefully, they will apply their critical abilities not only in the classroom but also when they access web pages outside the classroom. And they will see technology not just as "technology" but also as an expression of continuously changing social practices.

Notes

[1] "Evaluating Internet Sources" from Purdue's OWL provides a very useful introduction to analyzing web sources <http://owl.english.purdue.edu/handouts/research/r_evalsource4.html>.

[2] Should students be familiar with postmodern ideas and Foucault's comments on authorship, it might be interesting to explore NARTH's absence of the author and its later comments on relativism, pluralism, and truth.

Works Cited

Baron, Dennis. "From Pencils to Pixels: The Stages of Literacy Technologies." *Passions, Pedagogies, and Twenty-first Century Technologies.* Ed. Gail E. Hawisher and Cynthia L. Selfe. Logan: Utah State UP; Urbana, IL: NCTE, 1999. 15–33.

Boreen, Jean. "Surfing the Net: Getting Middle School Students Excited about Research and Writing." *Weaving a Virtual Web: Practical Approaches to New Information Technologies.* Ed. Sibylle Gruber. Urbana, IL: NCTE, 2000. 78–90.

Borgmann, Albert. *Technology and the Character of Contemporary Life.* Chicago: U of Chicago P, 1984.

Bruce, Bertram C. "Speaking the Unspeakable about Twenty-first Century Technologies." *Passions, Pedagogies, and Twenty-first Century Technologies.* Ed. Gail E. Hawisher and Cynthia L. Selfe. Logan: Utah State UP; Urbana, IL: NCTE, 1999. 221–28.

Chapman, David. "A Luddite in Cyberland, Or How to Avoid Being Snared by the Web." *Computers and Composition: An International Journal for Teachers of Writing* 16.2 (1999): 247–52.

Feenberg, Andrew. *Critical Theory of Technology.* New York: Oxford UP, 1991.

Kellen, Katherine. "Expanding Our Reach: Writing HTML Commands to Create Student Hypertext Projects." Unpublished Manuscript.

National Association for Research and Therapy of Homosexuality (NARTH). Home page. 18 July 2001 <http://www.narth.com>.

Quéau, Philippe. "E-Heritage." UNESCO Report, 2001. 17 July 2001 <http://www.unesco.org/webworld/points_of_views/200601_queau.shtml>.

Romano, Susan. "On Becoming a Woman: Pedagogies of the Self." *Passions, Pedagogies, and Twenty-first Century Technologies.* Ed. Gail E. Hawisher and Cynthia L. Selfe. Logan: Utah State UP; Urbana, IL: NCTE, 1999. 249–67.

Tawfik, Mohsen. "Is The World Wide Web Really Worldwide?" UNESCO Report. 1999. 16 July 2001 <http://www.unesco.org/webworld/points_of_views/tawfik_1.html>.

Teaching with the World Wide Web: Transforming Theory, Pedagogy, and Practice

CAROLYN HANDA
Southern Illinois University—Edwardsville

An exciting, versatile medium to use in a classroom, the World Wide Web can serve a variety of functions for teaching writing and literature. It presents a space where students can share their work with each other and with an audience beyond their immediate classmates and teacher. Today it is also a fairly comprehensive research tool for both students and teachers. In addition, the many pages available on the Web provide fruitful material for critical study and in-class discussions ranging from examinations of successful page and site design to semiotics and rhetorical efficacy. Most important to remember is that each of these functions reflects a different pedagogical purpose, a different teaching philosophy. Although this chapter will outline several techniques for using the World Wide Web, instructors must constantly consider the pedagogical effects of the ways in which they use the Web and the degree to which those classroom activities fit into a coherent overarching plan for the semester. Teachers must always ask themselves what pedagogical purpose each specific use of the Web serves and how it fits into their overall sequence of assignments. Using the Web just for the sake of using it without being able to articulate to students what pedagogical and course purposes the use serves, and how to incorporate such a use into the overall design of the course, could prove confusing to students, if not counterproductive to the course's goals in the end.

Web-Based Pedagogy

Interestingly, the Web's ability to display information in ways that draw on graphic design techniques, video clips, and sound bites has dominated the many other ways in which it can be used. This ability to include images has led to its being heavily adopted by commercial interests because organizations can use the Web for worldwide digital advertising, chiefly the Information Superhighway's equivalent of roadside signs and malls—company web pages and online shopping. Focusing on this aspect, however, is not the way we should necessarily approach using the Web to teach unless we understand how digital images, graphics, and sound could serve a clear pedagogical purpose. We need to ask ourselves what learning skills we might support and what learning situations we could create by adding web assignments to our curricula. Historian T. Mills Kelly did observe that "students who gain access to learning resources on the Web display a higher level of recursive reading than do those who use printed materials" (B9). For history classes which require massive amounts of reading, posting such information in bulletin board fashion on a class web site might encourage the type of thinking historians value, especially if the sources were also hyperlinked: "The thinking of students who put together sources that spanned two centuries, from Hobbes to Marx, had begun to change in important ways: from memorization and regurgitation (and forgetting) of facts to a recognition of the inter-relatedness of historical developments over time. The use of the Web helped students to see the past as a web of knowledge" (Kelly B9).

Analyzing and synthesizing material that spans centuries are certainly not intellectual abilities particular to history. Sometime during their two-semester sequence of first-year writing classes, students must learn how to analyze, synthesize, and categorize information as they come to understand procedures for locating resources, then incorporating information into the arguments they will make in research papers. Although the information for an English 102 research paper may not span centuries, it should span a range of views and of sources. Students must arrive at the same recognition of the "inter-relatedness" of information needed to support a convincing argument that Kelly describes.

The observation that these skills might be aided by the recursive, hypertextual nature of some web assignments is a pedagogical consideration to bear in mind when experimenting with assignments. Michael Joyce distinguishes between two uses of hypertext. The more recursive hypertext we have been discussing is the type Joyce calls "constructive" hypertext. The other he terms "exploratory":

> By exploratory use I mean to describe the increasingly familiar use of hypertext as a delivery or presentational technology. . . . Exploratory hypertexts encourage and enable an audience . . . to control the transformation of a body of information to meet its needs and interests. (41) (See Figure 1.)

Figure 1
Exploratory Hypertext

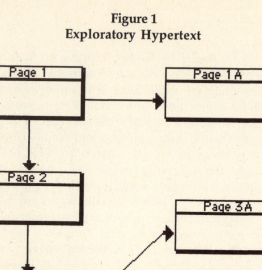

The other use, Joyce argues, is more unfamiliar and less widespread. This use is

> as an invention or analytic tool. . . . [C]onstructive hypertexts re-
> quire a capability to act: to create, change, and recover particular
> encounters within the developing body of knowledge. (42) (See
> Figure 2.)

One final distinction exists: "Just as exploratory hypertexts are designed for
audiences, constructive hypertexts are designed for . . . 'scriptor[s].' Scriptors
use constructive hypertexts to develop a body of information that they map
according to their needs, their interests, and the transformations they discover as they invent, gather, and act upon that information" (42).

Figure 2
Constructive Hypertext

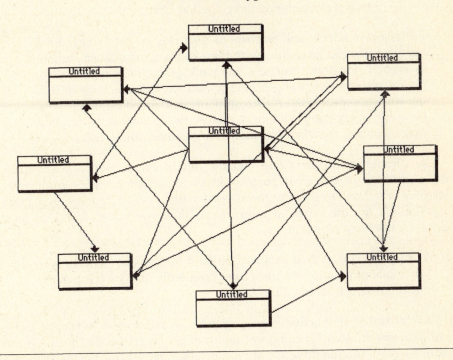

In other words, constructive, or recursive, hypertext encourages a nonlinear movement back and forth between linked pieces of text and related subjects among those texts. Hypertext, by its very nature, offers multiple avenues within one text to other texts, offering readers irresistible temptations to jump from one text to another. When students make these jumps in a constructive hypertext, they begin to see connections among ideas, among points of view. Writing teachers might envision a preliminary assignment for a research paper that asks students to reproduce, on separate web pages, three or four short sources for a research paper, and on a separate web page, a summary of the similarities or contradictions among the stances of the pieces. The students could then establish hyperlinks from the summary page to spots within the sources that relate to the appropriate section of the summary (see Figure 5 again).

We should equally also bear in mind that web authoring packages cannot help but be designed to serve the prevailing methodology in the disciplines for which those packages might initially be intended. Take, for example, the web authoring package WebCT, which is currently used at many universities across the country. This package was developed for a pedagogical purpose almost antithetical to the one subscribed to by most composition instructors who teach process-oriented, collaborative writing classes or courses based on the theory that students learn from discussions with others and from educational situations that encourage them to think along with each other. Instead, the initial purpose of WebCT was to serve large, lecture-based science classes. Christy Desmet of the University of Georgia points out the "utilitarian nature of WebCT," which was originally developed at UGA:

> Professors of science and teachers of large classes, the first groups in our university to go on-line with their courses, introduced students to WebCT. For these teachers, the package includes templates for on-line quizzes, a grading program, and surveillance tools to track the students' progress. . . . The students associated on-line instruction with science and with large classes, two pedagogical situations that encourage frenetic note-taking and memorization. (57)

As Desmet also points out, writing and literature teachers, operating with a different pedagogical purpose in mind, adopted the program later after they were able to identify those parts which would be more pedagogically suitable for the types of interactions they wanted to foster in their classes. Desmet explains that

> WebCT also offers chat rooms, a bulletin board, and environments for collaborative projects, tools used frequently now by composition and literature teachers. (57)

Many of us realize that active, engaging projects, rather than lecturing, foster more effective student learning, yet many of us invariably fall back on the lecture model of teaching. We should understand that we can use the Web in a variety of ways, some of which are the online equivalent of lecturing, where students are made to sit passively and *look* rather than to sit passively and *listen*. Online work does not necessarily equal active learning. Newman and Scurry report that "a recent study by the Policy Center on the First Year of College . . . found that '[e]xtensive lecturing . . . was the pedagogical technique most often utilized in the classrooms of these first-year students, although only 21.4 percent of students feel that lecturing should be included in their coursework'" (B7–B8). The authors also provide a list of ways to use technology in pedagogically effective ways:

- Engage students in active learning.
- Connect learning with real life.
- Offer easy access to massive amounts of information.
- Allow faculty members to tailor teaching styles to each student's needs.
- Shift the faculty member's role from source of information to supervisor or coach of the learning process.
- Allow students to easily review previously covered material.
- Provide preliminary experience in a safe setting. (B8, B10)

Weighing this list along with the variety of theories and practices structuring the writing classroom (see Tate et al.) would make the application of the World Wide Web to the teaching of writing a more informed enterprise.

Displaying Course Materials

When teachers first consider using the Web for their classes, they usually think of posting their class syllabus, course materials, course description, and objectives, and sometimes ancillary readings. In a password-protected environment like Web CT, posting copyright materials for one group of students or posting the materials in a "read only" form without printing capabilities would circumvent copyright problems.

The advantages of posting materials on the Web are clear: The instructor can update material without having to reduplicate twenty to thirty or more copies, and students can access the material from any number of locations should they happen to forget or lose their syllabi. Instructors do need to remember, however, that once materials are posted on the Web, they are accessible to anyone, anywhere, unless they have been protected by password. Therefore, instructors must consider the appropriateness or risk of posting sensitive, controversial, or private materials. Instructors should realize that posting materials on the Web is tantamount to agreeing to share them with the world, so if they are reluctant to share their syllabi, course materials, and assignments globally, they should refrain from posting them. Instructors must also respect students' privacy by refraining from posting student work unless the student has give written consent to the instructor and understands how widely that work could be read.

One set of particularly well-designed and intelligently constructed class web pages can be found at <http://www.siue.edu/~jvoller/main.html>. The site belongs to Jack Voller, my colleague in the English department at Southern Illinois University—Edwardsville. The splash page gives a short, uncluttered list of major topics of information available for his current and potential students (Figure 3). Instructors who check Voller's classes for examples of online syllabi will find clear class descriptions, explanations of class projects, and a class calendar. Voller uses color quite effectively to highlight important areas of a syllabus, something difficult to do with paper syllabi. He also encourages collaborative out-of-class discourse by setting up a class listserv, with instructions for subscribing and a link for immediate posting also available through the syllabus itself. See <http://www.siue.edu/~jvoller/ghost.html> for one example.

Teachers in K–12 classes may not have course syllabi to post, but they could post pages that welcome students to their classes as a way of setting the tone for the semester or the school year. With the help of a digital camera, a teacher could take class snapshots and post them as a way of encouraging camaraderie and a sense of pride in the class. Lori Mayo, a teacher at Jamaica High School, a New York City public high school, has created just such a series of pages, among others, by using her students' yearbook photos. These can be viewed at <http://www.geocities.com/lorimayo_99/yearbook. html>.

Most important for class web pages is the instructor's sense that the materials posted should benefit students and help them to display what they know and what they are learning by being members of this particular class. Instructors need to bear in mind that there is no overwhelming curricular

Figure 3
Jack Voller's Webstuff

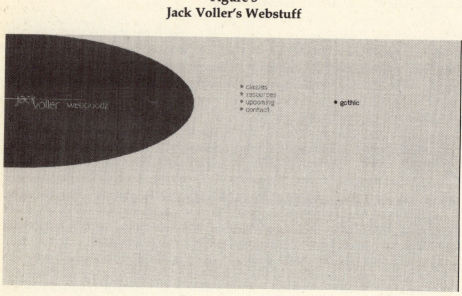

profundity in displaying a course syllabus and materials on the Web only for the sake of posting without giving any thought to how the online syllabus might differ from hard copy or to what different opportunities a web syllabus might present to students, just as there is nothing pedagogically ingenious about passing out insufficiently conceived hard copies of a syllabus and course assignments. What we do with all these materials, whether in class or on the Web, to engage students in their own learning and to push them beyond their current intellectual levels is what matters the most.

Collaboration on the Web

One of the most exciting uses of the Web for a writing class is its ability to provide space for students to collaborate. Collaborative web projects reflect classroom practices that arise from a social constructivist philosophy of knowledge acquisition and education:

> Knowledge conceived as socially constructed or generated validates the "learning" part of collaborative learning because it assumes that the interactions of collaboration can lead to new knowledge or learning. A fixed and hierarchical view of knowledge, in contrast, assumes that learning can occur only when a designated "knower" imparts wisdom to those less well informed. Implicit in these two views of knowledge are two definitions of language. Seen from the fixed and hierarchical perspective, language is a medium, the vehicle through which knowledge is transmitted. As such it remains on the margins of knowledge. The social constructivist view, by contrast, places language at the center of knowledge because it

constitutes the means by which ideas can be developed and explored. (Gere 72–73)

The pedagogical purposes for collaboration on the Web are several:

- Collaborative writing projects encourage students to work in groups, to put forth ideas, and yet to compromise—skills sought by many of today's employers. Collaborative projects posted on a class web site can become more than a line on a résumé. Potential employers can access the project via the Web and see, in effect, a portfolio presentation of the project, and one that the student will never have to hand-carry from interview to interview.
- Writing for the Web gives students a clear and immediate sense of audience. They quickly begin to understand that anyone in the world could conceivably view their writing, so they take much more care and pride than they usually do when writing papers that they perceive will only be read by their instructor, no matter how many times we tell them to write for a general audience.
- Writing collaboratively for the Web also removes the onus from individuals for finding and correcting grammar and punctuation problems. Students working as a group will much more freely stop to question problematic sections because they are acutely aware of the public audience for their work. The group will often more readily consult a grammar handbook or a person in class who has the sharpest editorial skills. Because projects are collaborative, students take less offense at or become less intimidated by grammar correction.
- Collaborative web projects also instill a sense of pride in the students. They should be able to see how their working together has enabled them to produce much more interesting and sophisticated work than they could do alone. Certainly they take pride in being able to show work completed by their class to friends and relatives across the country.
- Collaborative projects on the Web can also form part of an online portfolio for students trying to move to another level of education, whether it be from high school to college or from undergraduate to graduate school. They can discuss their experiences working with others and provide an interesting counterpoint to parts of their applications in which they talk only about themselves.

Collaborative projects do have their downsides, problems which instructors need to anticipate. Sometimes students are so accustomed to a competitive, self-serving type of education that they have a hard time not regarding collaboration as other people stealing "their" ideas. And there is the usual problem of students who don't shoulder their share of the load. Sometimes allowing students to grade the collaborative efforts of their peers and to suggest and then justify what grade they think that they themselves should receive helps mitigate the problem of laziness because students realize that a peer will know much more clearly than the instructor if they are not working up to par. The positive results of collaborative projects that work, however, far outweigh any possible negatives. I offer some of my former students' class web pages as examples. These were created by groups with varying degrees of computer skills. But as the semesters succeeded each other, students in later classes often did have more sophisticated web authoring skills. Today many students have created their own web pages. Also, web authoring packages are much easier to use than they were when my students created these pages in the late 1990s. Go to these sites for examples of collaborative class web pages:

- <http://arc.losrios.cc.ca.us/~handac/fall96>
- <http://arc.losrios.cc.ca.us/~handac/spring97> (See Figure 4.)
- <http://arc.losrios.cc.ca.us/~handac/fall98.html>
- <http://www.siue.edu/~chanda/fall99.htm>

Another type of collaborative web space can be found at Lingua MOO <http://lingua.utdallas.edu>. MOO spaces are usually completely text-based; users must master certain commands in order to move about the space and speak to others. And they must use a MOO/MUD client in order to enable their computers to manage the commands and the discussion. However, this version of Lingua MOO, developed by Cynthia Haynes and Jan Rune Holmevik, runs on a web site, so users can simply click on places in the MOO and travel there instead of typing in predesignated command strings. They do not need to download any special MOO clients.

As the welcome page of Lingua MOO states, the area is "a text-based virtual reality, where people can create their own spaces, work on projects, and interact with coll[e]agues from around the world in synchronous time." And while the MOO is primarily text-based, its web properties enable the use of graphics that can help users visualize the spaces they move through and create.

Individual Work on the Web

The Web is also a place where students can post individual projects. The project could be an end-of-term group of papers similar to a portfolio, which is sometimes called a "webfolio." Or it could simply be one project that the student feels is more representative of her or his work. Although webfolios are not collaborative in the same way that group-constructed web pages are, the public [nature] of the Web does create collaborative situations: Students see the stages and final products of their classmates' work, give each other feedback and support, and consider different ways to approach their own posted texts and web page designs. Ted Nellen and Lori Mayo discuss the personal learning that takes place for individual high school students when they develop their own webfolios: "Personal learning will occur when each student becomes responsible for the construction of hir [sic] own webfolio. The webfolio is important for each student because it can show a body of work, it can show progress through archiving features, and [it] can be evaluated upon performance by many people" (<http://english.ttu.edu/kairos/5.1/coverweb/nellenmayo/personal.html>). Nellen and Mayo's entire coverweb piece is

Figure 4
English 1A Homepage

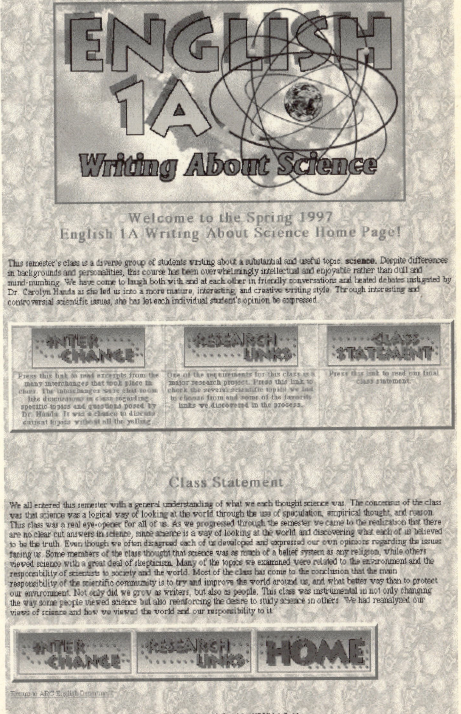

an excellent introduction to the practice and theory behind webfolios. See <http://english.ttu.edu/kairos/5.1/binder.html?coverweb/nellenmayo/index.htm>. For samples of Mayo's students' webfolios, see <http://www.geocities.com/lorimayo_99/work.html> and <http://www.geocities.com/lorimayo_99/work2.html>. Some samples of Ted Nellen's classes' webfolios are located at <http://mbhs.bergtraumk12.ny.us/work.html>.

Examples of college-level webfolios come from Claudine Keenan and Christy Desmet. Keenan taught previously at Pennsylvania State University, where her former students were some of the first in the country to create webfolios. See <http://www. lv.psu.edu/cgk4/015/015webs.html>. Christy Desmet, at the University of Georgia, assigns webfolios in a variety of classes: a freshman English 101 class (<http://virtual.park.uga.edu/cdesmet/eng 101/>), a literature class (<http://www.english.uga.edu/engl3k/fall98/assignments/portfolio/>), and some classes devoted to teaching writing for the World Wide Web (<http://virtual.park.uga.edu/cdesmet/class/engl 4830/work/portfolio.htm> and <http://virtual.park.uga.edu/cdesmet/class/engl4830/spring2k/work.htm>).

The Web as Springboard

Sometimes instead of busily writing for and posting material on the Web, we need to take time out to reflect critically on its parts and to discuss what we see there in terms of a writing class's goals. Existing sites provide great material for class discussions about intended audience versus actual audience, clarity of expression, the differences between reading from a screen and on paper, the importance of graphic elements, semiotics, rhetoric—both visual and verbal—and critical thinking.

Students could also be asked to contribute to these sessions by bringing to class the URL for one site which they feel is particularly effective or ineffective as far as audience appeal, clarity of information, appropriateness of information, levels of diction, organization of information, and graphics. Some of the typical search-engine sites provide interesting pages to analyze for audience appeal, clarity, and clutter. I know that when I first encountered this genre of web page, I had difficulty locating the space where I could enter my query. Even now I still feel disoriented by most search engines that I have never used before.

Instructors could prepare students ahead of time for evaluating web sites by discussing exactly which elements they want the students to consider as they make their evaluations and by distributing a checklist with plenty of space after each item for students to analyze the degree to which their particular web sites succeed. Such checklists (see the next paragraph for specific URLs) could cover tasks such as judging the credibility of a web page, evaluating the source's credentials, and gauging whether information is current and accurate. Instructors should conduct a few critical evaluation sessions before turning students loose on their own to demonstrate the kind of critical work expected on such an assignment.

A simple search for "web page evaluation" guides will yield hundreds of choices. The following are a few good ones to begin a search:

- "Evaluation Rubrics for Websites" at <http://www.siec.k12.in.us/~west /online/eval.htm>, which offers evaluation rubrics for primary, intermediate, and secondary grade students
- Esther Grassian's "Thinking Critically about World Wide Web Resources" at <http://www.library.ucla.edu/libraries/college/help/ cirical/index.htm>
- Allyn & Bacon's "Evaluating Web Resources" at <http://www.abacon. com/compsite/ resources/webevaluating. html>
- Steve Moiles's "Practice in Evaluating Websites" at <http://www.siue. edu/~smoiles/pract-eval.html>.

Using Existing Resources

Just the few resources mentioned throughout this entire chapter serve to remind writing instructors that they should never overlook the Web as a resource tool—both for themselves and for their students. Most important, they should realize that many tools already exist to help them find such resources. Steve Moiles, an instructor at Southern Illinois University— Edwardsville, has compiled such a resource at <http://www.siue.edu/ ~smoiles>. In addition to the evaluation guide mentioned previously, Moiles's web pages contain links to research-related sites, writing-related sites, and sites of interest to those who teach writing, such as a list of online writing labs (OWLs).

The Roan State Community College OWL at <http://www.rscc.cc.tn.us/ owl/owl.html> contains several useful resources for students. Notable among them is a guide to writing designed especially for nurses. And all new writing instructors, whether they use the Web for teaching or not, should know about the multitude of teaching resources available for information and for classroom use at Purdue University's Online Writing Lab at <http://owl.english. purdue.edu/>. Aside from providing the usual information services and hours, Purdue's OWL generously offers many different instructional resources, including handouts and PowerPoint presentations that both students and teachers can use. Among the handout topics are writing concerns, ESL help, guides for conventional English usage, and research formats. The PowerPoint presentations for students and instructors to view on their own computers or to download for class presentations fall under "Basic Writing Skills," "Research and Documentation Styles," "Grammar and Mechanics," and "Business Writing." Each category contains several different presentations.

Publishing companies also offer web sites with resources for students and for writing teachers. Houghton Mifflin offers composition resources for both students and instructors at <http://college.hmco.com/english>. The site offers a wealth of textbook companion websites, Teach with Technology information for instructors, premium sites that are online only in lieu of print products, an Internet Research Guide, and online tutoring service. Bedford/St. Martin's has several pages devoted to composition that contain resources for students as well as instructors at <http://www.bedfordbooks.com/composition/> in addition to companion sites for some of its textbooks. Bedford/St. Martin's also offers a resource called "Tech Notes," an email delivered newsletter and web site for writing teachers at <http://www.bedfordstmartins.com/technotes/>. Instructors must subscribe to the newsletter (there is a subscription link on the web site), but the site also contains archives of news, reading, and technology tips.

Another site briefly alluded to earlier is Allyn and Bacon's "CompSite" at <http://www.abacon.com/compsite/>. As the site itself says, "At Comp-Site you'll find guides, pointers and activity areas to help students with their writing projects. You'll also find materials for writing instructors, including Internet information, teaching tips, and collections of resources that can be adapted for a number of projects and assignments."

The Daedalus Group, creators of the Daedalus Integrated Writing Environment (DIWE) and Daedalus On-line, also has a Faculty Center online. Although the site is aimed primarily at users of the Daedalus system, it also contains teaching tips and professional resources of use to any writing teacher; the site is at <http://facultycenter.daedalus. com/>.

Instead of listing resources for writing teachers and students, some web sites offer places for teachers to take their classes in order to conduct online discussions, collaborate on projects, or set up discussion threads for topics to be covered during a semester. Because these are web spaces, the class does not have to be held in a computer classroom in order to use specific software. The Speakeasy Studio & Cafe at <http://speakeasy.wsu.edu> is "a flexible, interactive online space designed to enable the formation of community independent (to some extent) of the constraints of time and place." Teachers are able to set up forums or "tables" with set topics for students to discuss. Students may respond both to the instructor's prompt and to other students' comments. The discussion threads at first appear in an outline form, so students can easily see which comments and responses they want to read. Although this discussion is nonsynchronous, that is, it does not take place in real time as a chat room does, the Speakeasy Cafe does have a chat space where students can meet for real-time discussion when they go online at the same time. Information about becoming part of the Speakeasy Studio & Cafe, setting up "neighborhoods," and administering forums can be found on the web site.

One often-mentioned resource for teachers and students in literature classes is a site called "The Voice of the Shuttle" at <http://vos.ucsb.edu/>. Subtitled a "Web Page for Humanities Research," the site contains links to general humanities resources as well as more specialized areas such as classical studies, linguistics, and the literatures of several different countries. Another useful, attractive, comprehensive site for instructors in literature is a specialized site created by Jack Voller, "The Literary Gothic" at <http://www.siue.edu/~jvoller/> (Figure 5). The site contains information about authors, titles, and useful resources as well as some etexts unavailable elsewhere. Finally, one intriguing site is the "Favorite Poem Project" begun by Robert Pinsky when he was the thirty-ninth Poet Laureate of the United

Figure 5
Jack Voller: "The Literary Gothic"

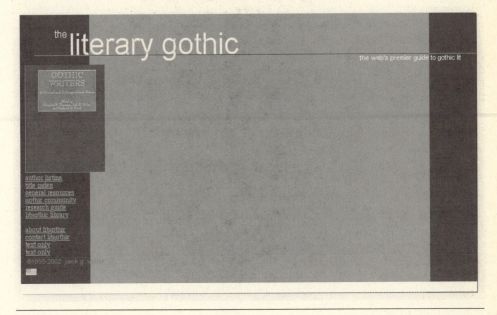

States. The site at <http://www.favoritepoem.org> contains short videos of a cross-section of Americans—young, old, famous, and average—each reading her or his own favorite poem and discussing the poem's emotional impact.

For new instructors, teaching with the World Wide Web could appear overwhelming because of the variety of ways in which they can approach such teaching and the wealth of resources available. In addition, constructing one's own class web pages can be daunting, not to mention time-consuming. But the sophistication of today's web-authoring tools, the innumerable guides and workshops available for those who would rather use HTML and JavaScript to create their own pages from scratch, the level of tech support available either online or in person at schools, and ultimately the pedagogical rewards for doing any part of these activities all encourage teachers to create an enriched learning atmosphere for all of those students lucky enough to encounter a writing teacher who uses the Web thoughtfully to guide individuals through the difficult process of gaining a better understanding of course materials and learning to think critically.

Works Cited

Desmet, Christy. "Reading the Web as Fetish." *Computers and Composition* 18.1 (2001): 55–72.

Gere, Anne R. *Writing Groups: History, Theory, and Implications.* Carbondale: Southern Illinois UP, 1987.

Joyce, Michael. *Of Two Minds: Hypertext Pedagogy and Poetics.* Ann Arbor: The U of Michigan P, 1995.

Kelly, T. Mills. "Before Plugging In, Consider Your Options." *Chronicle of Higher Education* XLVII.44 (13 July 2001): B9.

Newman, Frank, and Jamie Scurry. "Online Technology Pushes Pedagogy to the Forefront." *Chronicle of Higher Education* XLVII.44 (13 July 2001): B7–8, B10.

Tate, Gary, Amy Rupiper, and Kurt Schick. *A Guide to Composition Pedagogies.* New York: Oxford UP, 2001.

Web References

Allyn and Bacon, "CompSite":
    <http://www.abacon.com/compsite/>

———, "Evaluating Web Resources":
    <http://www.abacon.com/compsite/resources/webevaluating. html>

Bedford/St. Martin's [comp page]:
    <http://www.bedfordbooks. com/composition/>

Bedford/St. Martin's Tech Notes:
    <http://www.bedfordstmartins.com/technotes/>

The Daedalus Group, Faculty Center Online:
    <http://facultycenter.daedalus.com/>

Christy Desmet, English 101:
    <http://virtual.park.uga.edu/cdesmet/eng101

———, English 3k:
    <http://www.english.uga.edu/engl3k/fall98/assignments/
    portfolio/>

———, English 4830:
    <http://virtual.park.uga.edu/cdesmet/class/engl4830/work/
    portfolio.htm>

———, English 4830, spring 2k:
    <http://virtual.park.uga.edu/cdesmet/class/engl4830/spring2k/
    work.htm>

"Evaluation Rubrics for Websites":
    <http://www.siec.k12.in.us/~west/online/eval.htm>

Favorite Poem Project:
    <http://www.favoritepoem.org>

Esther Grassian, "Thinking Critically about World Wide Web Resources":
    <http://www.library.ucla.edu/libraries/college/help/critical/
    index.htm>

Carolyn Handa, English 101, fall 1996:
    <http://arc.losrios.cc.ca.us/~handac/fall96>

————, English 101, spring 1997:
   <http://arc.losrios.cc.ca.us/~handac/spring97>

————, English 101, fall 1998:
   <http://arc.losrios.cc.ca.us/~handac/fall98.html>

————, English 101, SIUE, fall 1999:
   <http://www.siue.edu/~chanda/fall99.htm>

Cynthia Hayes and Jan Rune Holmevik, Lingua MOO:
   <http://lingua.utdallas.edu>

Houghton Mifflin College English
   <http://college.hmco.com

Claudine Keenan's webfolios:
   <http://www.lv.psu.edu/cgk4/015/015webs.html>

Lori Mayo's students:
   <http://www.geocities.com/lorimayo_99/yearbook.html>

Lori Mayo's webfolios:
   <http://www.geocities.com/lorimayo_99/work.html>
   <http://www.geocities.com/lorimayo_99/work2.html>

Steve Moiles, "Practice in Evaluating Websites":
   <http://www.siue. edu/~smoiles/pract-eval.html>

————, "Home Page for College Writing":
   <http://www.siue.edu/~smoiles>

Ted Nellen's webfolios:
   <http://mbhs.bergtraumk12.ny.us/work.html>

Ted Nellen and Lori Mayo's Kairos Coverweb article:
   <http://english.ttu.edu/kairos/5.1.binder.html?coverweb/
   nellenmayo/index.htm>

————, Statement on Personal Learning:
   <http://english.ttu.edu/kairos/5.1/coverweb/nellenmayo/
   personal.html>

Purdue University Online Writing Lab (OWL):
   <http://owl.english.purdue.edu/>

Roan State Community College Online Writing Lab (OWL):
   <http://www.rscc.cc.tn.us/owl/owl.html>

Speakeasy Studio & Cafe:
   <http://speakeasy.wsu.edu>

The Voice of the Shuttle:
   <http://vos.ucsb.edu/>

Jack Voller, main page:
   <http://www.siue.edu/~jvoller/main.html>

————, English 309:
   <http://www.siue.edu/~jvoller/ghost.html>

————, The Literary Gothic:
   <http://www.siue.edu/~jvoller/>

with eyes that
think,
and compose,
and think:

ON VISUAL RHETORIC

ANNE FRANCES WYSOCKI
Michigan Technological University

By composing these pages as I am doing, I am hoping that their appearance strikes you as odd, perhaps even out of place, in an academic setting—**and that perhaps you will then question how and why academic pages are given the usual visual rhetorical treatment they are (which is, that is, as though there is nothing visually rhetorical in them)**—and that perhaps you will begin considering what kinds of constraints are placed on academic (and other) argument by the "appropriate" page layout we have inherited. Perhaps you will consider then what new kinds of arguments are possible (or what arguments are out there that we might not have thought were arguments) when we work while being aware of all the visual expectations and assumptions we have inherited—including the ones about what counts as "visual."

I am arguing, then, that learning to analyze and compose rhetorically effective visual communication is not (simply) a matter of working only with whatever it is we have named "images."

Effective visual rhetoric requires trying to understand and work with (or sometimes against) the expectations and assumptions and values of one's audience concerning ALL the visual aspects of a text.

WHAT (then) is visual rhetoric?

1   If rhetoric, to turn our eyes all the way back to Aristotle, is the use of the available means of persuasion to achieve particular ends, then whenever the means of persuasion include visual strategies, there is visual rhetoric at work.

Traditionally, when rhetoric was concerned primarily with a speaker and an audience looking at each other through the particularities of a time and place, rhetorical studies addressed the speaker's choices of bodily gestures and facial expressions as persuasive strategies. Now, when texts on paper—and on different kinds of screens—are objects of rhetorical study, the range of a rhetor's strategic choices can include every aspect of a text that is visual: A text's composer can choose her paper or the background color of her web page or the angle for her video shot; she can choose (or not) to include in her text photographs or drawings or shapes or tables or graphs or animations or type; if she chooses to use type, then she must also choose specific typefaces as well as the specific colors and sizes of the type; she chooses the size and shape of paragraphs or other graphical elements, chooses elements to repeat in order to create a visual sense of unity among pages (and chooses whether to create such a sense of unity), and so on.

2   If, however, we look at rhetoric as it was reinvigorated during the twentieth century through attention to the workings of culture, then rhetoric must consider more than a rhetor's choices in building any one argument. When, for example, we examine the situation of a speaker arguing that a city-state should prepare for battle rather than sue for peace, we can study the speaker's choice (perhaps) of using an inductive rather than a deductive logical structure or of a stern instead of grieving face; we can also, however, consider that such a speech is only possible in a culture that believes in and values the efficacy and validity of inductive and deductive argument, the efficacy of argument in general, the importance of public speech—and decision—making, the inclusion of certain people as (and exclusion of others from) "the public," the importance of individual opinion, and so on. We can, that is, consider how this speech is possible only because it makes sense within webs of particular cultural values; in addition, we can see

how the speech reinforces those values and hence works to persuade its audience not only toward battle but also toward upholding and carrying on the values which the speech articulates. Given this widened notion of persuasion, then, anything we make for each other—furniture as well as speeches, monuments, city-states, and printed texts[1]—is rhetorical: It is subject to careful analysis and composition because it shapes the values and behaviors that fit us into the structures and habits of our places and times.

We can therefore consider, as one particular example, how the visual presentation of this book, *Teaching Writing with Computers*, fits into and reinforces our cultural practices of authority, standardization, and mass production. Imagine that the book you now hold in your hands was presented on motley pieces of newsprint and notepaper, each chapter written in different colors and different handwriting (some of this handwriting being large and loopy; some small, tight, and left-leaning) or with every page looking like the first page of this chapter. What would you think of this book were it to call such visual attention to itself? Consider this imagined other book, and consider what seriousness and authority you would grant it; consider then how important is the repetitive visual presentation of the pages of this book as they are actually printed, the repetition tied to and impossible without a cultural taste for mechanical standardization and reproduction, . . . and ask yourself what other values you see adhering to the visual presentation of this book as it is now, in your hands.

1+2   As we analyze and compose texts, then, I want us to be aware not only of the particular visual strategies that a composer chooses when constructing texts aimed at persuading audiences toward specific ends; I want us also to be aware of how the strategies that we choose reinforce (and can perhaps help us be aware of and question) values, habits, and structures of our places and times.

WHY should we consider visual rhetoric when we think about teaching writing with computers? I think there are at least three reasons:

1   **Given our current cultural and technological situation, readers expect the visual aspects of texts on computer screens—but also now on paper—to be given more attention than they were afforded in the past.**

Computer technologies have ended up being designed to give writers more control over the appearance of their texts. The technologies of the printing press, on the other hand, help to shape and are shaped by a division of labor: Someone writes a text, and someone else decides which typefaces in what sizes, what column and page sizes, and what paper to use for making the text presentable in reproduction. Using computers to prepare texts for paper, writers can (to the extent that they are aware that such choices are strategic) make those decisions themselves; using computers to prepare online texts, writers can make not only those decisions but also decisions about colors, the arrangement of paragraphs, visual connections among screens, the inclusion of animations or sounds, what sorts of interactivities to use, and so on.

In a recent first-year writing class which I taught, students recognized that not making those decisions caused their web texts to look unprofessional. These eighteen- and nineteen-year-olds realized that relying on the defaults of HTML (the middling grey background, type of all the same size running page-edge to page-edge) would make it appear as though they—the composers—didn't know what they were doing. The matter of ethos thus made its way easily into our discussions when one woman, who was writing about euthanasia, asked for advice from the class. After looking at the first draft of her web pages, she said that she couldn't simply use the default grey background of web pages (even though grey was an appropriate color for her topic) because her readers would think she hadn't made a choice and hence would think she didn't know anything about HTML and web page design—and therefore wouldn't take her seriously about anything else. After a class discussion about the sense we get of a writer from the appearance of a text, she decided to use a dark brown-grey for her background.

Learning to analyze and use visual rhetoric can help people in our classes compose effective texts on and for computer screens and paper.

2   Our culture throws more visually shaped texts at us than we grew up learning to expect or to be comfortable analyzing.

Many writers argue that we need in our teaching and analyses to be aware of a recrudescence of the visual.[2] We have lived through a century or so of texts that were shaped by a belief that the body and the material—and hence the visual—could and ought to be transcended or ignored. Compare, for example, the lack of illustration and tiny type of late-nineteenth-century newspapers with the features of today's newspapers, especially those online; look at how academic texts and journals rely solely on type, rigidly aligned and organized, and on every article's looking the same. Now, however, we see texts (the nightly news, graphic novels, scientific visualizations, three-dimensional animated courtroom simulations of crimes, web pages, music videos, magazines of all genres, advertising) that require us to be attentive to how different meanings or emphases result from different visual arrangements.

To be responsible teachers, then, we need to help our students (as well as ourselves) learn how different choices in visual arrangement in all texts (on screen and off) encourage different kinds of meaning making and encourage us to take up (overtly or not) various values.

We need to learn how to analyze and create texts that do not ignore the visual if we are to be responsible and appropriately critical citizens.

3   **We can use the visual aspects of texts (both in analysis and making, on screen and off) to learn about and perhaps to make changes in other values at work in our culture.**

Most of us have been taught—and teach—that the proper way to write an article is to arrange words on an $8\frac{1}{2}$ x 11-inch sheet of paper with one-inch margins and first indents to indicate a paragraph. The paper will be white, the ink will be black, and the typeface will probably be Times or Helvetica. If the article is published, someone else will choose the final visual flourishes that help the text "go public" in reproduction. We, the writers, don't need to make those choices about how the text looks because—we have learned to believe—its meaning exists completely apart from its appearance. Form, here, is separable from and has nothing to do with content.

The "rhetoric of neutrality" is what Robin Kinross calls this attitude. Although Kinross is writing specifically about printed train schedules and stationery for industrial organizations when he names the "rhetoric of neutrality," his argument holds across genres of composition. Our belief that meaning can exist apart from the material embodiment of printed timetables, pages in bound books, or screens on computer monitors is woven into a belief that what we think has nothing to do with our messy, gendered, raced, aging, nationalized, digesting bodies.

We have seen this attitude come under criticism in the later decades of the twentieth century, not least in rhetoric and composition studies. We have recognized that what has long seemed to be simply the proper way to write—the arrangement of words into their most seemly order—is very much a matter of taste, as the particular argumentative moves of some bodies are made into the natural order that all bodies are supposed to follow . . . and we have recognized how this process of naturalization privileges those who are fortunate enough to be born into the bodies that are brought up into the appropriate tastes. We have also recognized how this process cuts off and silences others. Many in rhetoric and composition have worked hard to open up our practices so that we can learn to hear those who have been silenced so that others do not always have to change their ways—if they want to be heard—to fit our particular structures and ways of understanding.[3]

This work of opening up the practices of rhetoric and composition has involved learning to see what we have taken for granted. We have had to learn how (for example) standardized spelling, paragraphing, avoiding using *I*, and to-the-point argument are not god-given practices and that those who have been raised with other tastes are not stupid. We have learned, also, that when we open up our argumentative practices, we learn more about ourselves and about what it is that we take for granted; we learn new and potentially productive ways of thinking and of considering each other and what is around us.

We come back, then, to what I have been arguing from the beginning of this chapter, that the visual arrangement of the arguments we present each other—whether on paper, on screen, or through other kinds of architectures and constructions—is very much tied up with the attitudes we have about what the proper relations should be among thinking, texts, our bodies, and each other. Analyzing and experimenting with the visual rhetoric of our texts can thus help us see—literally—aspects of our culture, structures of thinking and relationships, that we have learned or have been taught to take for granted. Analyzing and experimenting with the visual rhetoric of our texts can help us perhaps develop new thinking and relationships that might help us better achieve our ends.

WHAT DOES IT LOOK LIKE to use concepts of visual rhetoric in writing classes?

Earlier I mentioned web pages in which one of my students from a first-year writing class wrote about euthanasia. Figure 1 is the first page of her series: You cannot see the color here, but the background is grayish-brown; the type is black except for the deep grey underlined links. As I mentioned earlier, this student recognized that, even though it might be an appropriate color for an argument about euthanasia, the default grey of web pages—if used here—would indicate to her readers (as everyone else in the class acknowledged) that she was probably unskilled with web pages and hence also unskilled in argument. (We discussed in class whether this was a fair assumption, and although people in the class acknowledged that it probably wasn't, they agreed that it was an operating assumption for most people whom they knew—just as, someone pointed out, turning in a badly typed, rumpled paper assignment resulted in their teachers' lowering the grades of their paper arguments.) And so the student needed to choose another background color. She

Figure 1
Student Euthanasia Page

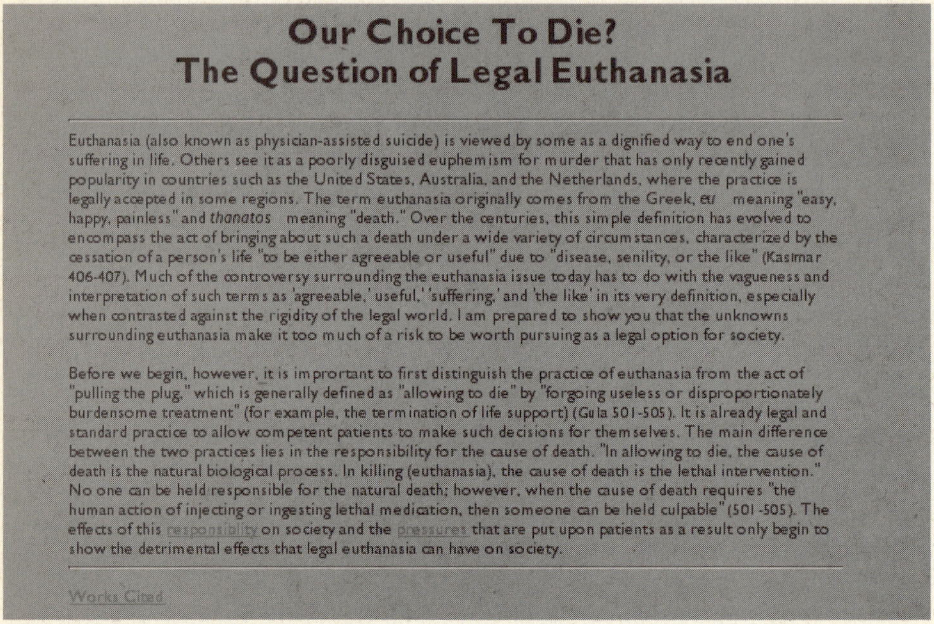

Our Choice To Die?
The Question of Legal Euthanasia

Euthanasia (also known as physician-assisted suicide) is viewed by some as a dignified way to end one's suffering in life. Others see it as a poorly disguised euphemism for murder that has only recently gained popularity in countries such as the United States, Australia, and the Netherlands, where the practice is legally accepted in some regions. The term euthanasia originally comes from the Greek, *eu* meaning "easy, happy, painless" and *thanatos* meaning "death." Over the centuries, this simple definition has evolved to encompass the act of bringing about such a death under a wide variety of circumstances, characterized by the cessation of a person's life "to be either agreeable or useful" due to "disease, senility, or the like" (Kasimar 406-407). Much of the controversy surrounding the euthanasia issue today has to do with the vagueness and interpretation of such terms as 'agreeable,' 'useful,' 'suffering,' and 'the like' in its very definition, especially when contrasted against the rigidity of the legal world. I am prepared to show you that the unknowns surrounding euthanasia make it too much of a risk to be worth pursuing as a legal option for society.

Before we begin, however, it is important to first distinguish the practice of euthanasia from the act of "pulling the plug," which is generally defined as "allowing to die" by "forgoing useless or disproportionately burdensome treatment" (for example, the termination of life support) (Gula 501-505). It is already legal and standard practice to allow competent patients to make such decisions for themselves. The main difference between the two practices lies in the responsibility for the cause of death. "In allowing to die, the cause of death is the natural biological process. In killing (euthanasia), the cause of death is the lethal intervention." No one can be held responsible for the natural death; however, when the cause of death requires "the human action of injecting or ingesting lethal medication, then someone can be held culpable" (501-505). The effects of this responsibility on society and the pressures that are put upon patients as a result only begin to show the detrimental effects that legal euthanasia can have on society.

Works Cited

considered using white, which would have made her pages look as much as possible like paper pages, but she decided (given the options) that white was too bright and harsh for her topic. She instead chose a color that looked somber, reflective, and quiet, like a monk's robes, indicating the mood that she felt toward and around her topic and that she wanted her readers to feel as well.

This student also decided to present her arguments on multiple screens, organizing her concerns so that each screen focuses on a particular step or subargument. She chose to do this—as did most members of this class—after the students had compared and contrasted their first drafts and had seen how arguments which were broken up over several screens helped them, as readers, see more readily (both physically and conceptually) and grasp and retain an argument's parts.

There are other aspects of this web page that I could analyze in terms of how the visual appearance of a page works as part of the overall argument. Consider, for example, the size and centering of the title, the use of margins and text alignment, or the student's choice of using serif instead of sans serif type or of not including photographs, drawings, or background texture. But more important to notice for my arguments here about visual rhetoric are the ways in which traditional rhetorical concepts—ethos, logos, pathos, audience, and intention—wind in and out of the visual considerations the author gives these pages. She uses the visual aspects of her pages as strategies to direct her audience's attentions, to persuade them to consider and perhaps take up her position; she uses the visual aspects of her pages in awareness of some of the conventions she has inherited, conventions that shape attitude and practice.

She is aware, for example, of how her visual choices give her author-ity—or not—in the eyes of her readers, and she has thought about the kind of appearance—that of a serious, thoughtful, reflective person—she wishes to present of herself in this argument, through words and visual presentation; these are all matters of ethos. She has also chosen to ask her readers to take on similar attitudes while reading, recognizing that the somber grey-brown, fully justified text and lack of photographs or drawings ask her readers to approach these pages in a still and intellectual manner; these are matters of pathos. Finally, she has chosen how to arrange her screens visually so that her readers might most readily grasp the structure of her arguments and see their order and progression; this is logos. In addition, this student considered carefully how she wanted to present an argument that she hadn't seen on the Web; she was aware of the extent to which the Web is made up of visually busy and active pages, and she wanted to create a place where the values of quiet, careful thought about others would be visible and perhaps taken up in addition to her particular arguments about euthanasia.

Other students approached the visual presentation of their pages dif-ferently, as one would expect: The composer of Figure 2 had been very upset by the killings at Columbine High School and other schools. She decided that she wanted to try to get others to feel her distress and to use that distress

Figure 2
Student School Violence Page

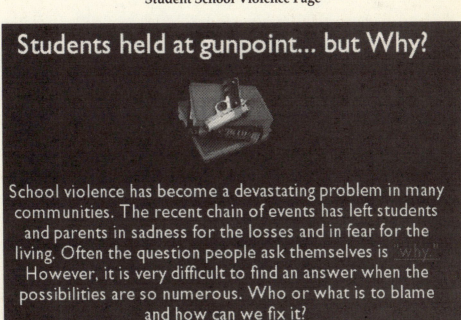

Students held at gunpoint... but Why?

School violence has become a devastating problem in many communities. The recent chain of events has left students and parents in sadness for the losses and in fear for the living. Often the question people ask themselves is "why". However, it is very difficult to find an answer when the possibilities are so numerous. Who or what is to blame and how can we fix it?

to motivate them to think about what could be done to prevent other deaths. As she considered how to present her arguments on the Web, she decided to "call out" to her readers visually, to create both a sense of urgency and of seriousness; she wanted to make visible the starkness of the shootings as well as the possibility of change. In the first of her series of web pages, shown here, she uses almost harsh black, white, and red; one illustration; and large, centered type to communicate the emotional urgency which she hopes others will share with her. She has chosen to make only one word a link in order to focus her readers on what is to be the central consideration of her writing.

Another student took on the topic of overpopulation in developing countries. Figure 3 is the first web page of his series. Here is logos (this student hopes) made stark and absolutely visible. This student did not want his readers to get caught up in the potentially messy and value-laden emotions of this topic. Instead, he wanted to emphasize for others what seemed to him the inescapable logic of his position, and so he has put at the top of each page the enthymeme he sees—and wants others to see—that should lead us (he thinks) to the appropriate response to overpopulation. There is no color used other than black and white, and the site has no illustration or photograph that might bring emotion into play. Instead, readers click on the parts of the enthymeme to read evidence in support of each structuring claim. This site's interaction—what is clicked and what information the clicking brings to a reader—requires hands-on interaction with the site's logic.

Although we could say much more about each of these pages, what is important here is to see how each writer grapples with the elements of her or his argument. These writers work to choose strategies—including visual ones—that make sense against a cultural background of argument, logic, emotion, thought, writing, and the conventions of the Web.

Figure 3
Student Overpopulation Page

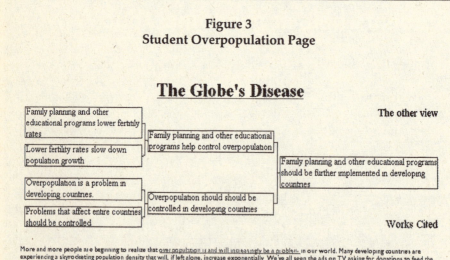

The Globe's Disease

More and more people are beginning to realize that overpopulation is and will increasingly be a problem in our world. Many developing countries are experiencing a skyrocketing population density that will, if left alone, increase exponentially We've all seen the ads on TV asking for donations to feed the children. Those donations are a wonderful way to treat the symptoms of overpopulation, but to really fix things we have to consider the cause. There are more people in many developing countries than their food supply can support. Family planning and other educational programs should be further implemented in developing countries so that overpopulation can be more controlled.

HOW can we go about incorporating the study and use of visual rhetoric in writing classes?

Given what I have written so far, I hope that you understand why I think learning to be a thoughtful and critical analyst and user of visual rhetoric means **learning to be a close and question-filled observer of the varied visual practices of where and when we live.**

I hope, then, that you understand why I do think the following approaches cannot stand alone when we address visual rhetoric in writing classes.

not PHYSIOLOGY alone

Learning to be a thoughtful and critical analyst and user of visual rhetoric is not primarily a matter of learning about the physiology of the eye. I do not question that the physical workings of our sight help shape our perceptions. The shape of our eyeball, its focusing mechanisms, and the arrangement of photoreceptors at the back of our eyeball, for example, all help determine how wide a field of vision we have and just how much we can see of a page held at a certain distance. Such perceptions, however, are inseparably woven into our understandings of what matters to us as we move through our days. The first printed manuscripts—Gutenberg's *Bible*, for one— look heavy and awkward to us because of their large physical size, and their pages look hard to read not only because they are printed in another language but also because they are printed in a heavily stroked, ornate typeface that is large and arranged in close lines.

Gutenberg's *Bible* was not the result of Gutenberg's being lazily inattentive to studies on how the eye moves when it reads, on which typefaces are most readable, or on the most easily held sizes of books. Such studies (which, of course, didn't exist in the fifteenth century) ask us to be concerned with the efficiency and speed of a person's reading a hand-sized book silently to himself, but Gutenberg produced his Bible at a time when different values accrued to reading: The manuscript was a large, decorated, expensive object meant to be placed on a lectern; it was meant to be read aloud and slowly to— and discussed with—a group of others occupied with the work of writing or contemplation; it was printed in a typeface that reproduced what was considered to be the most traditional handwriting used by the best-educated people of the time.

not GRAPHIC DESIGN / VISUAL COMMUNICATION / INFORMATION ARCHITECTURE alone

Just as the workings of physiology are often presented as universal guidelines for making decisions about the visual arrangements of a text, so too are tenets of graphic design, visual communication, and information architecture. If you look through manuals or textbooks of visual design, you will usually find instructions for how to make layouts that are clear and concise, or that use an eye-catching photograph, or that are balanced or with an obvious path or hierarchy for a viewer's eyes to follow, or that allow someone to move through a computer screen without needing to think about what to click—but rarely will you find questions about why those particular values should ground the choices a designer makes. You will rarely find questions about potential consequences of our being grounded in those values. In such books you are not likely to find descriptions of how graphic design developed as a discipline because of advertising, in support of creating the hungry eyes of consumer desire. You will learn that information architecture developed to help consumers use various technologies—computers, chain saws, city layouts—easily, quickly, and without needing to think much about the technology, but you are not likely to find consideration of what might be the consequences of visual communication that (for example) continually shapes its users to be passive recipients of the technology.

RATHER, here are approaches that build on each other to help composition students become effective analysts and composers of visual rhetoric:

ⓢ   **Encourage students to see the larger visual context in which the rhetoric of individual visual texts works.**

Being attentive to the constructed visual environment—the outsides and insides of buildings, campus layouts, packaging, magazines, computer screens, how we dress—can help us tease out how our visual tastes and understandings have taken shape, overtly and not. Having a sense of what these tastes are and how they have been developed—against a background of larger cultural values—not only helps us analyze the visual aspects of texts but can also help us determine if we want to continue supporting practices of which we may disapprove—and can help us think of strategies for changing practices.

Here are some activities and questions that can help students (and us) gain a better sense of how we learn to see and judge what is around us:

The world of products and signs: If you ask students to choose a two-hour stretch of a weekend day and to record every visual text they see in that period of time—that is, if you ask them to write down every time they see something that has been designed to catch their eyes and persuade them toward some action or thought—they will come back to you complaining that they simply could not write everything down. A morning shower means, minimally, printed containers for shampoo, conditioner, antiperspirant, and moisturizer, and getting dressed can mean names on shoes, T-shirts, and hats. A drive to the market requires a long catalog of street signs, license plates, the names on the backs of cars, billboards, the lines on the ground in parking lots, and neon signs for stores—and that is before the market with its aisles of packaging, sales announcements, and magazine racks.

Why do they think that they encounter so many things that ask visual attention of them? How do they decide what to be attentive to? What sorts of things draw their attention immediately—and why? What sorts of actions and ways of thinking do they think they learn from this kind of visual environment? (For example, do they look carefully at everything they see, or have they learned to make quick judgments about what they see?) Do they think that the geometric/linear patterns they see—in parking lots, on store shelves, in a city grid—might have any effect on their sense of what makes for proper order? How might their actions be different if the visual environment were different? (For example, ask them to imagine that magazines, television, or web pages contained no advertising or that there were simply fewer constructed things to look at.)

The personal world of appearance: If you ask students to describe the cliques in their high schools and how they knew who belonged to what cliques, the result will include a catalog of visual clues about clothing choice and hairstyles.

How did they learn to dress as they did in high school? Did someone teach them overtly, or did they somehow learn to pick up on what was "in" or "out"? Do they still find themselves avoiding certain kinds of clothing or hairstyles because of what happened in high school? How do they think these tastes will affect them later in life? What other sorts of visual tastes do they see themselves as having acquired in similar ways? Do they care (for example) about the furniture in their dorm rooms, apartments, or homes? Do they care about showing off their CD collections, or cars, or . . . ?

The built environment: Ask students to describe their favorite places to study or hang out with friends, and then ask them to try to describe the ways in which those places are arranged that makes them comfortable or conducive to conversation. Ask them if they've ever felt—in a public space—that they weren't wanted, without anyone's having to say anything. How did they know, and what did they notice about the place that led them to respond as they did?

How do they think they've come to associate comfort and conversation—or discomfort—with the arrangements they've described? How did they learn what kinds of spaces were meant (or not meant) for them? Are there any connections that they can make between the design of physical spaces and the spaces that they see on computer screens—or between physical spaces and printed texts of any kind—in terms of visual arrangement?

The world of computer technologies: If you ask students to redesign computers for people who are blind, the exercise can help them think about just how much computers—including monitors, keyboards, and mice—have been designed to emphasize sight instead of other senses. Ask them then to consider what sight helps us to know (about things at a distance, for example) as opposed to senses like touch (which requires closeness) or smell (which does not give us a sense of sharp boundaries between objects, as sight does).

How do the rectangularity and verticality of most computer monitors shape how students see what is onscreen and the kinds of arguments they can make onscreen? What kinds of different arguments might be possible if computer screens were round, or tall and narrow? What if computer screens were like big, flat tables that we moved around? What if we moved into arguments (as in immersive virtual reality) rather than looked at them on the flat surface of screens?

Given that computer monitors are designed primarily for one person to sit in front of, how do students think they could design screens that would help pull multiple people at once into looking at what is on the screen? What sorts of screen arrangements could help people think or feel that they were looking into rather than at the screen—and how would this shape their sense of the argument?

What previous communication technologies (television, film, printing, handwriting, typewriters, and so on) do students think have shaped the way that computers have been designed and have shaped the way that we design computer screens? Why? What does this tell them about a general audience's expectations of how things onscreen should work?

Just how much of the shape of web pages comes from the shape of paper pages in the West (consider the left-to-right and top-to-bottom orientation, and so on)? What differentiates web pages from paper pages (consider the ease of color use, interactivity, how far to the bottom and to the right one can scroll, and so on)? How might the Web be different if it had been designed within cultures that read with different orientations? What does thinking about such questions tell them they need to learn or be attentive to if they are to design screens that are rhetorically effective for the audiences that they are most likely to encounter? By thinking about such questions, can they think of screen designs that might help them create new or different kinds of arguments? How would they have to design such new or different arguments so that the arguments wouldn't seem too far out of the ordinary to the audiences whom they are most likely to address?

The following questions can help students generalize from their observations:

How do these various aspects of their visual environment affect how they get along with others? (For example, do they make assessments based on clothing?) How do all the things that they are asked to see and interpret—consciously or not—in a day shape what they think is worth taking seriously or not? What do they have to know and understand in order to negotiate all the visual texts they encounter? What values (consumerism, quick judgment, individuality, the top-to-bottom hierarchy of arguments, and so on?) seem to them to be at work in what they have observed? In what ways can they imagine changing the built, visible environment to encourage a change in actions and values of those in it?

⑥ **Help students understand that the visual aspects of texts are rhetorical, that is, that they are designed by people who choose among different possible strategies to achieve different possible ends, within the context of cultural expectation and practice.**

Because we have all grown up in densely visually constructed environments, usually with little overt instruction in or awareness of how the construction takes place, it is easy to think of the visual elements of texts as simply happening or appearing—as though (as a group of teenagers once told me) television sitcoms were the result of a camera crew following a typical family through their days.

To help students (and ourselves) learn how the visual aspects of texts function rhetorically, take a visual text—any web page or software interface, any advertisement, any television newsscreen—and ask students how the text would be different if it were changed in some way. *How would it be different if (for example) the red in the text were replaced with green, if the classical-looking typeface were replaced with something hand-painted, if the white woman were replaced by a black man, if the photograph of the mother and child were replaced by the large words "Love is gentle," or if the text were a billboard instead of a web page?* Asking such questions helps us see how the overall effect of a text would change—which helps us see the original overall intended effect. Trying to identify everything about a text that could be changed also helps us see just how wide the range of possible strategies is in different kinds of visible texts—and helps us think about our own choices of strategies when we compose visible texts.

You can also present visible texts from other times—Victorian advertising that will probably looked cluttered and overly wordy to us, a page from an eighteenth-century novel whose type will look tiny and messy and whose punctuation might seem odd, a piece of royal furniture from seventeenth-century France—and ask students what values they see at work. What were the audiences of these texts supposed to take away from the texts? What values and practices would have been taught or reinforced by these texts? Seeing how the visual aspects of texts have been shaped in other times—and in other places—can help us gain perspective on the values and practices in the texts of our own time and place, and can help us see the strategies at work in them.

Ⓢ   **Teach visual strategies, terminology, and guidelines in context.**

The observational activities that I described earlier—asking students to see how many visual texts they encounter or to consider how they make clothing choices—help students develop a sense that visual rhetoric doesn't appear out of nowhere but is instead tied to everyday practices and their supporting cultural values.

You can use the same kinds of observational activities with the kinds of texts students are more likely to come across and create in academic settings, applying the same kinds of questions as those which I described earlier but also helping students develop a sense of the particular strategies that are appropriate in particular rhetorical situations. For example, ask students to collect pages from manuals and textbooks (on paper and onscreen), and then ask them questions about the values and practices encouraged by the visual arrangements they see. *Do they see an approach to thinking that breaks a topic up—dissects it—into smaller sections, or do they see other kinds of thinking being encouraged? Does the visual appearance of the pages make them feel that they can approach the topic confidently, or do they feel nervous about the topic just by looking at the pages? At what age group and level of education do the pages seem aimed?* Then ask them to identify (although these observations will frequently come out of discussing the previous questions) the particular visual strategies that they see tied to the observations they have made. *What size page, choice of typeface, placement of tables, use of color (including black, white, and grey), size of type or amount of type on a page, or level of indexing contributes to the overall sense they have of a page or text? How might they change those visual strategies to make a text more inviting, more gentle, or more targeted toward a younger or older audience?* Try this collection exercise with different kinds of texts—a genre of web pages (pages of health advice, science magazines, or children's educational pages) or one kind of phonebook ad (for lawyers, perhaps, or for health services)—and you will help students see how strategies vary across genres and media, across audiences and intentions. This exercise will help students make thoughtful and appropriate choices about the visual strategies they choose when composing their own work.

These observations can provide openings, then, for discussing terminology and guidelines that appear in design books and manuals.

After observing how different are the design strategies we have learned to expect in phonebook ads for lawyers as opposed to the pages of grammar textbooks (for example), students will be better able to judge how to apply and use common terminology like *contrast*, *hierarchy*, or *balance*; they will then be better able to modify or oppose the concepts they learn in order to create visual communication that is most appropriate to its audience and situation.

⑥ **Encourage students to use technologies awarely as they compose arguments so that they can develop a wide understanding and repertoire of—and competence with—rhetorical strategies.**

Some of the questions that I have listed previously—the ones, for example, that ask students to consider how computers emphasize sight or how the size and resolution of most computer screens make it hard for more than one person at a time to look at what is onscreen—can help us recognize constraints on thinking and action that common practice and the design of the technology have made invisible or natural. Through questioning how the design and use of our technologies might shape and so limit our thinking and arguments, we can develop fresh—and more critical—approaches to what we compose.

To help students think about how communication technologies might shape their arguments—including their uses of visual rhetoric—and to help them understand how the specific rhetorical choices of their arguments do function, you can use the following approaches. Once students have begun defining their intentions and their audiences for a composition (onscreen or off), and once they have begun to describe or sketch out the concrete steps they might take, ask them to do the following:

- *List every (visually) rhetorical choice they make as they compose.* To help students do this, you will often have to help them see that what might not seem like a choice really is. For example, any time that they do not change a default setting as they compose a web page, they are making a choice that will have consequences on how their audiences read their work—as illustrated in my earlier discussion of the student who realized that she could not retain the default grey of web pages. Help students learn to detect as many of the choices as possible that they do have as they compose—choices of individual words, of color, of using a photograph instead of an illustration, of paragraph order and shape, of margin size, of using a single long text instead of multiple pages of smaller texts, of using text rather than or alongside drawing, of which elements to align with each other (and how)—and you will help them develop a wide repertoire of possible strategies to chose among as they compose.

If you ask students to do this individually, with their own compositions, have them come together then as a group to list everything that they have considered. They will come up with a useful checklist of invention strategies for the next time that they compose or revise.

- *Justify every (visually) rhetorical choice they make as they compose.* By having to describe why they think a particular strategy—used alone or in concert with other strategies—will help them achieve their intentions with their particular audiences, students gain more conscious control over the strategic choices that they make. If you ask students to write up such a list of justifications immediately after they have generated the first draft of a composition, you will help them reflect on their choices and later develop plans for revision.

- *Design their argument for a different audience.* When students have to take a web site composed for adults and reshape it for teenagers (for example), they have to reconsider a tremendous range of visual and verbal aspects of the text. Such reconsideration can help them see how their choices of strategies are tied to audience expectations and can therefore help them make the most fitting choices.

- *Redesign their argument for the same audience.* Once students have a solid draft of a web site or other text, ask them to describe what reading their text will be most like for their audiences—that is, will their audiences experience the text as being most like a standard academic text, like a magazine page, or like moving fearfully through the tunnels of a vast castle (as with many computer games)? Ask them then to choose some other broad approach (for example, that moving through their texts will be like being in a laboratory, or a bustling city market, or a snowed-over street) and to redesign their texts to try to develop that experience for their audiences. This doesn't mean that students need to make the text "literally" simulate that environment as they would in (for example) virtual-reality environments or graphical computer games. This also doesn't mean that students need to actually build the texts which they describe. It is enough if they sketch out what they might do and tell how they believe their readers will respond to the shapes they will give their texts. But if students do try to change—as much as possible—the (primarily visual) experience audiences will have of their texts, they will gain a sense of how their rhetorical choices shape the relationships audiences develop with texts. They will also gain a sense of the wide range of possibilities there are—and that are often unused—for ways in which composers can approach audiences.

- *Watch how others move through their arguments.* Writing studies teachers often ask their students to do protocol analyses—to watch carefully, that is, as others read their papers, having those others speak aloud what they are thinking and understanding (or not understanding) as a paper is read. Such analysis is also highly useful for helping students learn how others move through and understand texts that are given more visual attention than the typical academic text. Having a reader describe what she sees first—and why—in a text and how she interprets a composer's color choices or choice and placement of a photograph can help a composer not only understand how to make more effective rhetorical choices but also understand more clearly how conventions of visual composition function in our place and time.

- *Design with their audiences. Participatory Design* is the name given to a set of practices that were shaped, primarily in Scandinavia, in the development of computer-based systems but that have spread to other areas of design.[5] These practices are grounded in beliefs that the typical author/designer–audience relationship—in which the author/designer imagines the audience and constructs texts or other artifacts abstractly for that audience—results in products that are, at best, not as useful as they could be for audiences and, at worst, disrespectful of audiences, rendering them passive consumers. When, instead, the audience for a text (which could, for example, be a web site about an elementary school or a nonprofit organization) is included from the beginning in discussions and decision making about the design of the text, then the text will be more useful for that audience and will better achieve its rhetorical ends. In addition, audiences are encouraged to develop more critical questioning of the texts (or other products) that they use.

- *Imagine that the technology being used were designed differently.* If the usual desktop computer were designed to have a monitor that was like a large, flat table (for example), how would that design change the ways in which students would shape their texts visually? What would they do differently, and why? What do these other possibilities help them see about how they were thinking about their audiences and the arguments that they were making? Given the constraints of the particular technology that they are using, can they take advantage of any of the other possibilities they describe?

Ⓖ **Encourage students to make arguments that differ from what we have become accustomed to seeing.**

If you encourage students to explore new kinds of visual arguments—for example, to produce term papers that contain no words or that do not follow the standard one-inch margin, one typeface guidelines or that are comprised of many short, word-free web pages—they will be in a better position to consider the constraints and consequences of the visually presented arguments we encounter day to day. They will, therefore, be in a better position to continue asking how tastes develop and how we learn to take certain visual structures and practices for granted, unquestioningly. You will be able to help them consider what is taken for granted in the kinds of visible arguments that we have learned to consider as natural and not worthy of question, and you will, perhaps, be able to help them consider how making new kinds of visible arguments might help them—and us—learn to be more responsive to the unfamiliar rhetorical strategies of others . . .

and perhaps then also be more responsive to others in general.

Notes

[1] In this chapter, I focus primarily on the pages we produce for each other rather than on furniture, architecture, or other kinds of visual texts since it is with pages that we are still most concerned in classrooms. To learn more about the rhetoric of other kinds of visual texts, see Blair and Michel or Foss.

[2] For various perspectives on how and why our culture has become more visual, and for a range of responses writing teachers might make, see Bolter, Lanham, Rutledge, or Stafford.

[3] Delpit and Grimm, for example, each lay out the process I have described, compellingly and in more detail.

[4] See Cooper for a thoughtful description of how most technical documentation asks its users to think of themselves and the relationship they have with the technology they are trying to learn.

[5] To read about the origins of Participatory Design, see Floyd et al. For an overview of Participatory Design practices, see Schuler and Namioka. To read a highly useful description of such practices at work in designing software for children (applicable, of course, to others), see Chapter 7, "The Activity of Innovation," of Druin and Solomon.

Works Cited / Further Reading

Arnheim, Rudolf. *The Power of the Center: A Study of Composition in the Visual Arts.* Berkeley: U of California P, 1982.

Bang, Molly. *Picture This: Perception and Composition.* Boston: Little, Brown, 1991.

Blair, Carole, and Neil Michel. "Reproducing Civil Rights Tactics: The Rhetorical Performances of the Civil Rights Memorial." *Rhetoric Society Quarterly* 30.2 (2000): 31–55.

Bolter, Jay D. "Hypertext and the Question of Visual Literacy." *Handbook of Literacy and Technology: Transformations in a Post-Typographic World.* Ed. David Reinking, Michael C. McKenna, Linda D. Labbo, and Ronald D. Kieffer. Mahwah, NJ: Erlbaum, 1998. 3–14.

Cooper, Marilyn. "The Postmodern Space of Operator's Manuals." *Technical Communication Quarterly* 5.4 (Fall 1996): 385–410.

Delpit, Lisa D. *Other People's Children: Cultural Conflict in the Classroom.* New York: New P, 1996.

Dondis, Donis A. *A Primer of Visual Literacy.* Cambridge, MA: MIT P, 1973.

Druin, Allison, and Cynthia Solomon. *Designing Multimedia Environments for Children: Computers, Creativity, and Kids.* New York: Wiley, 1996.

Floyd, C., W. M. Mehl, F. M. Reisin, G. Schmidt, and G. Wolf. "Out of Scandinavia: Alternative Approaches to Software Design and System Development." *Human–Computer Interaction* 4.4 (1989): 253–350.

Foss, Sonja K. "The Construction of Appeal in Visual Images: A Hypothesis." *Rhetorical Movement.* Ed. David Zarefsky. Evanston, IL: Northwestern UP, 1993.

Grimm, Nancy. *Good Intentions: Writing Center Work for Postmodern Times.* Portsmouth, NH: Boynton/Cook, 1999.

Kinross, Robin. "The Rhetoric of Neutrality." *Design Issues* II.2: 18–30.

Kostelnick, Charles, and David O. Roberts. *Designing Visual Language: Strategies for Professional Communicators.* Boston: Allyn, 1998.

Kress, Gunther, and Theo van Leeuwen. *Reading Images: The Grammar of Visual Design.* London: Routledge, 1996.

Lanham, Richard. *The Electronic Word: Democracy, Technology, and the Arts.* Chicago: U of Chicago P, 1993.

Nelson, Robert A., and Richard Shiff. *Critical Terms for Art History.* Chicago: U of Chicago P, 1996.

Rutledge, Kay E. "Analyzing Visual Persuasion: The Art of Duck Hunting." *Images in Language, Media, and Mind.* Ed. Roy F. Fox. Urbana, IL: NCTE, 1994: 204–18.

Schriver, Karen A. *Dynamics in Document Design: Creating Texts for Readers.* New York: Wiley, 1997.

Schuler, Douglas, and Aki Namioka, Eds. *Participatory Design: Principles and Practices.* Hillsdale, NJ: Erlbaum, 1993.

Stafford, Barbara M. *Good Looking: Essays on the Virtue of Images.* Cambridge, MA: MIT P, 1996.

Williams, Robin. *The Non-Designer's Design Book: Design and Typographic Principles for the Visual Novice.* Berkeley: Peachpit, 1994.

Teaching and Learning Visual Rhetoric

MARY HOCKS
Georgia State University

For most of my life, I was a horrible photographer. Fingers in the picture, blurred images, heads cut off, too much sky—these were standard fare for my pictures. Last year, I learned how to take pictures with a digital camera. The whole process of capturing and composing digital photographs has completely changed the way that I look at my own visual literacy. For the first time, feedback from the camera lets me use the display window to look at the frame and to see the results of my image production. Not only can I see and compose photos that please me, but I can also work with drafts of images because image-editing programs allow me to change and manipulate the picture endlessly. As I traveled down a western highway, thinking about how much I enjoy taking my bike to remote places, I tried a few shots with the camera and came up with the photo on page 203.

I learned to look by doing it and created a visual narrative for my cyclist friends to enjoy—something to imagine on hot work days in the city. As I captured the story of my travels, I also somehow discovered the (perhaps more interesting) paradox of being in motion and yet staying still. The image probably communicates this idea more eloquently than I could explain it. I could also have easily added captions, words, lighting, or other layers that would complicate the meaning of my picture. I could choose to lay bare the various layers that make up the overall effect or leave it as simply a holistic image. The ability to alter images (and include words with them) not only creates what Mitchell calls a new "truth" to the picture, but it also adds the experience of reflexivity and reflection to the process of photography. The combination of learning how to look, experimenting, getting feedback from technologies, interacting with audiences, and having the tools for revision taught me something—to construct visual meanings and compositions with confidence. This is what good learning practices are supposed to do—engage us in an exploratory process that allows us to experiment. My goal in this chapter is to encourage teachers to teach and learn visual meanings with their students.

Figure 1
Western Highway Photo

Visual Literacy and Rhetoric

Many of us trained in the traditional humanities are still educating ourselves about the visual elements of teaching writing, particularly on computers. Trained in words, how confident do we feel about our own visual literacy practices? We may be uncomfortable with, or even suspicious of, our students' using visual elements in their work. Or we may be tempted to turn to a verbal parallel before we try to experiment with visual techniques in our own work. The traditional definition of *visual literacy* assumes that visual displays constitute a language. *Literacy* could thus be defined as making meaning through images. This analogy to alphabetic language has been central to most definitions of *visual literacy*. Images were considered referents of linguistic concepts or facts; images worked as symbols or signs that pointed back to meaning making in alphabetic systems. Other definitions of *visual literacy* have concentrated on formal elements of visual compositions—elements like balance, hue, saturation, texture, and scale. Visual literacy, in these terms, is taught as design—learning to recognize and apply basic visual elements to compositions. People who teach visual communication have often drawn on a traditional formalist approach to visual design that seeks to make us more sensitive to elements of color, arrangement, scale, and other aspects of visual style.

Two schools of thought inform the current thinking about visual literacy: The first asserts that images function in a manner similar or parallel to words—they create meaning through their syntax and proximity and have a distinguishable grammar (i.e., Dondis). The other dominant theory is that images work far differently than words—and that they are seductive or even dangerous in their abstract and imprecise mode of signification (i.e., Postman). These distinctions between "visual culture" and "print culture" that separate image and word within humanities scholarship are symptomatic of what Bruno Latour calls modernist thinking—the binary-based thinking that posits radical paradigm shifts from one communications medium to another or from one form of writing technology to another. When brought into the online environments of our computer classrooms, visual literacy falls short of describing the interactive environments of many new media and new technologies (see Hocks; Kendrick and Hocks). Thus, if we want to help our students explore the integrated and visual nature of electronic writing and design, we ought to stress the continuum between visual and verbal forms of expression. We can also experiment with creating visually rich documents ourselves. By doing so, we move beyond literacy and formalism to teach with a broader understanding of visual rhetoric.

How do we begin thinking about a visual rhetoric? Rhetoric is a dynamic system of strategies employed for creating, reacting to, and receiving meaning. Because rhetorical practice is fundamentally collaborative and dialogic, no individual rhetor can operate in isolation. When we bring this understanding of rhetoric into the digital classroom—with its screens and visually based information technologies—the visual elements of writing buried in every writing technology we know come into dramatic focus. We can begin by simply looking at the computers around us and analyzing them as intensely visual artifacts. The screen itself is a tablet that combines words, interface icons, and pictures; also, the screen invokes other modalities like touch and sound. Every element of the computer contributes to gain our attention, to teach us, to frustrate us, to pull us into dialogue with information and with people online. Visual rhetoric, like verbal rhetoric, is a system of ongoing dialogue among rhetors, audiences, and dynamic contexts, but it focuses on the multiple modalities and contexts of meaning available to us in the world. Those contexts include the changing digital technologies that we encounter in the computer classroom.

*   *   *

Students in English courses have always produced lots of writing, but until fairly recently, they had little choice about what those productions looked like and who read them. Students today are often steeped in the visual and electronic culture in which they have grown up, and they will think visually and beyond mere text when they work on documents in computer classrooms—they are likely to include different colors, font styles, or backgrounds on web pages, animated graphics, background music, or video clips. What students don't always realize is that anything presented on the screen is rhetorical. What they have chosen, selected, and designed to create an effect puts them into a critical dialogue with other students, with the teacher, and with like-minded folks in cyberspace. As Anne Wysocki explains in another chapter of this book, approaches to visual rhetoric are multidisciplinary, but critical reflection on the rhetorical and cultural contexts of all things visual is the most important lesson for learning visual rhetoric. Students can be taught to critique the visual world around them and to make apparent what has been transparent in the printed pages and online conventions we have inherited. They can study audience, style, and argument in all kinds of visual media and become better cultural critics and rhetoricians. In class, students and teachers can learn together as we train our eyes to see our visual culture more critically. Students bring an impressive repertoire of looking into our computer classrooms, and we would do well to draw on what they know as we teach them to hone these skills toward specific rhetorical purposes. We can learn a lot about visual practice in everyday life from our students, and we can prompt them to be more reflective about what they do in our courses.

*   *   *

When teaching in a digital environment, we have the opportunity to teach students to look critically and reflectively at media forms and to conceive of themselves as designers of their own histories and cultures. This kind of approach to pedagogy both acknowledges the fundamental role that technologies play in our understanding of critical literacy and drives the use of new communication technologies toward student-centered learning goals. Design processes allow writers to engage in the construction of knowledge because design allows the interplay between the visual and the textual to create one semiotic space. Teaching the process of design allows students to help shape the social and cultural environment in which they find themselves. Both Nancy Kaplan (2001) and Randy Bass (1999) have argued persuasively that the design of electronic artifacts is an essential part of enacting disciplinary knowledge in English Studies because those artifacts will determine how knowledge will be received and consumed. Through designing digital documents and then testing to determine how people see and read them, our students develop an awareness of themselves as active producers of knowledge in their discipline or profession and as agents in the world around them. The process of designing something that enacts their own experiences—and by doing so, to think outside the box and also *about* the box—is an essential step for teaching students how to use visual rhetoric.

*   *   *

In the following section, I offer some examples teachers can use to develop students' understanding of visual rhetoric by analyzing and engaging in the design processes that digital technologies make possible. These assignments are appropriate for introductory composition courses that make use of digital technologies both inside and outside the classroom. I ask my first-year composition students to produce new media documents like digital narratives, speculative designs of activist technologies, and community web sites. I do so because I want them to work conceptually with experimental spaces that are motivated by classroom and public audiences and that engage them concretely with various kinds of media.

Assignments

The following assignments assume that students have access to visually rich tools for image production, onscreen presentations, and web page design. However, I have tried to emphasize the kind of learning that takes place during the design process and, when possible, to suggest a range of tools for completing the assignments. Even as the technologies and the media forms change or become more accessible year after year, students can still develop rhetorical and compositional techniques from the following assignments.

Interactive Digital Media Critique and Design Projects

Multimedia design projects are common in writing classes that aim to incorporate a Professional Writing approach, i.e., an approach informed by writing practices used by working professionals outside the university. The field of technical and professional writing has contributed greatly to our understanding of how to teach electronic technologies in meaningful ways. First-year through upper-division writing classes can meaningfully and successfully borrow from professional writing to introduce students to contemporary writing situations. Document design and usability—the testing of those documents with actual users throughout the design process—are essential steps for creating any kind of interactive media.[1] This assignment thus has two parts—a rhetorical analysis of new media documents and a design project. Students first analyze and critique professionally produced examples of digital interactive media—for example, CD-ROMs, DVDs, and web sites. Once students have practiced thinking critically and rhetorically about these new media, they then develop a design for a project aimed at a particular audience or an actual client. When students work on these projects, they can gain experience developing various digital production skills as tools become available to students in their classrooms and on their desktops. For example, students in my classes can select pictures and artwork, record music and voice-overs, and scan-and-enhance images. The tools are not the focus of what students learn from these projects, however. Production experiences on collaborative projects teach students two important parts of the process for digital writing: the conceptual design process and the team model for production.

Students must first learn to think through the design choices and information strategies for a particular audience. A very simple step for beginning this audience-based analysis is to have them start to analyze the ads, the colors, and the interactive links that surround a favorite web site. Whose interests does this particular site seem to represent? What immediate visual cues tell you what the site's content tries to capture? What other contexts or networks of information surround the site? What are the links, buttons, and banners persuading you to do? This kind of analysis teaches students to treat the Internet as a type of media open for analysis much as they might analyze the audience of a particular television program, but with particular attention given to the interactive elements of the online medium. This analysis encourages them to be sensitive to how the visual, verbal, and interactive elements of web sites are rhetorical—that they aim toward cultural values used to persuade and capture the attention of audiences.

So that their vision is not limited to the point-and-click conventions of web-based documents, I also help students learn to analyze CD-ROM or DVD media so that they can understand how the look and the dominant visual metaphors create the cultural and literal meanings of those pieces of media (see Wysocki's "Impossibly distinct" for an excellent example of this kind of analysis). Any CD-ROM or DVD would work as a discussion starter (and choosing one which picks up on other themes in a particular course is recommended). For my purposes here, I refer to one CD-ROM that I have used: *Out of Bounds*, a presentation about southeastern artists created for display at a museum during the 1996 Olympic Games in Atlanta.[2] This project was a collaboration between faculty and students, and it featured key artists from the region by focusing on their identities and their diversity.

In class discussion, students and I talk about how this screen uses a "Hollywood Squares" visual approach, a reference to the television show and a reminder of the consistencies between older and new media. The head-shot photos here are colorized, creating color schemes that correspond to all content associated with each artist. Along with being a navigational aid, the color schemes give an artistic ethos to the presentation. At the same time, the project has a fairly linear structure and arrangement of a large amount of

Figure 2
DVD Screen: *Out of Bounds*

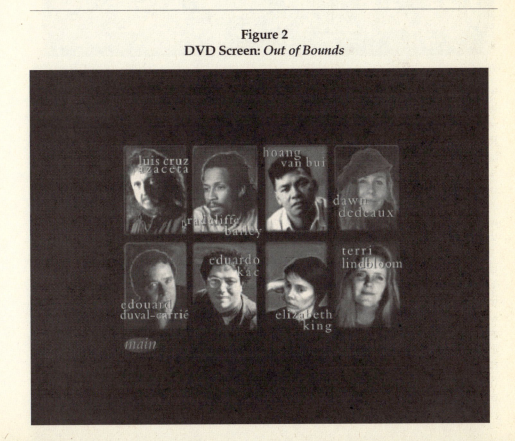

Figure 3
DVD Screen: Radcliffe Bailey

information. One clicks on these head shots and associated text to move to the next levels of information. The next layer takes one to the artist in his or her studio, which situates a context for that person's work and artist's statement. Radcliffe Bailey, for example, stands in a rich environment of civil rights activism.

As is visible on this screen, a collection of media is available from the options listed on the photo of each person's studio. As is often the case with such projects, most of this media were "found" and collected by the team. The artists' own slides and media spots were incorporated into the project, as in this video clip about Elizabeth's King's sculpture.

Students explore the meanings conveyed by the still and moving images, layers of image and text, colors, and color schemes in this CD-ROM project. They come to understand how this museum piece was composed to appeal to an international audience that visited Atlanta. A number of videos by the show curators are included that help place this artifact in its setting and help capture the rich dialogue among museum visitors, artists, and art interpreters. Thus, by situating this piece as a communicative act and a public display during a particular historical context, students can focus on the rhetorical contexts of audience and setting. Students also study the style of this piece— particularly how the depth and scope of information get represented visually on each screen through links and buttons.

Figure 4
DVD Screen: Elizabeth King

In addition to requiring that they read the rhetorical context of the piece, this assignment asks students to study the production process of the team that creates this kind of project, highlighting it as another kind of composition. Because I have copies of the actual production documents and meeting notes from the team which created this particular work, my students study the documents from the group's meetings to see how the paper version became a fully functional interactive media piece. With this access to the meeting notes, students can see how elements of the project came together, what was left out, how the authors decided to incorporate existing media and works by artists, and other important design decisions. The same kind of process can be accomplished by having students interview or email professionals who work in this industry or by contacting a campus web site's production team and asking questions about how the site was produced. Once students begin to look more critically at the visual elements of these kinds of projects, they can plan out a project in small groups in which they design some kind of interactive media for a particular audience. They typically choose a web site for a community or a campus organization, but I encourage them to remember the other digital interactive media and to think broadly about visual elements and especially about interactivity. I do this so that they will not limit their designs to their own production skills or to the technologies available in our classroom. This process of speculative design really encourages students to think both creatively and rhetorically as a group while paradoxically not limiting them to time and place.

The next step in the process is to teach students to storyboard their projects. Storyboarding is a visual technique borrowed from documentary video production in which every shot is planned out to correspond to a narrative script. In multimedia productions, storyboarding refers to planning and sketching out each screen of the digital production. To teach students the storyboarding process, I give them sheets of paper and ask them to draw every media element, each navigational link, and all text that appears on the screen. They also note the colors, fonts, and any other graphics that will be used on each screen. This process makes them pay careful attention to detail, to spatial placement, and to screen real estate as well as to the consistency of the interface. It also forces them to narrow the scope of their projects in collaboration with one another. They can literally test the navigation on these sheets of paper by having other students punch the "buttons" and move to the next paper screen. They think carefully about what other users will see and how they will interact with the information in their projects. As students learn to storyboard a sequence of screens, they think broadly about how visual information gets structured and impacts the design. Their design skills can be minimal (stick figures are allowed) because storyboarding teaches students to *think through* the elements of design and navigation that meet the audience's needs. Students discuss or interact with the target audience, and as a group they develop a set of hand-drawn storyboards and decide how to organize the content of the site.

The analysis and speculative design process can be accomplished in a few weeks, and students don't need any specific technical skills to complete the assignments. If you teach web authoring in your class, you can have students create five live web pages as a prototype to show to the clients or to the class, explaining along the way the design and content choices they have made. Students have the client or another class team approve the paper storyboards before they develop online documents. I teach students how to use a scanner and an image software program to create each screen as a still image first. Those layered graphics then can be imported into a web authoring program and combined with links and other interactive features of the program. This actual prototyping of the project takes a few more weeks to accomplish, but it is well worth the time and effort if your ultimate goal is to have students present a working prototype to an audience.

These kinds of design assignments can be used successfully in professional writing courses at all levels of the university. In our technical writing and business writing courses, for example, we use case-based assignments and service learning projects to teach students web design.[3] We often have students create projects for a real client—a community client, an employer, or a student organization or program on campus. Such a project constitutes about a third of the course work for the semester. Each group of students writes a number of documents together, and they receive feedback as they move through the design process. They initially write a proposal or project description and receive commentary from the instructor. If the project is being developed for a campus unit or a community client, they also get initial input from these other audiences for the project. Each group then develops a plan or schedule for its project which includes a description of the project's scope and a set of handdrawn storyboards. These storyboards are submitted to the instructor and to other groups in the class for feedback and approval. Each group then begins to develop a prototype of its project using a web-authoring tool. Usually, one person is assigned to do the time-consuming work of acquiring and editing graphics while another person develops specific web pages. Ideally, the different group members will draw on their strengths to help one another and complete the project on time. The project is presented orally with use of an overhead projector to the class and sometimes to the client for whom it was created. Building the real audience into the entire life of the project—even if the audience is the other students in the class—will make these successful rhetorically based writing projects. I have increasingly found that these professional writing practices offer a valuable rhetorical development process to students in writing-intensive courses across the disciplines.[4]

Multimedia-supported Oral Presentations

Models from writing-intensive and technology-enhanced classes across the curriculum provide another very useful kind of example for those of us who want to teach visual rhetoric and develop our students' visual literacy. Students in upper-level English courses in Victorian and Modern British Literature at Spelman College use the Writing Program's computer classroom to develop visual literacy and rhetorical skills by working with film and multimedia to enhance their study of literature. In these classes, the ultimate goal of the teacher is to have students read fiction and poetry, view and analyze film adaptations of novels, and apply postcolonial literary theory to their study of literature. Students then develop a multimedia presentation of their work to deliver orally to the class. The final presentation captures students' research throughout the semester and can be thought of as a multimedia research essay. This is in some ways more rhetorically sophisticated than a traditional research essay assignment, however, because it asks students to pay attention to the visual features of their documents as they construct their online presentations to deliver to a live audience. It thus combines the multiple rhetorical modes of oral, written, and visual communication for an audience of peers. This kind of visual presentation is very easy for students to learn to create and is easily transported into the writing classroom.

In this series of assignments, using film as the basis for developing visual literacy provides excellent groundwork for students' understanding of visual rhetoric. As with the professional writing design projects, students engage in the dual rhetorical processes of critique and design. First, they learn to interpret visual messages and cultural ideological meanings conveyed by the way in which a scene in a particular film is staged and shot. They become more sensitive to the affective dimensions of the narrative by analyzing the music, the acting, and other elements of the film. Because their classes took place in a multimedia-equipped computer classroom, students could then use multimedia tools to capture pieces of the film and to combine them with their own ideas and analyses. Their ultimate goal was to make an oral presentation using PowerPoint, a standard multimedia presentation package, to organize their ideas and their selections of examples from the media that they had studied. The professor, Pushpa Parekh, advised the students to "work on creating aesthetically pleasing but also intellectually stimulating and substantive presentations." She specifically emphasized that these projects should "strengthen and augment our perceptions, analyses, and experience of literary works." These projects become online literary essays that these students present to one another orally and use to engage each other in dialogue about the relationships between older and newer media and between visual and verbal meanings.

Students typically need about a week to learn the software program and to begin to use the features that allow them to place pictures, text, and other media into the PowerPoint slide. Many design decisions are preset into the templates provided by the software, so I always follow up by asking students to examine those preset options critically and to think about other ways of arranging the material to make it more effective. If we don't want student learning to be limited by the conventions and the practices they know from the software that they use, we have to think about what the software offers them, the assumptions built into the interface, and what we can do through speculative design to encourage their imaginations to get outside of those widely used software programs.

Let's see how students accomplish doing this by way of an example. The project by four students entitled "Imprisonment: An Examination of Sociopolitical and Psychological Imprisonment in Victorian and Modern British Literature" demonstrates how a group of students used video, text, and graphics to create an online literary essay. These students covered a wide range of issues explored in the class focusing on gender, class, and the impact of colonialism. For example, students discussed cultural themes such as "The Cult of True Womanhood," summarizing its main features for the class and choosing an appropriate graphic from the Internet of a nineteenth-century woman to reinforce that concept.

The students here have carefully selected photographs and graphics that tell the story of the cultural climate surrounding female identity and that reinforce and emphasize the cultural history that serves as a backdrop to these texts. They have also arranged a traditional linear structure for their presentation in the title and on the right side of the screen. In this case, the teacher emphasized visual literacy by having students look at visual records and images of female identity as they related to topics in literature and culture. She emphasized visual rhetoric by having students engage in the complementary processes of critique and design, in which they actually made these projects the centerpiece of in-class oral presentations and dialogues about the literature and films studied.

These kinds of multimedia projects provide an excellent opportunity for students to combine the visual, oral, and written impact of their academic

Figure 5
"The Cult of True Womanhood"

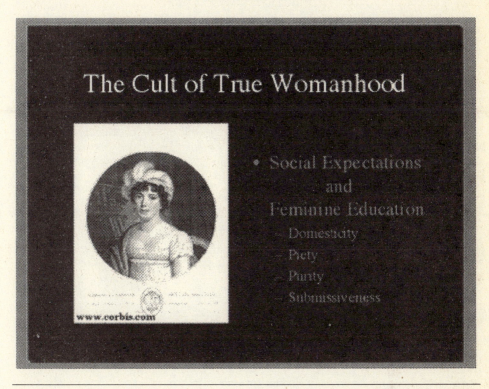

arguments for a live audience. For example, students learn to make arguments by analyzing the visual assumptions offered in a film. When analyzing the film *A Passage to India*, these students addressed the audience with the question "Can You See the Difference?" They used this question to engage the audience in a visual exercise on seeing race/class distinctions in the scene in which cars visually separate the British from native Indians, and classes from one another. In another example, students created an argument by juxtaposing two maps representing India at different points in time to demonstrate British colonization. The combination of their title and the maps provides the following visual demonstration of the theories about the colonization of India.

Building visual arguments, analyzing film clips, and arranging these materials into a presentation for the class helped these students understand and acquire visual literacy. According to the professor, as a result of having worked on these projects, students understood more clearly and became more actively involved with the important ideas and skills of the course. But more significantly, displaying and discussing this information engaged the students in a critical dialogue about colonialism in several modes. This kind of multimodal rhetorical learning is well suited to the electronic environments our students now use to compose and to communicate with one another.

Figure 6
British Colonization of India

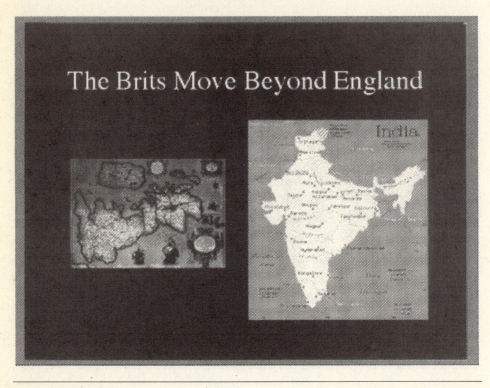

Conclusion

Teaching visual rhetoric, in my view, is intimately tied to the ways in which we define and practice literacy education. The very terms used to talk about various literacies—print and visual—have changed with the advent of electronic composition, authoring, and design. In computer classrooms and other online environments, students will increasingly be using new communication technologies and information technologies to engage in all parts of the research and writing process. Using even the most basic computer technologies for writing, for communicating electronically, and for navigating through online information involves them in a multisensory experience. The modern computer with its information technologies demonstrates how meaning is not just verbal or visual but rather is multimodal. To use these new technologies effectively, writers have to consider and use practices that are not just verbal but also visual, spatial, audial, and gestural—in short, multimodal practices of making meaning (Cope and Kalantzis 26). Teaching multimodal literacy advocates that texts cannot be truly separated from their use in lived practice (Kress 187). These writers from the New London School make a powerful case for teaching students to think through and design their own work using these technologies, and to pay attention to the practices behind the technologies. A student-centered pedagogy asks students to work within their own cultures and discourses by using experimental forms to learn actively from one another and to engage with the world around them. Visual literacy, then, is really inadequate for describing the kind of active, multimodal learning that we want to encourage in our students. Visual rhetoric—when understood as the dialogical processes of critique and design in contexts that deconstruct the visual world and the technologies surrounding us—goes much further in helping us teach students the rhetorical and compositional abilities that they can use for years to come.

Notes

[1] The textbooks *Dynamics of Document Design* and *Technical Communication*, for example, both include extensive chapters on interactivity and usability design testing, including testing for hypertext and other online documents.

[2] Two of the designers from the Georgia Institute of Technology who created this project, Thomas Winn and Mary Anne Stevens, gave me these materials and insights into the process.

[3] These assignments are developed by Jeffrey Grabill and Elizabeth Lopez, based on their own research and on models they have adapted from Purdue University's Technical and Professional Writing program.

[4] See Hocks, Grabill, and Lopez for a discussion of how professional writing approaches can intersect effectively with a WAC program.

Works Cited

Bass, Randy. "Story and Archive in the Twenty-first Century." *College English* 61.6 (1999): 659–70.

Cope, Bill, and Mary Kalantzis, eds. *Multiliteracies: Literacy Learning and the Design of Social Futures.* New York: Routledge, 2000.

Dondis, Donis A. *A Primer of Visual Literacy.* Cambridge, MA: MIT P, 1973.

Hocks, Mary E. "Toward a Visual Critical Electronic Literacy." *Works and Days* 17.1 & 2 (Spring/Fall 1999): 157–72.

Kaplan, Nancy. "E-Literacies: Politexts, Hypertexts, and Other Cultural Formations in the Late Age of Print." Online. <http://raven.ubalt.edu/staff/Kaplan/lit/One_Beginning_417.html>.

Kendrick, Michelle, and Mary E. Hocks. Introduction. *Eloquent Images: Writing Visually in New Media.* Ed. Mary E. Hocks and Michelle Kendrick. Cambridge, MA: MIT UP, in press.

Kress, Gunter. "Multimodality." *Multiliteracies.* 182–202.

Lannon, John M. *Technical Communication.* 8th ed. New York: Addison, 2000.

Latour, Bruno. *We Have Never Been Modern*. Cambridge, MA: Harvard UP, 1993.

Mitchell, William J. *The Reconfigured Eye: Visual Truth in the Post-Photographic Era*. Cambridge, MA: MIT UP, 1992.

Postman, Neil. *Technopoly: The Surrender of Culture to Technology*. New York: Knopf, 1992.

Schreiver, Karen E. *Dynamics in Document Design*. New York: Wiley, 1997.

Tufte, Edward. *Visual Explanations: Images and Quantities, Evidence and Narrative*. Cheshire, CT: Graphics P, 1997.

Wysocki, Anne Frances. "Impossibly distinct: On form/content and word/image in two pieces of computer-based interactive multimedia." *Computers and Composition* 18 (2001): 209–34.

SECTION V:
ASSIGNING AND ASSESSING STUDENT WRITING

Variations on a Theme: The Technology Autobiography as a Versatile Writing Assignment

KARLA KITALONG
University of Central Florida

TRACY BRIDGEFORD
University of Nebraska at Omaha

MICHAEL MOORE
Michigan Technological University

DICKIE SELFE
Michigan Technological University

Autobiographies and other narratives make good assignments in writing courses because they encourage students to reflect on how their own attitudes and beliefs develop, both socially and individually. The four of us have been assigning technology autobiographies—narratives in which writers explore their relationships with technology—for the past several years. Because we all have access to technology-rich laboratory and classroom environments and tend to choose technology-related themes, our courses often attract technology-savvy students for whom technology is taken for granted, invisible, a mere backdrop to their lives. Writing technology autobiographies encourages them to reflect upon their own (and sometimes upon other people's) experiences with technology, which leads them to think critically about technology. In the process, the invisibles can become visible, the implicit can be made explicit. Useful and engaging writing often results from such reflection. In this chapter we demonstrate how we adapt a single, basic technology autobiography writing prompt as an assignment in a wide range of writing classes and illustrate ways in which that writing assignment deepens our own and students' understanding of technology.

219

Theoretical Background for the Assignment

We have been influenced in this project by the trend in composition studies—and in academia as a whole—to pay attention to the local and to build upon all stakeholders' perspectives. This trend has resulted in significant scholarship on narrative as a means for exploring literacy development (Bloom; Brandt, "Accumulating," *Literacy as Involvement*, "Sponsors"; Eldred and Mortensen; Isaksen; Lynch; Soliday). Narrative writing assignments in a variety of classes are motivated by teachers' recognition that "facts are constructed when we interpret the world; they are not discovered in a preexisting reality separate from the observer" (Bloom 61). Bloom acknowledges the importance of individual style—how a story is told—noting that "stories are sensitive to the way in which the storyteller crafts them" (Bloom 61). He further suggests that narrative writing assignments illustrate the social nature of knowledge: "[N]o story is constructed by one person alone." Moreover, stories are not stable, unified truths: A "story, as a social construction, can appear to change as if transformed into a different story when the narrator's voice alters. Such altering may occur as the narrator's subjectivity shifts, fragments, and becomes refigured" (Bloom 61–62).

Influenced by work such as Bloom's, we wanted to help students recognize that their experiences with technology are not merely insignificant threads in a larger fabric of social narrative about technology, but that they can, through their own ways of telling, influence the stories told about technology in Western technoculture. In short, by telling their stories, we believe, students can facilitate deeper social and individual understandings about technology. We observed, also, that teacher-scholars in English studies productively integrate the work of colleagues from other disciplines. For example, the work of ethnographers such as Clifford Geertz, James Clifford, and John Van Maanen has found a place in our discipline, as has the work of usability specialists such as Alan Cooper and Donald Norman and cyber-ethnographers Bonnie Nardi and Vicki O'Day, all of whom pay avid attention to participant observation and the narrative constructions that result.

Although we have been encouraged and influenced by a relatively broad cross-disciplinary interest in and attention to narrative, our basic technology autobiography prompt is modeled on the examples set forth by teachers who have used and written about literacy autobiographies (Brandt, Soliday, Eldred, and Mortensen). For these teachers, the value of the literacy autobiography is the way in which it helps reveal deeply personal but largely unspoken reading and writing practices and contexts that students bring with them to the classroom. We assign technology autobiographies for much the same reason: In writing narratively and autobiographically about their own relationships to technology, students reveal both idiosyncratic and culturally embedded responses to rapid technological changes. As teachers in technology-rich teaching environments, we not only want, but also *need*, to understand the range of these responses so we can construct effective teaching and learning environments that work for the majority of students.

About the Assignment

Formally, the four of us began assigning technology autobiographies in first-year composition and other types of classes about four years ago. Informally, we had begun to collect short autobiographical writings about individuals' relationships with technology somewhat earlier (see <http://www.hu.mtu.edu/~kitalong/adept/>). We have found the technology autobiography assignment to be readily adaptable; we have assigned these autobiographies to students at six different institutions in several different kinds of classes and curricular contexts (see Table 1).

Whenever we assign technology autobiographies, we begin with essentially the same assignment, which consists of a series of basic questions (see Table 2). Although we try to keep this set of questions constant, we each devise our own variations on the assignment to accommodate the particular goals of different classes, as the examples provided later in this chapter illustrate. As teachers, the data we gather about students through variations of the technology autobiography assignment are beneficial in several ways.

First, the information students provide in their technology autobiographies helps us determine the level of software and hardware knowledge students possess when they enter our classes. This information enables us to assess individual students' technical skills and content knowledge early in the semester, which, in turn, allows us to adjust course content a bit to accommodate the students who actually show up, instead of working solely from our assumptions about the students' abilities and needs. In one of Karla Kitalong's composition courses, for example, almost two-thirds of the students revealed significant skill and experience in web development. For Kitalong, then, it made sense to shift the pedagogy away from the teacher-centered HTML demonstrations that she had planned and toward small-group learning, with the more experienced students helping their peers.

To get at specific aspects of technology knowledge, we sometimes assign variations on the technology autobiography assignment. For example, technology autobiographies assigned in a service-learning-based composition course might ask students to explain their experience with, attitudes toward, or concerns about technologies used in the service context. Similarly, when the course's focus is on film or the visual arts, students can be asked specific questions about their experiences with film or digital camera technology. In our own technical communication curricula, autobiographies assigned in a publication management class can ask students to highlight any prior experiences they may have had with the publishing industry while those assigned in a technical communication pedagogy course can elicit students' teaching experiences. Regardless of the particular focus of a course, we have found that such variations on the technology autobiography assignment allow us to understand the range of experiences and attitudes represented in the present class while also helping us amass a repertoire of examples and resource people for future courses.

Table 1. Contexts for Assigning the Technology Autobiographies

Clemson University:
- First-year composition
- Publications management (graduate technical communication majors)

Michigan Technological University:
- First-year composition
- Technical communication service course (undergraduate; several sections)
- Publications management (undergraduate technical communication majors)
- Literacy, society, technology, and education (graduate course)

University of Central Florida:
- First-year composition (honors and regular; multiple sections)
- Visual communication (undergraduate technical communication majors)
- Technical communication service course (undergraduate)
- Technical communication pedagogy (graduate)
- Digital literacies for the liberal arts student

University of Arizona:
- First-year composition
- Creative nonfiction (undergraduate)
- Developmental writing (undergraduate)

Breadloaf School of English:
- Literacy, electracy, democracy (graduate and teacher training)

University of Nebraska at Omaha:
- Technical communication service course (undergraduate)
- Introductory technical communication certificate course (undergraduate and graduate)

Villa Julie College:
- first-year composition (undergraduate)
- technical writing (undergraduate)
- literature and technology (undergraduate)

Table 2. Basic Questions for Technology Autobiography Prompt

- Recall your earliest experiences with technological devices or artifacts.
- What were they?
- What do you remember about using them?
- What were the popular gadgets in your house while you were growing up?
- What does it mean to be technologically literate?
- Whom do you identify as being most technologically "literate" in your life?
- How does your technological literacy measure up to others'?

- What technologies are on your desk at home?
- What technologies are you carrying now?
- What technologies are on your technological "wish list"?
- Do you think there are social consequences or potential impacts on your lifestyle that depend on your technological capabilities?

- How do you expect to deal with new technologies in the future?
- What advantages—and what problems—do you see with the way you approach technology?
- What is your preferred way of learning new technologies?
- In what ways does good documentation help you adapt to technological change? What type of documentation helps most?

Technology autobiographies not only reveal an analytic view of individual students' available technology skills, values, and attitudes, but they also allow us to envision the bigger picture. By collecting technology autobiographies across classes and curricula, we gain access to a comparative body of knowledge about students' technological patterns and habits of mind, written in their own words. Barton and Barton call this big picture a "synoptic" view and note that it encourages comparison, contrast, and pattern seeking, all of which produce a different kind of understanding than does the individual, in-depth analytical view (Barton and Barton 141). To date, we have employed the synoptic view in our composition courses largely to understand generational differences in technology-related behaviors, habits of mind, and attitudes and to examine institutional structures surrounding technology. Other teachers might wish to take up gender, race, or class-based differences.[1] For technical communication students, this collective data has proven useful in audience analysis, usability testing, and user-centered design. Together, then, the analytic and synoptic views describe more fully students' approaches to technology and enable us to collaborate with students in the design of technology-rich composition and technical communication classes (Kitalong, Selfe, Moore, forthcoming; Selfe, unpublished ms).

On a more pragmatic level, a final benefit accrues from our collection of technology autobiographies. As teachers in technology-rich environments, we often struggle with how best to integrate tools or skills into classes already packed with important content. Two of us (Kitalong and Bridgeford) have found that the technology autobiography provides a convenient and non-threatening context within which students can practice software skills and explore typical genres. In short, the basic technology autobiography assignment has evolved into other creative forms that can be integrated into a variety of classes. In the next section, we will outline specific adaptations of the assignment that accommodate a wide range of teaching goals and learning objectives.

Variations on the Theme

Depending on the type of class, we each freely vary the basic technology autobiography assignment so that we can collect the kind of analytical data we need to design the most effective learning environment for our students while simultaneously retaining the essential questions with which we collect the synoptic data—the components of the big picture—that have become so crucial to our ongoing research. We have used many of the examples that follow in our technical communication courses; as you will undoubtedly recognize, the assignment can be adapted for use in many different types of writing classes.

Intergenerational Technology Understanding

A serendipitous occasion in Michael Moore's introductory technical communication course several years ago led to a fascinating new variation on the basic technology autobiography assignment. Most of his students were engineering majors who had enrolled only because the course was required. Undaunted, Moore began the class by assigning students to write what we consider the "standard" technology autobiography, using the essential questions outlined in Figure 2. Once he had collected their writings, Moore engaged the students in an in-class discussion about genre and convention, asking questions such as the following:

- Why did most of you submit your TA in the standard essay genre—$8\frac{1}{2}$-inch x 11-inch paper with one-inch margins?
- Do you ever feel free to work beyond those conventions?
- Do you think this genre is humanities-specific; that is, where do you see the narrative or essay genre in engineering?

To spur students toward thinking about the group projects that comprised the major component of the course, Moore then engaged them in responding to the following discussion prompts, variations of which might work well in a service learning composition course.

- What attitudes and assumptions about technology in general and communication technologies in particular do you see in your own autobiography?
- Can any of these attitudes and assumptions help you configure your project(s) for this class? For example, can you gain insights about what to do about differing levels of expertise among and between group members? About group or audience members' ambivalence toward technology?
- Should you ask your clients or target audience members to write technology autobiographies?

In the process of explaining the technology autobiographies, Moore had told the class about a book chapter several of us had written (Kitalong, Selfe, and Moore, forthcoming), mentioning his desire to collect autobiographies from parents and others. One student, Jeff Good, said he would ask his dad to write a technology autobiography. Another jokingly volunteered his mom to do the assignment for extra credit. Moore followed up by recasting the original assignment as a letter to parents so that interested students could solicit these optional intergenerational technology autobiographies. As a result, Moore collected a surprisingly large number of technology autobiographies from the parents of his students, many of whom seemed eager to participate and flattered at having been asked.

The synoptic view afforded by reviewing the parents' writings alongside those of his students revealed to Moore a series of economic metaphors—the "coin" people attach to ownership of technology and expertise in its use. Moore immediately saw a connection between the economic associations expressed in the collection of intergenerational technology autobiographies and Brandt's observation that the literacy interviews she conducted were "filled with examples of how economic and political forces, some of them originating in quite distant corporate and government policies, affect people's day-to-day ability to seek out and practice literacy" ("Sponsors" 172). Thus, Moore's own scholarship was enriched by his unplanned access to the multigenerational technology autobiographies of his students and their parents.

Moreover, Moore believes that teachers and students can explicate some of the privilege and entitlement that comes with access to technology (McGee) when they focus on the economic metaphors embedded in the TAs. In fact, he observes that value judgments such as "efficiency," "fast," "advancements," "easier," and "innovation" are all imbued with economic qualities. Attempts in composition studies to analyze unequal access to technology and other resources in terms of race and class can also provide a good analytic lens for reading and building on TAs in ways that can help interrogate the sometimes-invisible structures of privilege (Isaksen), thereby promoting a critical link between technology and literacy. Another possible trajectory combines discussions of students' and parents' experiences, attitudes, and assumptions with critical approaches to computer-mediated pedagogy. For example, many of the TA responses that Moore received reflected a normative, white, heterosexual, mostly male ideology and world-view. Moore then encouraged the students, now armed with their parents' perspectives as illustrated in their TAs, to pay another level of attention to the technological ideas with which they had grown up.

Subsequently, Karla Kitalong developed an assignment, the intergenerational technology biography, for her culturally diverse first-year composition course, the theme of which is "Technology, Identity, and Community." After writing a "standard" technology autobiography, each student interviews an individual at least ten years older or younger than she or he is, and then writes a research essay based on that interview. These essays benefit students by affording them an early introduction to the art of conducting informational interviews and citing primary sources. In addition, since the students are, perhaps not surprisingly, often unaware of the circumstances that drive life decisions, they gain a great deal from their interviews with parents, grandparents, aunts, uncles, and neighbors who grew up in places like Puerto Rico, India, Tibet, South Africa, Hong Kong, the Philippines, Algiers, Taiwan, and many parts of the United States and Europe. The hardships of immigration, exile, death, poverty, illness, and adversity—often masked by the ordinary routine of daily life or forgotten in the face of success and triumph—are recalled in the pages of an intergenerational technology autobiography.

By recasting these narratives as coherent papers, students not only learn about the technological influences on another person's life but also learn something about themselves. Those who have chosen to interview children marvel at how readily "youngsters" learn to use tools and how deeply they comprehend the issues that accompany a technologically enriched lifestyle. As they research and write their intergenerational technology biographies, then, students come to understand their own technology learning patterns better. Simultaneously, they begin to recognize that even seemingly mundane lives have almost inevitably been enriched, complicated, or irrevocably changed by technology, an insight that broadens their definition of *technology*. Finally, their work adds in unexpected ways to the synoptic view of how individuals accommodate themselves to technology.

A New View of Audience Analysis

Reading technology autobiographies can provide insights into the practice of audience analysis. We have used this approach with technical communication students in particular, but any students who are asked to consider the rhetorical triumvirate of audience, purpose, and context could make use of technology autobiographies in this way. In a publications management class, Dickie Selfe and Michael Moore ask technical communication majors to produce documentation for the department's computer lab; because all the students enrolled in the class are also avid users of the lab, they read each others' autobiographies to gain insights for audience analysis. Similarly, students assigned to write "real-world" documents like newspaper editorials could benefit from understanding the views of a representative sample of their peers.

The teacher of the class can also use this assignment as a form of audience analysis. When Dickie Selfe taught a graduate publications management class during a sabbatical year at Clemson University, he asked students to write what he calls TAPAs—Technology Autobiography/Publication Autobiographies. The publication autobiography component of the assignment helped students to articulate what they already knew about the publishing industry and publications management. These autobiographies also helped Selfe assess the students' knowledge and identify students who might be willing to share their knowledge with others in the class. Even if students are reluctant to present information formally to the class about their areas of expertise, they may willingly answer informal questions, contribute useful resource material, or help identify potential guest speakers. Knowing a little more about their students' views and levels of experience before the course starts can also help teachers group students for peer review and small-group assignments.

In a technical communication pedagogy course, Karla Kitalong's University of Central Florida graduate students wrote TATAs—Technology Autobiography/Teaching Autobiographies. The TATAs were posted on WebCT, where each student read the others' work to gain insight into a range of different learning preferences. The TATAs also exposed the less experienced teachers in the class to insights gained by those with previous classroom experience.

Practice with Tools and Forms

Karla Kitalong has made the technology autobiography the primary context for visual communication students' tool instruction. Throughout the semester, as they learn, practice, and experiment with key design and layout software, understand the principles of typography, develop information graphics, and learn basic web design, Kitalong's students produce a half-dozen successive versions of their technology autobiographies. Although the assignment is intended primarily as a practical context within which students can learn about software, Kitalong has noticed that some interesting critical thinking takes place at the juncture of visual and verbal narrative.

The "self-portrait-with-technology" assignment, which is designed to provide students with Adobe PhotoShop practice, inspired Tim, an older student who has worked as a professional printer and a grant writer. In his self-portrait, he superimposed a 1970 image of himself and a downloaded mug shot of Bill Gates onto a clip-art image of Mount Rushmore. In revising his autobiography to accommodate the graphic, Tim expressed ambivalence about the easy relationship he now has with technology and wondered whether the 1970-era Tim would accuse the present-day Tim of selling out to commercialism. In the same class, Lydia's PhotoShop visual encapsulated a lifetime of technological and cultural transformation. A recent immigrant to Central Florida from her native China, Lydia blended three images in her self-portrait: a clip-art Chinese pagoda formed the backdrop for an image of baby Lydia in her mother's arms standing beside the young adult Lydia, originally photographed in front of her Orlando apartment building.

When Kitalong's visual communication students looked for statistics or numerical data to use in their technology autobiographies and employed Microsoft Excel to create a graph or chart, other critical thinking resulted. Donna, co-owner of a family business and the married mother of three, designed an information graphic to show what percentage of women self-identified with each of four working-woman roles. She then revised her text to acknowledge that on the one hand, she herself is a "June Cleaver" in that she believes in the "traditional roles of stay-at-home-moms and breadwinner dads." On the other hand, she also sees herself as a "Mother of Invention," one who shares home and family responsibilities with a supportive husband. By positioning herself against statistics about women's attitudes toward work, Donna pointed out that many women are hybrids—not easily compartmentalized as one "type" of working woman. For her, as for many other working women, technology is a tool to be used to achieve "balance between home and work," to juggle the sometimes competing "roles as wife, mother, entrepreneur, and student."

After writing a traditional first draft, another student, Hayley, constructed her final technology autobiography to resemble a chronological résumé. In the introduction, she wrote, "My résumé promises its readers that [I have] the ability to use a variety of technologies." After telling several compelling stories about her technology adventures and misadventures, she ended by saying, "Whether or not I am judged by the skills listed on my résumé, it is important to note that my résumé does not mention my most important skill— that of being a mother." Like Donna, Hayley hopes to use technology to allow her to blend home and work more successfully. Hayley learns new technologies not just to improve her technical communication career prospects but also to make aspects of her life easier—managing household affairs; teaching her three-year-old son his letters and numbers; compiling, editing, and producing her church's newsletter; and keeping in touch with family, friends, and babysitters.

Tim, Lydia, Donna, and Hayley were exceptional students in many ways, but Kitalong particularly noted the ambivalence they expressed about their own relationships with technology. The freedom to experiment with visuals and layouts helped the students hone their software skills; simultaneously, it demonstrated to them that integrating the visual with the verbal can generate new knowledge and insights.

Indirect Access to Technology Perceptions

Tracy Bridgeford has developed the most unusual version of the technology autobiography assignment—she asks technical communication students to write technology biographies of characters in a novel that is included in her course reading. In the technology biography, students describe and analyze a particular character's world-view and relationship to technology. In addition, they connect that character's perspective with their own technological attitudes, preferences, and habits of mind. This variation on the technology autobiography assignment affords an indirect entry point for students to consider how technology shapes their own and others' perceptions. Bridgeford uses this assignment in a technical communication course, but teachers who assign literature or literary nonfiction in their technology-intensive composition courses might also find it a useful alternative to standard literary analysis assignments.

Each of Bridgeford's technical communication classes revolves around a particular theme such as environmentalism. She identifies several technical documents that, upon first reading, seem straightforward, objective and neutral; environment-related examples might include the Environmental Protection Act of 1970 plus related documents such as grant application forms, reports, descriptions, processes, and procedures. In presenting these documents as technical communication exemplars, she calls students' attention to attributes such as style, tone, clarity, audience, content, organization, formatting, and production methods. To encourage them to think about the sociopolitical contexts surrounding a particular type of document, she also selects a novel on which she bases individual and in-class exercises. In courses with an environmental theme, for example, she might assign Scott Russell Sanders's *Terrarium*, a dystopian novel depicting a futuristic, overpolluted Earth that has become inhospitable to humans.

Students do a variety of assignments based on the novel. For example, they may write a progress report addressed to a specific character in which they evaluate problem-solving methods, summarize information, or describe collaborative methods. Or they may write technical process descriptions, procedures, or instructions for mechanical or cognitive operations depicted in the novel; write and produce fact sheets based on events in the novel; or construct a glossary that guides a particular audience to an understanding of terms necessary for comprehending events that occur in the story. The technology biographies in which students articulate a particular character's relationships to technology fit into this series of assignments.

Bridgeford's technology biography assignment prompt includes three questions:

- What is the character's relationship to technology? In other words, describe what technology figures in the character's life and work and what role that technology plays.
- What does this character's relationship to technology indicate about his or her world-view? In other words, how does this character's relationship to technology determine (at least in part) how the character understands his or her world?

Using these initial questions, Bridgeford guides students to describe their chosen character's relationship to technology; in so doing, she alerts them to ways in which that relationship may be indicative of the world-view to which the character subscribes. Finally, her third question directs students to describe their own relationships to technology.

- What does your choice of character indicate about your own relationship to technology and world-views?

With this final question, she invites students to consider how an individual's relationship to technology influences his or her world-view and to extend that consideration by articulating the features of their own relationships to technology.

Bridgeford has found that she must make clear to students from the outset that technology biographies are not narratives about technology but rather narratives that interpret how technology shapes world-views. With this assignment she tries to encourage students not to simply describe but also to interpret how technology shapes their selves and their worlds.

Conclusion

When we first started assigning technology autobiographies in our classes, we thought that it was important to keep the assignments as similar as possible so that we could collect comparable bodies of data. Indeed, it is important to have a synoptic view—to gather more-or-less equivalent blocks of data that can be compared across space and time. As we have shown, however—and as Lynch, George, and Cooper attest—"emulating others' classroom practice is tricky" largely because "you always need to determine what exactly in the practice is appropriate and applicable to your own teaching situation" (411). Even though we developed these assignments together, we are four different people who teach in very different institutions and have different pedagogical ambitions. Therefore, our individual "takes" on the assignments have diverged. When it makes sense to do so, we still keep the same basic questions, but we add and subtract as needed to fit our own agendas.

As you can undoubtedly tell, we find that assigning technology autobiographies has many benefits for us as teachers and scholars. We'll close by emphasizing that having our students write technology autobiographies benefits our students almost as much as it benefits us. First, the technology autobiography provides an opportunity for students to reflect on their own attitudes and practices concerning technology. We have found that even within the technology-rich institutions and curricula in which we teach, students seldom consciously reflect on their relationship with technology other than to consider how best to engage with it as a tool. Given a reason to articulate their definitions of technology; to recall their earliest experiences with technology; and to examine the evolution and current state of their technology attitudes, habits, and practices, most of them gain new insights that they are quick to share with us. In fact, Michelle and Mary Ellen, two experienced teachers who enrolled in Karla Kitalong's technical communication pedagogy course, devised their own version of the technology autobiography, which they termed the TATL (Technology Autobiography/Time Line). In this version, students combined narrative and self-reflection with historical research to produce information graphics that depicted their personal technological history.

Moreover, students benefit from reading the technology autobiographies of some or all of the other students in the class. After they have developed an analytic viewpoint on their own relationship with technology, they can move on to a synoptic or big-picture perspective by observing how their views and approaches are similar to or different from those of their classmates. We believe that such a comparative view may instill in students an increased confidence in their own ideas, help them gain insights into how others think, and suggest to them appropriate technology and content goals and visions that they may wish to set for themselves.

In short, as narrative tools for critical analysis, the autobiographies that students write and read as part of our technology-rich courses help them see themselves not as isolated individuals struggling with or enamored of technology but rather as participants in a larger technological culture. Narrative reflections allow us to collect and analyze comparative data. In addition, they offer students the opportunity to explicate their relationships with technology while also reinforcing the link between literacy and technology. In articulating their own attitudes, practices, and habits of mind concerning technology, students gain new insights into the role of technology in their world and learn new strategies for teaching and learning in a technological society.

Note

[1] See Moore's early attention to critical race theory and economic metaphors discussed later in this chapter.

Works Cited

Barton, Ben F., and Marthalee S. Barton. "Modes of Power in Technical and Professional Visuals." *JBTC* 7 (1993): 138–62.

Bloom, Leslie R. *Under the Sign of Hope.* Albany: SUNY P, 1998.

Brandt, Deborah. "Accumulating Literacy: Writing and Learning to Write in the Twentieth Century." *College English* 57 (1995): 649–68.

Brandt, Deborah. *Literacy as Involvement: The Acts of Writers, Readers, and Texts.* Carbondale: Southern Illinois UP, 1990.

Brandt, Deborah. "Sponsors of Literacy." *College Composition and Communication* 49 (1998): 165–85.

Bridgeford, Tracy B. "A Narrative Way of Knowing Technology." Paper presented at Computers and Writing. Muncie Indiana. May 2001.

Clifford, James, and George E. Marcus, eds. *Writing Culture: The Poetics and Politics of Ethnography.* Berkeley: U of California P, 1986.

Cooper, Alan. *The Inmates Are Running the Asylum: Why High Tech Products Drive Us Crazy and How to Restore the Sanity.* Indianapolis, IN: SAMS, 1999.

Eldred, Janet C., and Peter Mortensen. "Reading Literacy Narratives." *College English* 54 (1992): 512–39.

Feenberg, Andrew. *Critical Theory of Technology.* New York: Oxford UP, 1991.

Frantz, Andrea B. *Cases in Technical Communication.* New York: Wadsworth, 1998.

Garay, Mary S., and Stephen A. Bernhardt. *Expanding Literacies: English Teaching and the New Workplace.* Albany: SUNY P, 1998.

Geertz, Clifford. *Local Knowledge: Further Essays in Interpretive Anthropology.* New York: Basic Books, 1983.

Isaksen, Judy L. "From Critical Race Theory to Composition Studies: Pedagogy and Theory Building." *Legal Studies Forum* 24 (2000): 695–710.

Johnson, Robert R. *User-Centered Technology: A Rhetorical Theory for Computers and Other Mundane Artifacts.* Albany, NY: SUNY P, 1998.

Keller, Evelyn F. "Feminism and Science." *Feminism and Science.* Ed. Evelyn F. Keller and Helen E. Longino. New York: Oxford UP, 1996.

Kitalong, Karla S. "Beyond Tool Vision: A Software Odyssey for Technical Communicators." Paper presented at Computers and Writing. Muncie, Indiana. May 2001.

Kitalong, Karla S., Dickie Selfe, and Michael Moore. "Technology Autobiographies and Student Participation in English Studies Literacy Classes." *Teaching Writing in the Late Age of Print.* Ed. Jeffrey Galin and J. Paul Johnson. New York: Hampton Press, forthcoming.

Kynell, Teresa, and Wendy K. Stone. *Scenarios for Technical Communication: Critical Thinking and Writing.* Boston: Allyn & Bacon, 1998.

Latour, Bruno. *Science in Action: How to Follow Scientists and Engineers Through Society.* Cambridge, MA: Harvard UP, 1988.

Lynch, Dennis A., Diana L. George, and Marilyn M. Cooper. Afterword. "Moments of Argument: Inquiry and Confrontational Cooperation." *On Writing Research: The Braddock Essays 1975–1998.* Ed. Lisa Ede. Boston: Bedford–St. Martin's, 1999.

Lynch, Kimberly. "Participatory Literacy: Response on and between the Line(s)." *Issues in Writing* 7 (1994): 62–86.

Lyotard, Jean Francois. *The Postmodern Condition: A Report on Knowledge.* Trans. Brian Massumi. U of Minnesota P, 1985.

McGee, Michael C. "The 'Ideograph': A Link Between Rhetoric and Ideology." *Quarterly Journal of Speech* 64 (1980): 1–16.

Moore, Michael. "Literacy, Technology, and Narrative: How Students Perceive the 'Virtual.'" Paper presented at Computers and Writing. Muncie, Indiana. May 2001.

Nardi, Bonnie A., and Vicki L. O'Day. *Information Ecologies: Using Technology with Heart.* Cambridge, MA: MIT P, 2000.

Norman, Donald. *The Design of Everyday Things.* New York: Doubleday, 1990.

Savage, Gerald G., and Dale L. Sullivan. *Writing a Professional Life: Stories of Technical Communicators On and Off the Job.* Boston: Allyn and Bacon, 2000.

Selfe, Richard J. "Learning with Students: Technology Autobiographies in the Classroom and Curriculum." Unpublished manuscript.

Soliday, Mary. "Translating Self and Difference Through Literacy Narratives." *College English* 56 (1994): 511–26.

Star, Susan L. *The Cultures of Computing.* London: Blackwell, 1995.

Sullivan, Patricia, and Jennie Dauterman, eds. *Electronic Literacies in the Workplace: Technologies of Writing.* Urbana, IL: NCTE; Houghton, MI: Computers and Composition, 1996.

Van Maanen, John. *Tales of the Field: On Writing Ethnography.* Chicago: U of Chicago P, 1988.

Winsor, Dorothy. *Writing Like an Engineer: A Rhetorical Education.* Mahwah, NJ: Erlbaum, 1996.

Responding to and Assessing Student Writing: The Uses and Limits of Technology

CHRIS M. ANSON
North Carolina State University

Whenever administrators of writing programs are asked why they can't add more students to each section of a composition course, their answer usually points to the teacher's tasks of reading, commenting on, and evaluating student writing. Writing classes are necessarily small because writing must be *read*: because every student's work needs to be considered slowly, carefully, and insightfully, with a critical pedagogical eye that translates impressions (of the learner, of the text, and of their places in the course and curriculum) into wise pedagogical responses that then must be put into just the right language to encourage learning and rethinking. This responsibility, enacted on paper after paper written by two dozen students in each of three or four or even five courses per term, is what teachers take home with them after a day of classroom instruction, office hours, and meetings. It is a responsibility that translates a typical full-time teaching assignment into a commitment of between sixty and seventy hours of work per week (WPA 2001) and has led to the establishment of national labor standards for class size and course loads (CCCC 1991).

Amidst these realities, the allure of current and future technology is not surprising even in a praxis with deep interpersonal and humanistic roots. We like to believe that someday machines might relieve us of the need to read piles of students' writing. We could pontificate and guide and orchestrate—and leave the challenges of response and evaluation to a sophisticated piece of software with an inventory of deeply programmed suggestions expertly matched to a thousand linguistic and rhetorical features manifested in hundreds of thousands of possible student papers.

This chapter on the uses of technology begins with the claim that human response, at least but not always by teachers, and at least but perhaps not always in a face-to-face context, can never yield to machines if our goal is to help students to be more effective, insightful writers. By dispelling any hopes and quashing any myths about the potential of new technology to *formulate* responses, I hope to turn to the bright side of technology—to how we can put new technologies to work for us in the enhancement and situational extension of our expertise: reading students' work thoughtfully and providing careful, individual response to it and evaluation of it in ways that promote learning.

Why Computers Can't (Yet) Read Responsively

In an era of burgeoning new technologies, it may seem that the moment is not far off when a computer might be able to read an extended piece of discourse and do something intelligent with it. In reality, many computer programs now exist that can "do something with" a piece of text—even find the gist of a long news report and turn that report into a two-line summary suitable, perhaps, for a broadcast. Such programs have been under development for decades (see Shank and Abelson 1977).

But language is messy and complicated, and no computer has been able to come close to doing what the average teacher "does with" a piece of student writing. Even one of the oldest hopes for computers in the realm of natural language—simple machine translation—has remained quite limited to date, though programs continue to improve. Although most programs do well translating simple, very literal sentences from one language to another or providing the gist, say, of a foreign web site's contents, performing even slightly more complex tasks is far beyond their capacities. Consider a popular translation program, one sponsored by Babelfish at Alta Vista, which renders incomprehensible a line from a first-year student's paper when it is translated from English to French and then back to English:

> *Original:* It is ironic that some people on the religious right think it is fine to send a man to the gas chamber or fry him in an electric chair while these same fundamentalists blow up abortion clinics (and murder abortion doctors) because they think abortion is murder.

> *Translation:* It is ironic that certain on the religious line think it must send a man very well has the gas room or make it fry in an electric chair while these same fundamentalist makes jump of the private clinics of suspension (and assassinate doctors of suspension) because they think that the suspension is murder. (<http://babelfish.altavista.com>)

A similar translation program at Freetranslation.com produces an even more garbled response when the student's sentence goes from English to German and back:

Translation: It are belay send should roast ironically that some people thinks on the religious right that it with a fine of the gases chamber a man, or it in an electric chair during this same fundamentalists blow on abortion clinic (and murder abortion doctor) because they think, that abortion murder is. (<http://www.freetranslation.com/>)

If some of our most sophisticated programming is unable to "read" a line in English from a student's paper, translate it accurately into another of the dozen most-used languages in the world, and translate it back again into readable English, no computer system in our lifetimes will be able to read a student paper and offer more than rudimentary responses, such as preprogrammed comments on lexical density, sentence structures, or estimates about "support for generalizations" based on trigger words such as *for example.* Nor will any piece of software even begin to provide the sort of sophisticated "translation" of our interpretations and impression-based reasoning into advice and pedagogical forms of response for students that teachers of writing dole out on a daily basis (see Anson "Reflective Reading").

In the area of machine scoring of student writing, several powerful computer programs are now being marketed with the aim of providing a reliable way to numerically evaluate large samples of student writing. But critiques of their underlying goals and mechanisms have raised serious questions about their usefulness for classroom instruction. In an exploration of recently marketed essay-scoring programs such as WritePlacer Plus and the Intelligent Essay Assessor, Herrington and Moran show both the limits of the programs (which are designed mainly to score essays on simple criteria, not to offer richly contextualized responses to them or to explain in detail the many aspects of an essay that led to a score) and their theoretical insufficiencies. "The final and overwhelming problem with these programs," they explain, "is that students are writing to a machine, not to human beings" (496). Their own writing, done to test the programs under scrutiny, felt to them "reduced, degraded . . . not words that might have an impact on another person and in some small way change the world" (497).

But even if we could program computers to read and respond thoughtfully to student texts, they would no doubt apply the same static process to their reading. Students submitting drafts of papers to such programs would receive feedback that could look at their paper only through one lens, and even if several lenses could be programmed (*Thoughtful, Impatient,* and *Charitable,* say), it would be very difficult for a program to weigh decisions, speculate about effects, or do the complex work of reading as oneself and then responding by imagining the perspectives of various members of other audiences. These relativities of reading, these multiple subjectivities, represent astonishingly complex and sophisticated intellectual operations that can't even be simulated, much less produced genuinely, by machines.

Perhaps more significant for the teacher of writing is the inability of new machine-scoring programs to work with samples of writing composed for prompts other than those designed for the scoring (see Herrington and Moran 486). Every teacher brings to the task of formulating writing assignments a wealth of contextual knowledge about his or her students; their backgrounds; their awareness of local, national, and international issues; the position of their work within the course; and the ideas to which they have been exposed in readings, class discussions, and class presentations. Every assignment is unique and uniquely a product of a specific classroom, its assumptions and directions winding like vines into and through the knowledge of how students themselves are growing in the classroom. Teachers reading the results of such context-specific assignments and prompts are looking for evidence of intellectual processes far beyond the usual generalized categories sought by machine-scoring programs, such as "focus, organization, development and support, and mechanical conventions" (see Herrington and Moran 486).

This is not to say that advances and refinements in artificial intelligence should never invade the domain of teaching and learning. Quite the contrary: Some of our greatest insights into the ways that humans process natural language have come to us from attempts to get computers to do the same things we do (Shank 1982, 1999; Dillon, Revonen, Rouet, and Spiro 1996; Spiro 1980). For our own purposes as teachers, however, there are far more immediately useful things that computer technology can do to enhance the human responses we provide to students and find so important for their development, and it is to these we'll now turn.

Using Technology to Improve and Enhance Teacher Response

There is no question that computer technology has vastly enhanced the way that people work with text and use it to communicate with each other and to disseminate knowledge. Recognizing that fact takes just a glimpse back to the days when typing had one font (until removable type balls could be tediously swapped for every word in italics), when poorly planned footnotes ran off the bottom of the page, and when a fresh copy of a page had to be retyped for every revision or editorial change, no matter how small. Now, the revolution that began with word processing continues in the realm of the Internet, which allows text to be sent and received instantly and provides new opportunities for collaborative work on those texts to take place in a range of electronic venues.

In the realm of response to student writing, innovations in both hardware and software are giving us the means to vary the nature and medium of our feedback to students and the feedback they provide to each other. Described next are several methods, beginning with those that can enhance teacher commentary and moving to those that enhance peer commentary or provide students with other kinds of feedback from which they can learn. Some methods, such as macros, are not new; others are developments still on the horizon but soon to be available to teachers.

Reading and Responding Online

When students submit their work on computer disks or as attached files via the Internet, the medium currently restricts the way we might respond to that work. It's difficult to write anything in the margins of the student's text without taking time to reformat the paper so that it divides the text space; the best we can do is to add carriage returns and write comments, perhaps in a different font, in between lines or paragraphs, a process which ends up breaking the students' original text and intruding on it. The fastest and most efficient way to respond to students' papers by using conventional word-processing programs is to type end comments or to create a separate file of commentary. Such commentary benefits, perhaps, from compelling us to think globally and to distill our many impressions into a paragraph or so of advice or suggestions. What it gains from pulling us out of the realm of small details, however, it loses in not allowing us to connect comments directly to specific words, phrases, or sentences.

There is little question that the technology used for many palm-held devices will soon become more widely and cheaply available to students and faculty for the submission and evaluation of papers. These devices have touch-sensitive screens that allow text to be highlighted or annotated in handwriting. Connecting such devices to a microcomputer will allow us to download students' papers into the device, write on the electronic essays as if they were written on paper, and then send them back to students with our comments and annotations. The benefits of such a process, while not extensive, include speed, efficiency, and the ability of the writer to make revisions onscreen instead of working between an annotated printout and an original text file.

Embedded Commentary

Another increasingly popular computer enhancement to both formative and summative response comes from the feature in newer word-processing programs that allows embedded commentary. Typically, a student submits a paper in electronic form, on a disk or as an attached file. Opening the paper on his or her computer, the instructor then decides where to place remarks and suggestions. An "insert comment" menu opens a text box into which the comment is typed. Later, the student can look at the annotated paper, which contains only icons or highlighted words to indicate the instructor's commentary. As the student scrolls over or clicks on these highlights, the instructor's commentary appears somewhere on the screen, then disappears as the student moves elsewhere in the paper.

In Figure 1, a highlighted pop-up window is shown over a page of student text; the shaded word shows the position in the paper where the comment was inserted. This example was created using the "insert comment" feature of Microsoft Word.

Embedded commentary offers several advantages over traditional marginal commentary. First, comments can be tied to specific words or parts of a

Figure 1
Screen Shot of Pop-Up Revealing Embedded Teacher Commentary

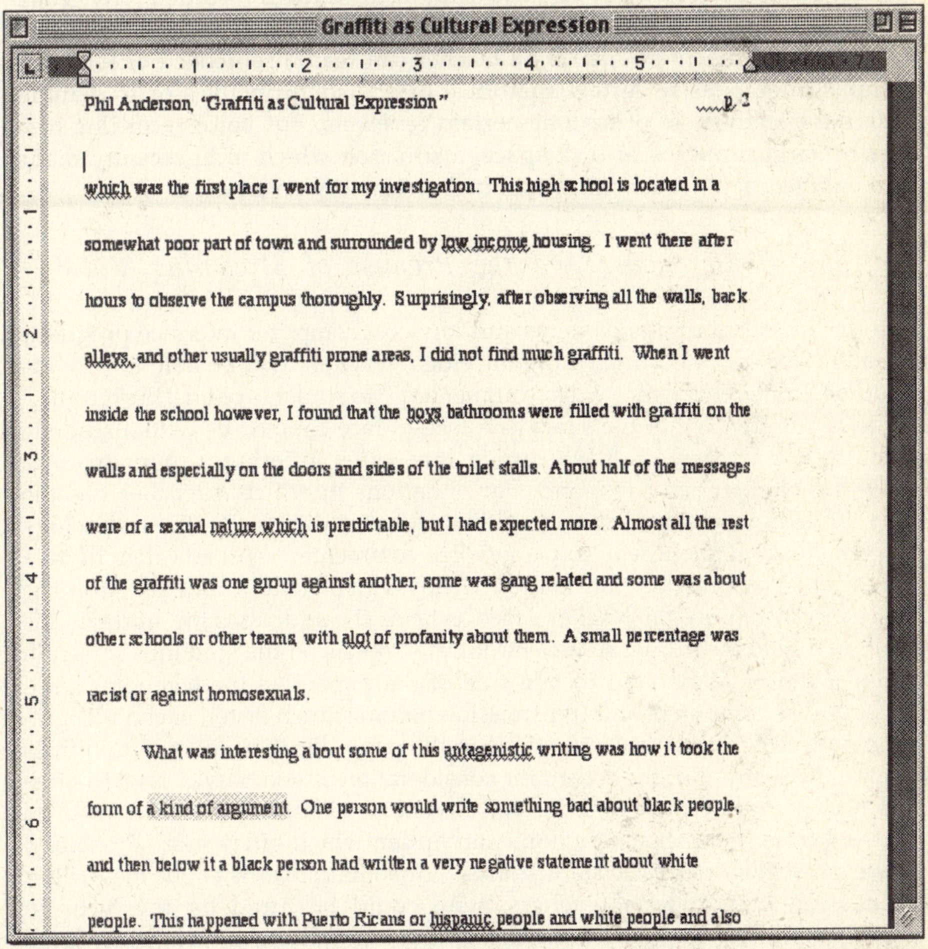

> **Graffiti as Cultural Expression**
>
> Phil Anderson, "Graffiti as Cultural Expression"   p. 2
>
> which was the first place I went for my investigation. This high school is located in a
>
> somewhat poor part of town and surrounded by low income housing. I went there after
>
> hours to observe the campus thoroughly. Surprisingly, after observing all the walls, back
>
> alleys, and other usually graffiti prone areas, I did not find much graffiti. When I went
>
> inside the school however, I found that the boys bathrooms were filled with graffiti on the
>
> walls and especially on the doors and sides of the toilet stalls. About half of the messages
>
> were of a sexual nature which is predictable, but I had expected more. Almost all the rest
>
> of the graffiti was one group against another, some was gang related and some was about
>
> other schools or other teams, with alot of profanity about them. A small percentage was
>
> racist or against homosexuals.
>
> What was interesting about some of this antagonistic writing was how it took the
>
> form of a kind of argument. One person would write something bad about black people,
>
> and then below it a black person had written a very negative statement about white
>
> people. This happened with Puerto Ricans or hispanic people and white people and also

[KG] You describe an interesting phenomenon in the graffiti you observed at Cranwell, but in addition to describing it, you might be able to do some deeper analysis if you pulled out some examples from your notes and included them in your paper, pointing to more specific characteristics.

---

text that precipitated them, showing the place at which a reader had a particular reaction. By providing marked or highlighted text, or discrete icons, embedded commentary creates a "hidden layer" of response that leaves the writer's text more or less intact and symbolically unmarred by the reader's own scrawl. Because comments appear one at a time, they are less likely to overwhelm or demoralize less experienced writers. Furthermore, because they're hidden from view, the writer needs to find and open each comment, a process which may encourage a more careful consideration of the responses. Comments can be removed from the paper during the revision process, a feature which may motivate the writer to make fuller and more considered revisions.

Embedded commentary can also come in the form of recorded (oral) voice responses instead of textual comments. The advantages of voice commentary are many (see Anson 1997, 2000); a teacher can read a sentence out loud, for example, to emphasize certain rhetorical or stylistic principles or to demonstrate the effectiveness of making certain revisions. But voice recording also takes up large amounts of disk space, a situation which until recently made them impractical for much more than making cursory remarks.

Electronic Conferencing and the Promise of Streaming Video

With the advent of digital cameras and low-cost computer interface programs that allow for quick editing of digital video, teachers will be able to provide one-to-one conferencing or "video commentary" to students online. Such conferencing is admittedly not the same as a face-to-face conference with a student; it's more like written feedback turned into video, offering a monologue to which the student can't respond. For situations in which a teacher has too many students to meet effectively with each one individually, the technology can provide an efficient way to personalize commentary and talk directly to a student about a draft or final paper. A tiny video camera that sits atop the computer can capture the teacher's face as he or she addresses the student. The resulting digital recording, sent electronically, opens on the student's screen in a small window above and to one side of the paper. As the technology improves and as computers and transmission become much faster, such videography may well be linked to animations in the paper itself, such as certain lines zooming to the front of the screen for consideration or text moves used to illustrate various principles of effective revision. "Conferences" can also be provided from the instructor's home, an option which offers more flexibility. (However, see my essay "Distant Voices" for some concerns about the further exploitation of part-time teachers, who could be hired by the hour to "telecommute" to campus as virtual graders of writing produced in large sections.)

The Perils and Possibilities of Macros

In most word processors, it's possible to create a "macro," a bit of text associated with a special keystroke or series of keystrokes, such as "F10" or "Control-Q-1." When the keystroke is used, that programmed piece of text is automatically inserted into a document wherever the cursor is placed. Early in the development of personal computers, the macro was sometimes used as an efficient means for offering commentary to students without having to retype the same message whenever the same concern arose. In some uses, macros were inserted into "boilerplate" text, much like canned holiday letters that leave blank spaces for the names of the recipients and a few remarks to deceive the reader into believing the letter is unique. The following are two sample macros (in italics) within the same piece of boilerplate commentary.

COMMENTARY A

Shaun: In responding to your paper, I've focused most of my attention on the four main issues we discussed and practiced in class. In regards to the first—overall coherence and organization of ideas—your paper *shows a clear and logical progression, with decent attention to the way in which one idea leads to the next and to the overall structure of the essay.* The second broad area . . .

COMMENTARY B

Becky: In responding to your paper, I've focused most of my attention on the four main issues we discussed and practiced in class. In regards to the first—overall coherence and organization of ideas—your paper *demonstrates an attempt to provide a coherent structure, but your transitions are somewhat weak so that it's not always clear how one idea moves into or relates to the next.* The second broad area . . .

In this example, both the possible advantages and the considerable limitations of the macro appear. Clearly, providing detailed commentary to students is made far less burdensome if the teacher can identify a particular strength or weakness and then offer the student several sentences or even entire paragraphs with the touch of a key. At the same time, macros must remain quite broad and unspecific because it's impossible to predict how a general criterion is or is not successfully met in a particular piece of discourse. Creating dozens of macros that anticipate many possible responses takes a long time, and the resulting chunks of text are hard to remember and apply quickly. Worse, in most writing classes students will soon realize that the responses they are getting are canned, and their effectiveness—as well as the teacher's credibility—may diminish.

Text Comparisons

Another feature of more sophisticated word-processing programs that is usually related to embedded commentary allows the writer or reader to compare two versions of the same text. After opening one version onscreen, the user accesses the "compare documents" feature and tells the computer the location of the document to be compared. The computer then opens the second document and highlights the changes made between the drafts, as shown in Figure 2.

Although this feature may not appear to fall into the realm of "response" to writing, it could be useful for teaching the revision process. Many inexperienced writers appear to lack an understanding of revision and the revising process (Sommers 1980). Using models of carefully and thoughtfully revised prose, teachers can visually display for students the extent and nature of changes that can occur between drafts. Students can be asked, during or after

Figure 2
Screen Shot Showing Tracked Changes in a Revised Draft

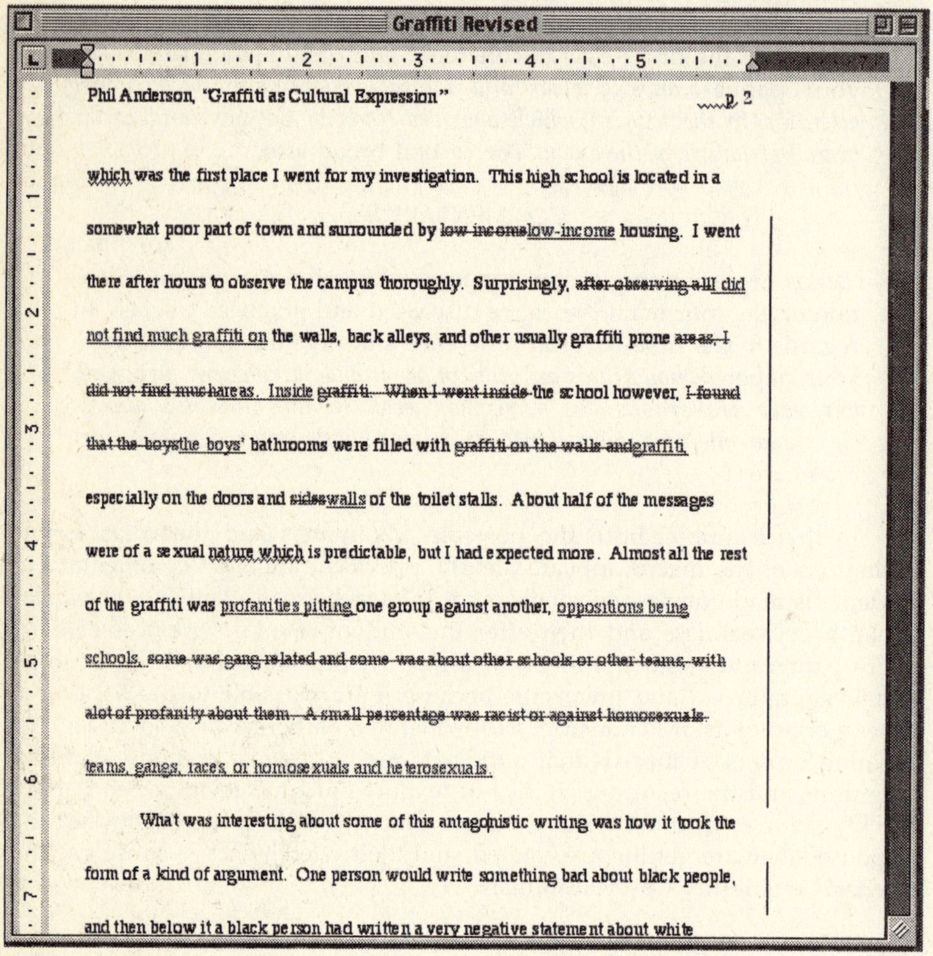

Graffiti Revised

Phil Anderson, "Graffiti as Cultural Expression"   p. 2

which was the first place I went for my investigation. This high school is located in a

somewhat poor part of town and surrounded by low incomeslow-income housing. I went

there after hours to observe the campus thoroughly. Surprisingly, after observing allI did

not find much graffiti on the walls, back alleys, and other usually graffiti prone areas, I

did not find much areas. Inside graffiti. When I went inside the school however, I found

that the boysthe boys' bathrooms were filled with graffiti on the walls andgraffiti

especially on the doors and sidoswalls of the toilet stalls. About half of the messages

were of a sexual nature which is predictable, but I had expected more. Almost all the rest

of the graffiti was profanities pitting one group against another, oppositions being

schools, some was gang related and some was about other schools or other teams, with

alot of profanity about them. A small percentage was racist or against homosexuals.

teams, gangs, races, or homosexuals and heterosexuals.

  What was interesting about some of this antagonistic writing was how it took the

form of a kind of argument. One person would write something bad about black people,

and then below it a black person had written a very negative statement about white

revising their own work, to provide a metastatement about the nature of their own changes after analyzing the draft comparisons provided by such programs.

Annotated Models for the Internalization of Criteria

Without clear expectations for their writing, students often have difficulty gauging their texts against any standards that might offer formative and productive feedback rather than the kind which is purely summative and evaluative. Annotated models are samples of writing (produced in response to a particular task or assignment) that contain expert reactions, advice, or reader-based commentary. By using some simple HTML formatting, an instructor can create a sample paper with "pop-up" annotations. As a student passes her cursor over a highlighted word or phrase, a window appears that contains some commentary about the word, line, or general place in the text.

The most effective annotated models are those that connect pop-up comments directly to stated criteria for successful texts in the genre being written or in response to a particular task. If the criteria are stated in several categories, students can click on one of the categories and go to a fresh copy of the model with annotations relating to the criteria under consideration. If the criteria are more "holistic" and generally descriptive, then pop-up comments can connect general impressions (triggered by certain features of the text) to the descriptive criteria.

Figure 3 shows a page from a sample paper in the genre of the article summary. The embedded comments relate to one criterion ("comprehension of the material") of five criteria on an analytical scale that is used to evaluate summaries, the others being "appropriateness of topic and reading," "sophistication of the discussion," "structure, length, and rhetorical quality," and "surface quality."

When provided in order to illustrate, define, or explain criteria, such annotated papers can help students to internalize certain features of successful performances, if only by exposure to and commentary on these features. Students can then transfer these new understandings to their own papers in progress. Computer technology offers a far more elegant and paper-saving way to display expert commentary than by circulating photocopies of annotated essays.

Technology Used to Support Peer Response and Evaluation

In addition to facilitating teacher commentary, computers have obvious and proven benefits in promoting peer response. Papers can be sent to peer groups easily and quickly, and the members of the group can respond in various ways described elsewhere in this chapter, such as through the use of embedded commentary. Teachers can examine peer responses against a student's revisions without having to cart home piles of drafts and other artifacts of peer work. Various uses of email, chat lines, forums, and listservs can also promote useful peer response, as has been demonstrated for more than a decade (Brown 1992; Bump 1990; Castner 1994). In recent years, more sophisticated programs have emerged to assist students in the process of providing peer response, such as Aspects <http://www.grouplogic.com/downloads/index.html>, Daedalus <http://www.daedalus.com/info/Overview.html>, Forum <http://www.foruminc.com>, and Norton Connect <http://www.wwnorton.com/connect/welcome.htm> (see Sands 1997 and Wooley 1996 for some comparisons). Research such as Honeycutt's study comparing asynchronous and synchronous networks (Honeycutt 2001) continue to explore the advantages and the shortcomings of various programs and media.

Figure 3
Screen Shot of Annotated Summary Showing One Set of Criteria

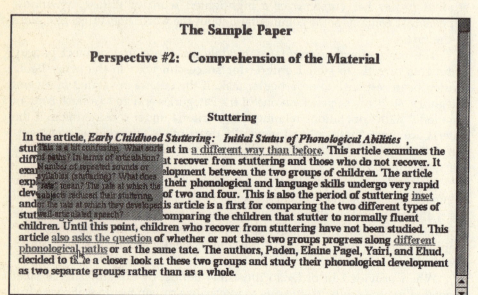

The Sample Paper

Perspective #2: Comprehension of the Material

Stuttering

In the article, *Early Childhood Stuttering: Initial Status of Phonological Abilities* , stut[...]at in a different way than before. This article examines the diff[...]t recover from stuttering and those who do not recover. It exa[...]elopment between the two groups of children. The article expl[...]their phonological and language skills undergo very rapid dev[...]of two and four. This is also the period of stuttering inset and[...]is article is a first for comparing the two different types of stut[...]comparing the children that stutter to normally fluent children. Until this point, children who recover from stuttering have not been studied. This article also asks the question of whether or not these two groups progress along different phonological paths or at the same tate. The authors, Paden, Elaine Pagel, Yairi, and Ehud, decided to take a closer look at these two groups and study their phonological development as two separate groups rather than as a whole.

Using Machine Text Analysis Thoughtfully

Finally, new computer technology is almost daily providing more sophisticated ways to identify certain textural features and characteristics for writers. These text-analytical programs are not new; very early in the development of personal computers, software companies began selling grammar programs or bundling them into word-processing software. The earliest provided primitive measures—they counted average sentence lengths or identified cases in which the writer had used a passive verb. Today, such grammar checks are far more sophisticated. MS Word, for example, offers instant checks on repeated words, unclear phrasing, jargon, sexist language, passive voice, sentence structure, relative clauses, verb agreement, and the like. Settings can be adjusted according to several "levels" of discourse or audiences, such as formal, technical, casual, or standard. Together with the ubiquitous spell checker and some other lexical aids such as thesauruses, these programs can locate trouble spots for writers quickly and efficiently.

As tools for developing writers, however, such programs also have their limitations. First, most of the problems the programs identify exist at an editorial level on the surface of the text: They deal with matters of style and some rudiments of grammar. Paying too much attention to the results can deceive students into thinking that once they have fixed the identified problems, they will have produced a successful text. Furthermore, no program can offer much help at the level of revision, which concerns large sections of a paper, issues of overall coherence and structure, persona, or sensitivity to audience.

At the same time, students can be asked to use these primitive grammar and style checks to learn something about their own texts, if only by having the computer ask questions about those texts. The robot-like application of rules also raises questions about when a decision, such as whether to use the passive voice or a very long sentence with many relative clauses, may be appropriate.

Conclusion

The few innovations described within this chapter will probably look primitive in a dozen or so years, the products of new technologies limited in speed, multimedia capabilities, and ease of use. But even more dazzling new media are still not likely to replace human response to student writing, response made by highly literate experts hired to help students to develop their literacies in multiple ways. Instead, these media and technologies will certainly enhance that human response, offering faster, more effective, and more meaningful ways to provide it and facilitate it. To ensure that what we do with new technologies is theoretically supportable, we need to accept progress with an experimental eagerness that allows us to assess the strengths and weaknesses of innovation and to use it when it best supports and enhances our work.

Works Cited

Anson, Chris M. "Distant Voices: Teaching and Writing in a Culture of Technology." *College English* 61.3 (1999): 1–20.

Anson, Chris M. "Reflective Reading: Developing Thoughtful Ways to Respond to Students' Writing." *Evaluating Writing: The Role of Teachers' Knowledge about Text, Learning, and Culture.* Ed. Charles R. Cooper and Lee Odell. Urbana, IL: NCTE, 1999. 302–24.

Anson, Chris M. "In Your Own Voice: Using Recorded Commentary to Respond to Writing." *Assigning and Responding to Writing in the Disciplines.* Ed. Peter Elbow and Mary D. Sorcinelli. San Francisco: Jossey-Bass, 1997. 105–13.

Anson, Chris M. "Talking About Text: The Use of Recorded Commentary in Response to Student Writing." *A Sourcebook on Responding to Student Writing.* Ed. Rick Straub. Norwood, NJ: Hampton, 2000. 165–74.

Brown, Lady F. "The Daedalus Integrated Writing Environment." *Computers and Composition* 10 (1992): 77–88.

Bump, Jerome. "Radical Changes in Class Discussion Using Networked Computers." *Computers and the Humanities* 24 (1990): 49–65.

Castner, Joanna. "Encouraging Peer Responding through InterChange." *Wings: A Newsletter for Users of Daedalus Integrated Writing Environment* 2.2

(1994). 25 July 2001. <http://www.daedalus.com/wings/castner.2.2.html>.

CCCC Executive Committee. "Statement of Principles and Standards for the Post-Secondary Teaching of Writing." *College Composition and Communication* 42.3 (1991): 330–44.

Dillon, Andrew, Jarmo J. Levonen, Jean-Francois Rouet, and Rand Spiro, eds. *Hypertext and Cognition*. Hillsdale, NJ: Erlbaum, 1996.

Honeycutt, Lee. "Comparing E-Mail and Synchronous Conferencing in Online Peer Response." *Written Communication* 18 (2001): 26–60.

Listserv of the Council of Writing Program Administrators. "Studies of Faculty Time," Discussion thread 9–13 Jan. 2001. <http://lists.asu.edu/cgi-bin/wa?A1=ind0101&L=wpa-l>.

Herrington, Anne, and Charles Moran. "What Happens When Machines Read Our Students' Writing?" *College English* 63.4 (2001): 480–99.

Sands, Peter. "Writing Software Comparisons." *Kairos* 2.2 (1997). 22 August 2001 <http://english.ttu.edu/kairos/2.2/reviews/sands/comparison.html>.

Schank, Roger C. *Dynamic Memory: A Theory of Learning in Computers and People*. Cambridge: Cambridge UP, 1982.

Schank, Roger C. *Dynamic Memory Revisited*. Cambridge: Cambridge UP, 1999.

Schank, Roger C., and Robert P. Abelson. *Scripts, Plans, Goals, and Understanding*. Hillsdale, NJ: Erlbaum, 1977.

Sommers, Nancy. "Revision Strategies of Student Writers and Experienced Adult Writers." *College Composition and Communication*, 31 (1980): 378–88.

Spiro, Rand. *Theoretical Issues in Reading Comprehension: Perspectives from Cognitive Psychology, Linguistics, Artificial Intelligence, and Education*. Hillsdale, NJ: Erlbaum, 1980.

Woolley, D. R. "Choosing Web Conferencing Software." *The 1996 International University Consortium Conference on WWW Course Development and Delivery*. 1996. 26 April 2001. <http://thinkofit.com/webconf/wcchoice.htm#goodconf>.

Evaluating Academic Hypertexts

CHARLES MORAN AND ANNE HERRINGTON
University of Massachusetts at Amherst

If we use the Internet at all, we are used to reading some sort of hypertext, whether it be a school's home page with links to departments, faculty, and administrative offices; a store's home page with links to the products that it sells; or a museum's page with links to holdings and a calendar of exhibits. What makes each of these a hypertext are the internal and external links. Students know this territory perhaps better than we do; web pages are out there as a "prose model," and even if we are not yet ready to assign hypertext projects, our students may ask to submit a hypertext composition for an assignment we had conceived of in terms of a conventional, non-hypertext composition. Just as it is harder and harder to forbid the inclusion of graphics in students' papers or to limit the percentage of research that students do on the Web, so also is it becoming harder and harder to forbid hypertext compositions. As an alternative to proscribing academic hypertexts, we suggest it is more interesting to think about permitting or even encouraging student writing in hypertext, writing to be read on web browsers and, of course, evaluated for a grade. When we do, we face the problem of evaluation. What is a "good" academic hypertext? The genre is evolving. Online journals such as *Kairos* present models of academic hypertext, articles that their authors will claim credit for in their personnel files. Students will not likely know of these online journals, much as they will not know of the print journals in our field. But they will know about commercial web pages, and they will draw on these as models.

In this chapter, we focus on the issue of evaluation. (For those wanting to learn more about developing hypertext/hypermedia assignments, we refer you to the De Witt and Strasma collection.) The issue of evaluation has been on our mind because recently each of us has been faced with the challenge of trying to evaluate a hypertext composition alongside conventional, non-hypertext compositions, all submitted for the same assignment. Both of us struggled with two questions: "What criteria should we use when evaluating academic hypertexts?" and "Is it possible to evaluate hypertext and non-hypertext compositions using the same criteria?"

For one of us (Anne), this was a first experience reading a student-composed, academic hypertext. And the experience was quite disorienting. Although the hypertext had an informative purpose to which she was accustomed, reading it was, for her, like being placed into an entirely new culture where she did not know the customs. So that she would have a record of the experience, she kept a reading log. Looking at it now, she sees her preoccupation with finding her way through the text, something that is not on her mind when she is reading a linear text. Here are a few of her log entries:

> Where to begin? . . . I'll read about site design first. . . . Now, where to go next?. . . The site map is sure different from the linear outline for a text essay. . . . I'm feeling that this is disjointed. . . . Wish all the sections took me back to the home page. . . . Ah, this section is more essay-like. . . . And that's it? Essay-reader that I am, I wanted a closing of some kind or feeling of closure.

The attention she had to give to navigating this new kind of text distracted her from attending to its substance and the logic of its linked structure. It also made her painfully aware that she did not have much basis for evaluating the hypertext because of her lack of familiarity with the conventions of this hypertext genre and lack of consideration of appropriate criteria. Thus, her interest in this present inquiry.

For Charlie, the experience was disorienting, too; though he had read student hypertexts before, they had been voluntary, "extra-credit" projects, and he had not felt the need to evaluate them carefully against traditional academic essays. Now, faced directly with the question "Is this hypertext composition better than, equal to, or less good than this traditional research paper?" he found himself wishing for the familiar features and navigating conventions of the traditional essay:

> Because I'm doing this at home, some of the far-flung web sites download very, very slowly—-looking at gravestones from the New London burial ground, I'm on the world-wide wait, which means that I can write in this journal as I wait! This was a good 45-second download, a real interruption in the "reading" process. Beautiful images, though. And now I can't get back to the home page! So type in the address again—-all continuity gone.

The difficulty we found in evaluating hypertext projects in the same "stack" as traditional research papers is a difficulty other teachers also face. In an article in the Spring 2001 issue of *Kairos* on an online distance-education Women's Studies course that she taught, Lisa Hammond Rashley writes, "I found some difficulty in the course learning how to evaluate online work. . . . In the case of the research papers . . . when I had to measure traditional papers . . . against a hypertext presentation, the task became a much more complicated one." She presents this note as a preface to one student's traditional research paper. She also provides a link to a specific hypertext presentation written by another student.

Since these two samples are publicly available, we decided to use them for an experiment in developing criteria that could be used for a specific assignment for which both hypertext and non-hypertext compositions were submitted. We also chose them because we found both interesting and well researched. Our purpose was not so much to evaluate each piece as to see whether we could develop criteria for doing so. The two pieces we chose are a hypertext essay, "Gender Socialization," by Shannon York, and a piece that is simply titled "Traditional Research Paper" by Marcy Keown. Both can be found at <http://english.ttu.edu/kairos/6.1/binder.html?response/wost/>. We will refer to York's piece as "the hypertext" and to Keown's as "the traditional essay."

We need to say something about our reading process, to "come clean," before we begin. First, each of us, independently, decided to begin with the traditional research paper. This choice, which reveals something about our own amphibious situation here—our instinctive preference for the old element—certainly conditioned our reading. If we had begun with the hypertext piece, our reactions would certainly have been different, although our evaluation of the two pieces might have been the same. Second, each of us, independently, chose to read the traditional research paper as it was presented to us, onscreen, feeling that since it had been published onscreen, in *Kairos*, it should also be read onscreen. Doing this created problems for us: The lack of page numbers made it difficult to refer to specific points in the text, the small type-font made screen-reading difficult, and scrolling sometimes made us feel "lost" in the paper. Perhaps by choosing to read the traditional piece online, we were not being entirely fair to its author—unless she had known that it would be published online after she wrote it.

Developing Criteria

We worked inductively to develop criteria and, initially, independently: Each of us read and developed criteria for first the traditional and then for the hypertext essay. Finally, we worked together to sort out and shape criteria that applied to both essays and that were distinct. Both the traditional and the hypertext essays were recognizably arguments; each had a point to make, and each supported that point with evidence. Therefore, the criteria that we ordinarily use in judging academic essays in this genre seemed to apply across the media: "Focus and Central Claim," "Evidence of Constructive Thinking," "Organization/Coherence." Both pieces had been researched, so "Documentation" was also a criterion for us. Because both were substantially "written" pieces, "Syntax/Style" and "Grammar/Proofreading" became criteria for us as well. But there was a criterion that we invoked in judging the hypertext that was unique to the hypertext: "Graphic Design." This included the visual elements of the hypertext: choice of fonts, page layout, choice of colors. In the narrative that follows we present our process as well as our product to suggest the value of this inductive process and to demonstrate that we did find criteria that applied to both texts, although, as our narrative will illustrate, the ways in which we applied these criteria were affected by each medium.

FOCUS AND CENTRAL CLAIM *(applies to both traditional and hypertext essays)*

Since both the hypertext and the traditional essay were presented as arguments, both of us were poised to look for "focus and central claim," and, indeed, we found these elements in both pieces. Both of us felt that the traditional essay's claim was more focused and clear, although it was one that the writer wrote herself into in her second paragraph. The hypertext's first page, its "beginning," included three question/answer sections that were to serve as background for the reader, a personal statement by the author, and links to five other pages. Its thesis, that gender roles are socially constructed, was embedded in the question/answer sections and in the personal statement. It felt to us that the thesis, cast in hypertext, had somehow been exploded and distributed. It was, in this form, more difficult for us to grasp.

CONSTRUCTIVE THINKING *(applies to both traditional and hypertext essays)*

This is a criterion that we apply because both pieces had been "researched": that is, they contain the author's voice and the voices of authorities selected and brought in as part of the research process. Both texts conveyed a sense that each author had a stake in her essay and a position of her own that she was trying to communicate. Beyond that, we asked ourselves, "What has the author made of her research?" Both pieces, in our view, did not make full use of their sources, both bringing in a great deal of research (here may be another criterion, "amount of research") but neither fully taking command of the source material and making it her own.

ORGANIZATION/COHERENCE *(applies to both traditional and hypertext essays)*

We applied this criterion differently as we moved from the traditional essay to the hypertext. To both of us, the traditional essay seemed well organized. It moved in a line: claim, evidence, conclusion. The hypertext was harder to judge with this criterion. In some ways, it seemed to be a linear essay transported into hypertext, with an introduction and conclusion. This led us to feel that the author was not fully utilizing the potential of the medium. In a few sections, the hypertext seemed to be a list of items collected but not integrated—like a collection of shells found at the beach. When looking at the organization of the traditional essay, we looked, of course, at units of text: paragraphs, the introduction, the conclusion. Was there forecasting? Was there summary? Did transitions and repeated key-words help us see the whole as we read a part? When looking at the hypertext, we found ourselves looking at the "menu" of links we could go to on the first page, at the means of navigation provided us by the author, and at the integrity and coherence of each page and of the full site.

SYNTAX/STYLE *(applies to both traditional and hypertext essays)*

Both are adequate, similar, equivalent. *Grammar and proofreading:* Each has a few errors, but not that many.

DOCUMENTATION *(applies to both traditional and hypertext essays)*

Seems fine for each.

DEGREE OF DIFFICULTY *(applies to both traditional and hypertext essays)*

Here we invoke William Faulkner, who is alleged to have preferred magnificent failure (in his view, his novels) to cautious success. Has the author tried to do something difficult? How far has she stretched? Looking at both the traditional and the hypertext essays prompted us to consider not only the degree of difficulty of the issue that each author addressed but also of the composing task, including the relative difficulty of working with the technology being used. Not surprisingly, the question first arose for the hypertext: How well does the author use graphics, colors, type-fonts? How effective are the pathways of links that are created? That parallel graphics questions did not arise for us when reading the traditional essay is perhaps because it did not violate our expectations (e.g., did not use 16 point type) and did not include figures or complex appendices.

In relation to the hypertext, we wondered whether composing in hypertext presents difficulties that composing on paper does not: choices of color, graphics, type-fonts, navigation systems, front pages. Should we give this author credit for attempting the difficulties of composing in hypertext? Should we expect the author to be a sophisticated web-designer? Should we take off points if she's not? And, if we applied this criterion to the hypertext, should we also apply it to the traditional essay? As we discussed this question, we realized that when we use this criterion as teachers, we draw on both our sense of the task being attempted and our knowledge of the skills of the particular authors.

GRAPHICS (FONTS, COLOR, PRESENTATION) *(applies to hypertext only)*

Here is a criterion that applies to the hypertext only. Given the difficulty that the hypertext author faced here, we found ourselves feeling that there really is a virtue to the traditional research paper: It eliminates this area of difficulty. Those who argue for school uniforms say that such a policy will help students concentrate on academics and not on dress. Given our experience here, we can imagine a similar argument for the traditional, paper-based essay. On this topic Anne wrote, "Well, I guess [it was] good that she experimented with font and colors, but I found them distracting in a few instances. The lime green against the sort of terra cotta color was a real glare." Charlie complained that the author had violated conventions of web design: She had used the blue that is conventionally assigned to links for some sections of text, making Charlie move his mouse over this text looking for a link. Both Anne and Charlie found problems of salience on the hypertext pages. What was one supposed to focus on first? Second? It was impossible for us to say whether the problems of salience were problems of graphical representation or problems of "fuzzy thinking" (see *Focus and Central Claim*).

On balance, we felt that some common criteria could be used to evaluate the two compositions since both were written in the genre "academic argument," but if we had applied those criteria without considering variations prompted by the different technologies, our evaluation would have been flawed. Working inductively with actual texts helped us see those differences as well as the commonalities. Using the previously mentioned criteria, we concluded that both the traditional essay and the hypertext were good arguments although the traditional essay was, in our view, a somewhat better argument. The hypertext did not make good use of color and graphics, and it violated at least one convention of web design. As we have noted, it is really difficult for us to separate this problem from the "follow the argument" problem—that is, color and graphics could have been used to establish coherence or line. Because they were not used to do so, should we attribute this flaw to the hypertext author's inexperience with the medium? Or should we attribute it to her inexperience with the genre of argument? We are not able to decide.

What We Have Learned

Our experience in reading and evaluating these two pieces, the hypertext and the traditional essay, has made us more aware that when we permit or encourage our students to compose academic hypertexts, we need to be clear about what it is that we want and expect, and we need to communicate these criteria clearly to our students. Our criteria for reading traditional research essays have a long history in American education. They are practically tacit to us and are often familiar to our students, who have written high school essays in their preparation for college. Our criteria for reading academic hypertexts have no history at all, however, so we'll need to discover and create these criteria as we go. And we'll need to publish them for our students, or, perhaps better, to engage in discussions with our students about the criteria by which they would want their hypertexts judged.

If you have not read any hypertext compositions that fall within that broad and fuzzy category called "academic writing," we encourage you to do so. Although it may seem that hypertext compositions are exotic creations that will never gain currency, some academics as well as students are composing them on their own initiative as well as upon the invitation of their teachers. Reading a few of these academic hypertexts will help lessen the sense of disorientation that a first encounter may prompt. For us, the experience of reading academic hypertext for this article has helped orient us to this new world of composing and reading. Reading a few academic hypertexts will demonstrate, we believe, the possibilities for thinking and composing offered by the capability of creating links and including images and sound along with print. A good place to start is with issues of *Kairos*, including the student samples we have drawn on from the WOST course. Doug Brent's hypertext argument, "Rhetorics of the Web: Implications for Teachers of Literacy," will also inform you about hypertext as well as give you the experience of reading a richly developed hypertext. As you read, we encourage you also to think about the nature of these hypertexts in relation to non-hypertext compositions. Reading hypertext with non-hypertext in mind not only serves to familiarize you with some of the various hypertext genres and approaches to composing hypertext; it also helps bring into relief our expectations for non-hypertext academic writing and some of the conventions and associated evaluation criteria that we take for granted. We believe such self-reflection is valuable for any teacher. For us, it prompted critical examination of the ways of thinking and shaping information that we value and, following from that, the conventions for composing which we value.

But to return to our specific focus, evaluating academic hypertext compositions, we close with some suggestions derived from our experience in our classrooms and our experience with this project.

THINK GENRE. To name a piece as hypertext is no more informative than to name it a paper text. What kind of hypertext? Institutional home page? Personal home page? Academic argument? Compendium? Anatomy? Encyclopedia entry? As Brent points out, hypertext genres are still evolving and consequently are not yet stable. That leaves more room for creativity for the composer; it also means readers/evaluators need to be flexible and open to new kinds of texts. Still, as a reader, thinking in terms of genres and, at the least, purpose and audience provides a way of orienting yourself in this new technology. Some genres are unique to the Internet—for example, the personal home page. Yet even these can be thought of in relation to such print genres as résumés and narrative personal statements. (Hesse views them as having features of a directory as well as of an essay narrative.) Other hypertext genres parallel print genres such as the novel and various persuasive genres, but with differences. The point is not to try to fit a given hypertext into the mold of traditional print genres but to use the genre conventions with which you are familiar as one way to get a handle on the hypertext—both how it is similar and how it is distinct. For an evaluator, this flexibility about genre conventions is particularly essential so that you do not inappropriately use a print genre convention and criterion (e.g., linear development of points) when evaluating a hypertext.

The samples of student essays included in the *Kairos* article about the WOST course suggest some of the variation that you might encounter in student work. The "Gender Socialization" hypertext is an issue-focused research argument while another hypertext, "Women in the Workforce," seems to have a more informative purpose and be in the manner of a compendium of encyclopedia entries or *Dictionary of National Biography* entries. As we have shown in our reading of the two research arguments, when the genre is the same, some conventions will remain the same across the different technologies while some others will change in their application.

DEVELOP RHETORICAL-TRAIT CRITERIA FOR EVALUATION. For a hypertext argument, even if it is one that aims to be exploratory and resist closure, most readers still expect claims to be made and supported. But for that hypertext argument, the development need not be linear; in fact, most advocates of hypertext composing extol the potential the technology provides for nonlinear, more associative means of development (Brent, Douglas, Duguay). For an informative text that is a compendium or an anatomy such as the "Women in the Workforce" hypertext, providing a rationale for the women included would be important as a criterion as would be providing an explanation in each profile of each woman's accomplishments in her field. Developing a sense of conventions and criteria may require reading of some hypertexts. If you have not yet begun to read and write hypertext compositions yourself before one of your students proposes submitting one to you, you might ask that student to develop some evaluation criteria to propose to you and to suggest a few hypertexts that she feels illustrate the type of hypertext she plans to compose. These suggestions will give you an idea of the kinds of sites with which the student is familiar, and you can then determine whether that is the sort of learning project in which you want the student to invest time for your course. If the sites are more like directory sites (e.g., an organization's web site), you may or may not consider creating such a site appropriate for your course.

FOLLOW PRACTICES THAT ARE APPROPRIATE FOR ANY ASSIGNMENT. First, decide the learning objectives for a "writing" assignment and the nature of the assignment (e.g., scope, purpose, kinds of thinking and activities in which you want students to engage). Then decide whether you wish to include a hypertext option. Establish your evaluation criteria in advance so that they can serve as a guide for the students in composing as well as a guide for you in evaluating. In "Losing Control: Writers, Readers, and Hypertext," Maureen Fitzpatrick, describes a course, Writing for Interactive Media. This *Kairos* article is a good source for examples of hypermedia assignments that are shaped to the goals of a particular course. The assignments include well-thought-out evaluation criteria that are presented to guide students as they compose as well as to guide the teacher in evaluating the hypermedia compositions. The examples also illustrate how certain criteria may remain the same across technologies given a common purpose. For example, for an informative assignment, the criteria include these that we would also expect for a print informative composition: "Is any of the information given unnecessary or unlikely/less likely to be useful? Is the information correct? Is the information useful?" The criteria also include ones distinct to the hypermedia technology: "Do media compete or complement? Can the user find the information [she wants] efficiently? Is it easy to get back to a place previously visited?" Alternatively, as we suggested earlier, you can collaborate with your students and negotiate these criteria. Doing so has the added advantage of prompting them to think more reflectively about the nature of the various sorts of composing that they do and the conventions of academic writing that they may take for granted.

Although we have stressed rhetorical criteria, we also recognize that in some instances one of your learning objectives may be that students should experiment with some new medium, using a number of its capabilities. In this case, the evaluation criteria might stress using the medium (e.g., making links both within a site and across sites, including graphics and sound), with less attention given to specific genre criteria. Here a difficulty for us would be in determining the student's initial skill level and somehow factoring that into the evaluation. One of Charlie's students last semester was a professional web designer who redesigned Charlie's course web site. Another student, for the same project, made her first PowerPoint presentation—on the uses of the comma. Charlie guesses that the redesign of the web site was less challenging for his experienced student than the presentation on comma uses was for his inexperienced student. How should such projects be graded? If one of your goals is to encourage students to experiment with the medium, then a criterion should be something like "Degree of Difficulty"—the amount of stretching and learning, in this case technological, that can be seen in the composition. Using this criterion, the first-time PowerPoint presentation would be more of an experiment for its author than the web-site redesign was for its creator, so it should receive the higher grade.

WHEN YOU ACTUALLY RECEIVE THAT HYPERTEXT COMPOSITION, DECIDE HOW YOU'RE GOING TO PHYSICALLY READ IT. Will you read it onscreen and take notes by hand? If you are a quick typist, you will likely find that handwriting is constraining, and if you want to have your comments in digital form at some point, you may resent retyping. An alternative is to keep both the hypertext and your word processor on the screen at the same time. This means splitting the screen, which is visually unfair to the hypertext, or "ALT-TABbing" between your browser and your word processor, which means that you have to read and write alternately. Or will you set up two computers—perhaps a laptop alongside a desktop, or two monitors for your desktop—and read hypertext on one while taking notes on the other? This seems to be the ideal situation because the hypertext is there on a full screen, and so are your notes and comments. But this configuration involves lots of expensive equipment and a desk covered with gear and wires.

TRY CREATING YOUR OWN HYPERTEXT COMPOSITION. When we evaluate traditional research essays, we can draw on our own experience and empathize with the choices the writer has made, the difficulties that she has faced. We are accomplished academic writers evaluating students' academic writing. If we have composed in hypertext, we become at least marginally accomplished hypertext authors who can empathize with the choices the author has made that are peculiar to this medium: link colors, background colors, navigation bars, and text fonts, sizes, and colors. When you compose in hypertext, you find yourself deciding, for example, "Will I let the reader wander through this hypertext? Or will I fix the reader's path with 'Next' and 'Previous' buttons? Will I provide a map of the hypertext, and if so, in what form? How will I use the first, 'home' page to introduce the hypertext? Will I have a 'summary' or 'conclusions' page—with links back to supporting evidence? Will I link outside my own hypertext to other sources, and if so, how will I maintain the reader's sense that she is still in my hypertext?"

We posed two questions at the start: "What criteria should we use when evaluating hypertexts?" And "Is it possible to evaluate hypertext and non-hypertext compositions using the same criteria?" Our short answer to the first question: Use criteria appropriate to the task since that task and the resulting composition will have been shaped by the technology. Our answer to the second question is an artful dodge. We cannot say for sure whether it is possible, or desirable, to evaluate hypertext and non-hypertext compositions with the same criteria. In our previous readings, we found ourselves using criteria that we would use in evaluating argument because that is what we thought we had before us. We also evaluated the hypertext according to criteria that are appropriate in judging hypertext. We suspect that our uncertainty about this question is not substantially different from the uncertainty we feel when we evaluate any group of non-hypertext compositions that are written for a variety of purposes and in various genres. If we were reading student work in a creative writing class, would we read a sestina against the same criteria we use when we read free verse? Or, even more radical, against the criteria we use when we read a short story?

Since we are ourselves, in this book chapter, writing a non-hypertext composition, we feel the need for a conclusion. Perhaps this need to conclude is because the convention is so ingrained in us—a thought that occurs to us because we have been moved by our study of student hypertexts to reflect on the conclusion as a convention of the academic essay—and (hyperlink here) on the idea of conclusions generally—in musical compositions but not, of course, in museum exhibitions! So if your students are composing a hypertext document for an academic assignment, use this opportunity to engage them in reflecting on the conclusion as a cultural construction. Ask them whether they feel that a conclusion is called for in a hypertext. Considering that question will quickly take you from considerations for evaluation to considerations of text values and taken-for-granted conventions. If so, in this case technology will have done what it seems always to do: It has made visible what was transparent, and has made us reflect on what we conventionally do.

Works Cited

Brent, Doug. "Rhetorics of the Web: Implications for Teachers of Literacy." *Kairos* 2.1 (Spring 1997). <http://english.ttu.edu/kairos/2.1/features/brent/bridge.html>.

DeWitt, Scott, and Kip Strasma, eds. *Contexts, Intertexts, and Hypertexts.* Cresskill, NJ: Hampton, 1999.

Douglas, Jane Y. "Will the Most Reflexive Relativist Please Stand Up: Hypertext, Argument, and Relativism." *From Page to Screen.* Ed. Ilana Snyder. Sydney: Allen and Unwin, 1997. 144–62.

Duguay, Kathleen. "Sites of Conflict: The Challenges of Hypertextualizing Composition in the College Writing Class." DeWitt and Strasma 15–38.

Fitzpatrick, Maureen. "Losing Control: Writers, Readers, and Hypertext." *Kairos* 6.1 (Spring 2001). <http://english.ttu.edu/kairos/6.1/binder.html?coverweb/fitzpatrick>.

Hesse, Douglas. "Saving a Place for Essayistic Literacy." *Passions, Pedagogies, and Twenty-first Century Technologies.* Ed. G. Hawisher and C. Selfe. Logan: Utah State UP, 1999.

Rashley, Lisa H. "Women's Studies 101 on the Web." *Kairos* 6.1 (Spring 2001). <http://english.ttu.edu/kairos/6.1/binder.html?response/wost>.